MW00966325

NOT BAD
FOR A
SERGEANT

NOT BAD FOR A SERGEANT

The Memoirs of
Barney Danson

With
Curtis Fahey

THE DUNDURN GROUP
TORONTO · OXFORD

Copyright © Barney Danson, 2002

All rights reserved. No part of this publication may be reproduced, stored in a retrieval system, or transmitted in any form or by any means, electronic, mechanical, photocopying, recording, or otherwise (except for brief passages for purposes of review) without the prior permission of Dundurn Press. Permission to photocopy should be requested from the Canadian Copyright Licensing Agency.

Design: Jennifer Scott
Printer: Transcontinental

National Library of Canada Cataloguing in Publication Data

Danson, Barney
 Not bad for a sergeant : the memoirs of Barney Danson / Barney Danson ; with Curtis Fahey.

Includes bibliographical references.
ISBN 1-55002-404-3

1. Danson, Barney 2. Cabinet ministers--Canada--Biography. 3. Canada. Parliament. House of Commons--Biography. 4. Retinal degeneration--Patients--Canada--Biography. I. Fahey, Curtis, 1951- II. Title.

FC636.D35A3 2002   971.064'4'092   C2002-902296-7   F1034.3.D35A3 2002

1   2   3   4   5   06   05   04   03   02

THE CANADA COUNCIL | LE CONSEIL DES ARTS
FOR THE ARTS | DU CANADA
SINCE 1957 | DEPUIS 1957

Canada

ONTARIO ARTS COUNCIL
CONSEIL DES ARTS DE L'ONTARIO

We acknowledge the support of the **Canada Council for the Arts** and the **Ontario Arts Council** for our publishing program. We also acknowledge the financial support of the **Government of Canada** through the **Book Publishing Industry Development Program** and **The Association for the Export of Canadian Books**, and the **Government of Ontario** through the **Ontario Book Publishers Tax Credit** program.

Care has been taken to trace the ownership of copyright material used in this book. The author and the publisher welcome any information enabling them to rectify any references or credit in subsequent editions.

J. Kirk Howard, President

The large print edition was made possible by the Donner Canadian Foundation and the CNIB.

Printed and bound in Canada.♲
Printed on recycled paper.
www.dundurn.com

The Canadian
National
Institute
for the Blind
Library for the Blind

Donner | Fondation
Canadian | canadienne
Foundation | Donner

Dundurn Press
8 Market Street
Suite 200
Toronto, Ontario, Canada
M5E 1M6

Dundurn Press
73 Lime Walk
Headington, Oxford,
England
OX3 7AD

Dundurn Press
2250 Military Road
Tonawanda NY
U.S.A. 14150

To Isobel, who has made my life vibrant,
and to our grandchildren,
Kate, Jeremy, Natasha, Emily, Kimberly,
Jeffrey, Elysse, Jake, Adrienne, and Sebastian,
who have made our lives complete

Most of this book was written before 11 September 2001, when the world changed irrevocably. The one exception is on pages 190 and 191.

An afterword, written a few weeks after the events of "9/11," offers some reflections on the new realities facing all of us.

Contents

Preface

First, a story. When I became engaged to Isobel, the woman who is still my wife some fifty-eight years later, her mother wanted to put an announcement into the local newspaper in England that her daughter was marrying Lieutenant Barnett J. Danson of the Queen's Own Rifles of Canada. The fact was, however, I was only a sergeant: I was about to go for my officer's training course and only afterwards could become a lieutenant. I didn't want to prejudge the outcome of the course — if I did that in a public way I probably would never even be considered — so I told my saddened mother-in-law to-be that she had to accept the fact that her daughter was marrying a sergeant — a damned good sergeant I thought, but definitely not a lieutenant, yet. This became something of a family joke.

Now skipping ahead some years — thirty-two years to be exact — Parliament had yet to be summoned after the election of 8 July 1974 in which I had been returned for the third time in York North. We were at our home in Toronto and I was in the garden, barbecuing a marinated flank steak. Isobel was anxiously calling from the kitchen, asking how I was doing. I kept reporting back that I still had a few minutes to go to get the coals just right (a marinated flank steak requires high heat but a short barbecuing cycle). In the middle of this process the telephone rang. I answered it and heard the prime minister asking if I would join the cabinet as minister of state for urban affairs. Rather than keep him on tenterhooks for any length of time, and endanger the flank steak too, I accepted immediately and ran back to the barbecue where the steak was beginning to burn. Isobel called out once more, "How are you doing?" Smugly, I replied, "Not bad for a sergeant."

The title of this book, then, derives from an experience in the Second World War. What is more, the book as a whole has its roots in that same period. For it was the war, more than any other event, that exposed me to the wider world and gave my life the shape it subsequently took, for better or worse. The war gave me confidence — I knew that, when the chips were down, I had been there — and introduced me to the woman who became my wife. For reasons that I will explain, the war also propelled me into the political arena, where ultimately, as minister of national defence in the1970s, I acquired a reputation — a good one, I hope — that still clings to me. Today, few people know that, before my entry into politics, I had a fulfilling and successful career in business. Most simply know me as someone who, one time long ago, was minister of national defence. That likely would not be the case were it not for my wartime experiences.

The Second World War was a defining event for me, as it was for many of my age. For most of us, the war represented our first time away from home and family. It gave us our first experience of travel across Canada and overseas, and our first exposure to a broad cross-section of society: farmers, miners, lumberjacks, rootless "hoboes," ex-convicts who generally kept their status secret but were known to the other former "cons" among us, "old guys," in their late twenties, or the still older ones we called "Pop," many of whom were trying to disengage themselves from family responsibilities, or failed marriages, or who found in the military something that had eluded them in the Depression — the job they needed to support their families. Many of us also encountered, for the first time, the full diversity of Canada's population. We met francophone Canadians, individually and in their regiments, aboriginal Canadians, who were adjusting to us as we to them and each of whom we almost always called "chief," and others from the whole range of ethnic groups which made Canada their home even in those times. Steeped as our society was in British Anglo-Saxon culture, we hadn't before realized just how culturally diverse Canada was — a diversity that is reflected in the names on tombstones in our war cemeteries. The war broadened our horizons immensely. This was certainly true for me.

Yet, for me as for everyone, the war also had a darker side. My three closest friends in my regiment, the Queen's Own Rifles — Freddy Harris, Gerry Rayner, and Earl Stoll — were killed within a few months of one another during and just after the Normandy invasion. Freddy (whose father, a doctor, was to deliver our four sons) was struck down on the beach on D-Day, 6 June 1944. Gerry, an Englishman who had come to Toronto via Trinidad to enlist, was killed by a sniper near Caen, on 18 July. Earl was hit by shrapnel at Boulogne and later, in particularly tragic circumstances to be related in the next chapter, bled to death, on 20 September, about a month after I myself had been seriously wounded. Still another very close friend, Harlan Keely, not in the Queen's Own but in the Irish Regiment of Canada, survived the Italian campaign but died in Holland on 16 April 1945, shortly before the European war ended.

These losses devastated me. I still remember VE-Day, when, with the memories of my dead friends still fresh in my mind, I could not bring myself to join the crowds rejoicing on Toronto's streets; instead, I returned to the office where I was then working to immerse myself in paperwork. Since then, hardly a day has gone by that I haven't thought of one of my friends; on some days, I have thought of all of them. And now, as I get closer to the time when I must at last follow them, I think of Freddy, Gerry, Earl, and Harlan even more often. Sitting with my albums of old fading pictures, I am reminded of the fun we had as young soldiers. We were a band of men who, in some special way, were closer than brothers.

The memory of my friends has been more than a source of sadness, however; from the beginning, it has also given my life a sense of purpose. Their deaths left me with an unshakeable determination to play a part in determining the direction our country was to take. For them and for so many others who never lived to become veterans, I resolved to do everything I could to make sure that their deaths had not been for nothing. The result, as I will try to explain in this book, was my first tentative approach to the world of politics even while I was overseas, followed by increasing political activity at a variety of levels through the late 1940s, 1950s, and 1960s, my election to the House of Commons in 1968, my two-year stint from 1968 to 1970 as parliamentary secretary to

Prime Minister Trudeau, and my appointment to the cabinet, first in 1974 as minister of state for urban affairs and then in 1976 as minister of national defence. Along the way, I met fascinating people at home and abroad, saw parts of the world I never would have otherwise seen, and in general led a life rich in challenges and full of rewards, both personal and political. I will tell all of this story here, beginning with my youth and then proceeding through my wartime experiences and my business and political career to 1979, when the voters forced me to look for another job. A concluding chapter explains what I have been up to since then.

When I began writing portions of this memoir, a friend asked who the hell would want to buy it. The question startled me at first, but it was a good one. I had no illusions of great financial rewards, nor do I have any now. First and foremost, I want my grandchildren to know something about the life I have lived, to have some sense of their own roots and of the values that drove me. I did not know any of my grandparents and the little knowledge I have of them comes from the few letters and photographs that have survived in our family. It is my hope that this book will compensate for the paucity of family history I inherited. I also hope to give readers some insight into my generation — its challenges, wars, and politics. If some historians find this of interest, I will be grateful. If others, too, find it interesting, I will be delighted.

A few words about how this book came into being. Any minister who keeps a detailed diary of daily activities not only takes himself or herself too seriously but has more time to spare than most ministers I have known. In my own case, while I always took my job very seriously, I never took myself seriously enough. Nor did I ever feel that I was a cog in the greater history unfolding around me. Consequently, I never kept a diary, an omission that I regret now. In writing my memoirs I was dependent on my memory and whatever could be gleaned from my collection of newspaper clippings and other assorted documents, my ministerial papers at the National Archives in Ottawa (MG 32, B 25, boxes 1B339), and the diaries kept by Eric Acker, my executive assistant at both Urban Affairs and Defence.

This was not the only challenge. I have been legally blind for some five years and now, at the age of eighty, it is almost impossible for me to write, or at least to read what I have written. I have been fortunate, however, to have the support of a superb writer and editor, Curtis Fahey, who conducted tape-recorded interviews with me and then had the incredibly difficult job of putting my story into words that sounded like mine. We worked together over his first large-print drafts until we were satisfied that we were as close to agreement as two independent-thinking individuals can be, one with a high degree of professionalism, the other with sometimes vague memories but also sufficient ego to start this project in the first place. At best, it has been a successful compromise for both of us, and, without Curtis, the task would have been impossible. Another indispensable person in the process was Sylvia Macenko, my special assistant who had the rare skill of being able to decipher my handwriting. Tragically, Sylvia died unexpectedly just as she was completing this final transcript. Aside from my personal grief for the loss of this vibrant, charming, and dedicated good friend, I had no idea where to turn to complete this work. Fortunately, Lesley Marshall, a close associate in our work with the new Canadian War Museum, immediately volunteered to help me out and her contribution was outstanding. Bringing a fresh approach, she corrected mistakes which had escaped us previously and made a number of insightful observations which were particularly valuable.

I have incurred many other debts in the writing of this book. In particular I wish to thank my wife, Isobel, who accommodated herself to my shifting moods in this process and who, over the last year, succumbed to the mess I made of our condominium, with papers and filing boxes wreaking havoc with her meticulous housekeeping. Most of all, I thank her for her unwavering support and encouragement. I wish to thank, too, Eric Acker, my former executive assistant at Urban Affairs and Defence, for access to his meticulously kept and, until now, highly classified diaries, and for his always wise advice, which helped me put my sometimes vague, sometimes false memories into context and with reasonable accuracy; General (ret'd) Paul Manson, former Chief of Defence Staff (CDS) and (as brigadier-general) program manager for the New Fighter Aircraft (NFA) procurement, for his considerable assistance during my years at Defence and subsequently as my successor on the board of the Canadian Museum of Civilization and chairman of the Canadian War Museum Committee; the Hon. Jacques Hébert, my collaborator in the founding of Katimavik, for chairing this most successful of all youth programs in Canada with dedication and passion throughout its all too short but dynamic history; Howard Nixon and Donald Deacon, who co-chaired Katimavik with Jacques Hébert, and Norman Godfrey, one of its most enthusiastic proponents, for their reminders of events in Katimavik's early stages; Peter Connolly, my first executive assistant, whose insider's knowledge of the system "on the Hill" helped get me started as a neophyte minister, for his always clear recollections of what really happened rather than what I thought happened; the Hon. John Roberts, a former colleague in cabinet, for his immeasurable help in putting events in context, as well as for providing an impressive literary commentary on my manuscript; Dr Jack Granatstein, distinguished historian and former director and CEO of the Canadian War Museum, for his encouragement and guidance; my good friend the Hon. Roy MacLaren for his wise advice; Lieutenant-General (ret'd) Bill Carr, former air force chief, for his help in triggering memories of our Arctic flights and of Operation Morning Light; Admiral (ret'd) Robert Falls, a former CDS and the first sailor to hold that appointment, for his thoughtful reflections on the time we served so closely together; General (ret'd) Ramsay Withers, a former CDS, for always willingly helping me to recall events of my days as minister of national defence; Major-General (ret'd) Andy Christie, who, as commander of the Special Service Force in Petawawa, for clarifying events relating to the CAST Combat Group and for providing precise details on this subject which many others involved had forgotten; Dr Ivan Head, principle foreign-policy adviser to Prime Minister Trudeau, for his insights into, and encyclopedic memory of, events and experiences during my time as Trudeau's parliamentary secretary; Bill Gilday and Charles Tretter, of the New England Governors' Conference, for their help on my Boston days and, more particularly, on the work of the Conference of New England Governors and Eastern Canadian Premiers; Idi Amin, for creating the havoc in Uganda which ultimately enabled me to visit that beautiful but tortured country; the staff of the Library of Parliament, for their superb service — always prompt, thorough, and courteous — in response to a myriad of enquiries; the embassies of Indonesia, Iran, Norway, and Russia, and the high commissions of India and Sri Lanka, for their considerable assistance and particularly for giving me the correct spellings of names of people and places I could only pronounce phonetically; Rabbi Arthur Biefeld of Temple Emanu-El, Toronto, and Kenneth Rotenberg and Ethel Rosenberg, for their assistance in recalling events in the development of this very special synagogue; Dr Peter Oberlander, former secretary of the Ministry of State for Urban Affairs, for his advice on Habitat, the United Nations Conference on Human Settlements in Vancouver; Dr Cornelia Oberlander, landscape architect par excellence, for reflections on her uncle Kurt Hahn, founder of the Salem School in Germany and then headmaster at Gordonston in Scotland, the inspiration for my concept of Katimavik; Major-General (ret'd) Gus Cloutier, now sergeant-of-arms of the House of Commons, for his invaluable help as my first executive assistant at National Defence; Vice-Admiral (ret'd) Ed Healey, program manager for the acquisition of new patrol frigates during my time at Defence, for help with the details of this important procurement; André Saumier, former senior assistant secretary of the Ministry of State for Urban Affairs, for his assistance, good advice, and considerable support during those days, and, more recently, for reading a draft of the chapter on my Urban Affairs years; and, for miscellaneous assistance, Dr Serge Bernier, head of the Directorate of History, Department of National Defence, and Dr Isabel Campbell, also of the Directorate; Ciunius Boyce of the Privy Council Office; Dean Oliver, senior historian, Canadian War Museum; David Meren, researcher; and all other friends who were so helpful but whose names I may have unintentionally omitted.

Finally, I wish to express my deep gratitude to two people who are no longer with us. The first is General Jacques Dextraze, my first CDS, a fighting soldier from the Second World War and Korea, whose crusty, "straight from the shoulder" advice and unquestioned loyalty were a constant source of strength during my time as minister. His presence was with me constantly as I struggled with the writing of this memoir, and I shall always remember him with respect and affection.

The second person is Pierre Trudeau. On 3 October 2000 I attended his funeral in Notre Dame Basilica in Montreal. I met many old friends and colleagues there, and in the course of the service I found myself thinking back to my days in the political trenches, working alongside a man who must surely rank as one of the most extraordinary prime ministers in our history. Pierre Trudeau could be exasperating at times, but I always got a great charge just from being around him. Charming, intellectually brilliant, with perhaps the most formidable memory I have ever encountered — he was, without a doubt, something very special. I wasn't alone in feeling this way, nor am I today. Indeed, the vast outpouring of emotion that greeted his death — which astonished those of us who remembered the days when he attracted as much antipathy as admiration — made it clear that he touched something profound within us as a people, and that we likely will not see his like again for a long, long time, if ever. I feel most fortunate that I had the opportunity to know him and to serve under him.

And so here it is, my autobiography. I hope that I may be forgiven for some vagueness in the narrative every now and then, and also for errors in detail. I hope, too, that I have been able to tell my story in such a way that my six precious granddaughters and four fantastic grandsons will better understand the kind of experiences that shaped "Grandpa Barney" and motivated him to do the things he did. May their own experiences be as rich and rewarding — in a world of peace.

Barney Danson
Toronto, August 2002

Chapter One
Youth, Marriage, and War, 1921–44

It was August 1944 in Normandy. Tens of thousands of German troops had escaped through the Falaise Gap and were in retreat while being savaged by our strafing aircraft (British Typhoons, American P47 Thunderbolts), artillery, and Vickers medium-machine guns. With the enemy just out of range of our Lee Enfield rifles and Bren light machine guns, the Queen's Own was ordered to move on 18 August from its overnight position at Damblainville southeast to Trun, our next objective east of Falaise, as we pursued the Germans towards Boulogne. As battalion orderly officer the previous night, I had kept myself awake with a steady diet of Normandy cider and the occasional shot of Calvados. This did not make for maximum alertness the following morning as we moved in fits and starts, on foot, in the scorching, dry August heat. Dust stirred up by vehicles clogged our nostrils, somewhat limiting the stench from slaughtered and disembowelled cattle and German transport horses that littered the road.

My platoon, like the rest of the battalion, was stretched out along a narrow dusty country road so that it presented a widely dispersed target for enemy artillery. We were exhausted after continually interrupted or virtually sleepless nights and pre-dawn "stand to," on the alert for any possible enemy counter-attack which would be most likely to occur at first light. We slumped down at each stop, taking the opportunity to rest, puff a cigarette, or even catch forty winks. In the midst of one of these pauses, a small procession wound its way down the road towards us. A crude and creaking horse-drawn farm cart carried a rough coffin topped with wild flowers. Straggling slowly behind it was the family of mourners: a clump of plainly clad Norman farmers caught between sides in the terror of war. Following the body of his wife was an elderly farmer in a rough tweed mismatched suit twisting a well-worn cap in his gnarled farmer's hands. The others shuffled along around him, seemingly oblivious to our presence but risking the dangers of a random shell to bury a loved one in these bizarre circumstances. While death was all around us, we felt like intruders on this simple family's grief. And then we moved on as they disappeared behind us and we were once more conscious of the stink of rotting animal flesh and the possible dangers awaiting us.

On the 19th we were ordered to halt and take up defensive positions on the high ground in an orchard just beyond the village of Grande Mesnil, roughly mid-way between Trun and Falaise. As we moved through the village, we were struck by the small First World War memorial in the town square. At its base were two fresh German graves marked with wooden Maltese crosses bearing the names and birth dates of the teenage victims; the main battle casualties are usually not much more than children.

Outside the village, I found a position in an orchard with a natural depression that I thought would reduce the amount of digging-in required, not an insignificant consideration given the hard, dry, flinty soil. Regrettably, the departing Germans had used it as a latrine and I didn't relish the thought of spending my time in that spot. To add insult to injury, they had used the surrender passes, dropped by Allied air forces to encourage the enemy to give up, as toilet paper. To my knowledge, this was the only beneficial use to which these passes were put.

Earl Stoll, who commanded the neighbouring platoon on my left, and I joined to coordinate the sighting of our positions. Earl, who was to die of wounds a few weeks later at Boulogne, was the last of my three buddies who had enlisted along with me and we had remained the closest of friends as we moved up through the ranks. Since I had only recently returned to the regiment after receiving my commission at the Battle Drill School in Vernon, British Columbia, and since I hardly knew our new company commander, "Hank"

Elliot, who turned out to be a first-rate person and distinguished professional soldier, I leaned heavily on Earl's experience. He was sceptical about my use of reverse-slope defensive positions, a doctrine I had learned from Eighth Army North African veterans and taught as gospel in Vernon. The principle was that, with reverse-slope positions, the enemy could not see you or accurately site their artillery on your positions; instead, he would have to come at you over the ridge of the hill, thereby exposing himself dangerously. The only difficulty was that you had to have scouts or observers to let you know what was going on ahead and if there was anyone coming. This was not a job anyone relished, and when I placed two men on a road fork a few hundred feet ahead, they were less than enthusiastic. Equally unenthusiastic was the French family in a nearby farmhouse that had no desire to have troops so close by to attract enemy fire. Keeping the men in position with a Bren gun and a PIAT (projectile infantry anti-tank), the latter inspiring little confidence in the holder and little fear in enemy tank crews, was not easy and they found more reasons to return to the main body for discussion than I could think of for sending them back.

Since we did not know how long we were to be in position before moving off, we didn't dig in deeply. Not for the moment anyway. We had our lunch of "compo" rations, which were pre-packed, measured portions of soup, meat of some sort, vegetables, biscuits, chocolate, jam, and tea. We were immediately joined by swarms of bees who shared our rations and occasionally became part of them. With everything but the tea ending up in a single aluminium mess tin, the bees added a flavour of their own. The tea, on the other hand, was so hot that you burned your lips and tongue on the mess tin, with the result that one had to wait until it was cold before drinking it unless you were smart enough to carry a tin mug for such situations. Lunch over, I sauntered down the hill to the carrier platoon, which, as part of the battalion's support company, consisted of armoured, tracked vehicles equipped with Bren light-machine guns. I wanted to pick up my battle-dress jacket, which I had thrown on a carrier because it was too hot to wear and too much trouble to carry; my glasses were in the pocket and I needed them for my map reading. Because the carriers were in softer soil and their vehicles allowed them to carry proper shovels, rather than the small, feeble entrenching tools we were given, they were dug in deeply.

When I returned to the platoon position, we were immediately assaulted by a whining, whistling, groaning, ear-splitting roar that I mistook for dive-bombing aircraft. The noise was followed by exploding bombs all around us. It was my first, and next-to-last, experience with the "Moaning Minnie," the multi-barrelled German mortar, Nebelwerfer, which, because of its high trajectory, had no respect for reverse slopes. The Germans must have guessed where we were since it was the only spot with a pre-built latrine. Fortunately, they didn't hit the latrine, not only because it would really have been messy, but also because some of the men had overcome their sensitivities and chosen the ditch rather than the neater but shallower models we had developed. After over four years in the army, we had become used to putting up with that sort of thing.

During a lull in the bombardment, I found my helmet and replaced the more comfortable beret I had been wearing. In the same lull, my batman/runner, with whom I shared a slit-trench (commonly known by the American term "foxhole"), had his entrenching tool working like an automatic digger. I never saw a hole dug so deep so fast, but as his head was disappearing underground and I was fastening on my tin hat, another barrage began to land. No sooner was my helmet on my head than I felt as if someone had taken a baseball bat or a sledgehammer, wound up, and hit me in the left eye. There was a momentary pause and the blood started to gush out of my mouth like Niagara. I could feel my strength draining away rapidly — I believed I was bleeding to death, that my time had come, not a total surprise for an infantryman for whom this possibility was a preoccupation.

I felt no panic; everything was happening too fast. My only reaction was one of acceptance that, as with all too many of my friends, my time had come.

Youth

The journey that took me to this somewhat grim moment in my life began in Toronto just over two decades earlier. I am named after my paternal grandfather, who died in 1919, two years before I was born. Barnett Danson emigrated to Toronto from Lithuania via England and Ireland in the 1870s and became a relatively prosperous menswear retailer, leaving an estate valued at, according to one newspaper at that time, $250,000, not an insignificant sum in 1919. He had five children in all — my father, Joe, my uncle, Leo, a son from an earlier marriage, Irving (who owned a men's cap manufacturing company in Montreal), and two girls, Rose and Florence — and Joe and Leo inherited the business. Apparently, Grandmother Danson was a retiring woman whose health prevented her from exercising any tight control over her sons, who enjoyed lively social lives in the Toronto of their days. Incredibly enough, my aunts were convent-educated (at St Joseph's, Toronto), in spite of the fact that the family were practising, but not Orthodox, Jews. All of them were warm, generous, and extremely honourable people, the latter quality apparently inherited from my grandfather and perhaps those before him. This sometimes manifested itself as self-righteousness and overblown pride, but they were unquestionably decent and generous people of great integrity.

The same was true of the other side of my family, which inherited little but guts. My maternal grandmother, Bertha Wolfe, American-born, was widowed when her husband, Max, died at the age of fifty-two, leaving her with nine daughters and two sons. Somehow this formidable woman supported and raised her large brood while operating a millinery store in Ottawa and then Toronto. She was the true matriarch whose table was always open to strangers, especially recently arrived and impoverished Jewish immigrants. This was an example followed by my mother, Saidie, particularly when boys and young Jewish men arrived in Canada to escape the vicious anti-Semitism of the Nazis in the 1930s. Until her premature death in October 1951, at the age of sixty — Father was to live much longer, into his early eighties — my mother was an energetic, extraordinarily unselfish woman who spared no effort in caring for others, whether they were family, friends, or strangers. Everyone she came to know was devoted to her; those who are alive today remember her still and speak of her glowingly.

Though both my father and my mother were remarkably kind and generous people, in most other respects they were quite different. Dad, always known as "J.B." to his children and grandchildren (the "B" standing for "Brass," his mother's maiden name), was an extrovert with an irrepressible sense of humour, a voracious reader, and something of a dreamer; he inherited none of Grandfather Danson's aptitude for business. Both he and Leo were devoted members of the Masonic Lodge, where their natural gregariousness found an outlet. Mother, for her part, did not have an extensive formal education. Nonetheless, she was a well-read, cultured person who always made sure that her children were exposed to the arts, especially music, and attended Toronto Symphony concerts at Massey Hall (even though the twenty-five-cent admission plus streetcar fare was not something we could easily afford). And, unlike my father, she was hardheaded, practical, and dynamic, a driving force in all her endeavours. Yet, despite their different temperaments, and despite the tensions that sometimes ensued because of the financial pressures of the Depression, my parents were deeply fond of one another, and the home they created for themselves and their children was a happy one.

There were four children in all — Bert, the eldest, was followed by Marilyn, me, and Bill — and each of us was born at Toronto's Grace Hospital, then located at the corner of College and Huron (the same family doctor, Dr Griffiths, delivered all of us). We were close to one another as youngsters and remain so to this day. Like all siblings, of course, we were both similar to and different from one another. Bert (who was to join the RCAF and marry my wife's cousin in wartime England) was more reserved than me but certainly no shrinking violet. He was also an excellent bugler and trumpeter. Marilyn, like our mother, was solid, warm, and so giving to her friends and community in later years that those who knew her invariably referred to her as an angel, a description I fully understand and wholeheartedly echo. Bill, four years my junior and, like me, a redhead — a feature we inherited from our mother — was thoughtful and more reflective than Bert and me and as good-hearted as Marilyn (he, too, served in the RCAF and received his bomb-aimer wing just before the war ended). Finally, there was me. Born on 8 February 1921, I combined my father's extroverted personality and some of his temper with my mother's more practical nature.

For many years, we lived on Jameson Avenue in the Parkdale district of Toronto. Today, Jameson is a haven for prostitutes and drug-dealers, but then it was a moderately elegant street and, being located near Lake Ontario, Sunnyside Beach, the Exhibition grounds, and High Park, was an almost ideal city environment in which to raise a family and especially a young boy. Our large Victorian home had been left to us by my grandfather, who had it duplexed so that we could share it with my aunt Rose. She had been widowed in the 1918 flu epidemic, and, to support herself and daughter, she supplemented her small inheritance by giving piano lessons. We had no Jewish neighbours close by, but there must have been a sufficient number of Jewish families in Parkdale to warrant a weekly visit from Mr Starkman the baker, whose horse-drawn wagon brought the heavenly delights of chala, rye bread, and bagels. Bagels were my passion — I was known as Barney Bagel in the family — and the attachment remains to this day, although bagels are not now the Jewish cultural preserve they were then. We were deeply conscious of our Judaism but never self-conscious about it. Indeed, there is a family story of me marching down Jameson Avenue waving a large Canadian flag and bellowing, "Hurrah for the Canadian Jews" — this while discrimination was rampant on the job market and Jews were excluded from many areas of social and economic life. My religious education, and that of my brothers and my sister, was provided by Holy Blossom Temple, a Reform Jewish congregation, then on Bond Street in downtown Toronto, with which our family had been closely associated for three generations. We usually made the weekly trip to Sunday school by streetcar; occasionally, however, a family friend, Mr List, obviously more affluent than us, picked us up in his elegant beige Durant — a forerunner of today's car pool.

I can't recall experiencing any anti-Semitism as a boy, but I certainly knew that I was vaguely different from non-Jews. They in turn viewed me as different, though to my knowledge this did not affect our relationships with each other. By the time girls had become a serious part of my life, I was not only attending Sunday religious school but was a member of a Jewish high school fraternity where parties and dates were strictly Jewish. Similarly, Christian friends would no more think of dating Jews than they would consider dating someone from another branch of their own faith; for example, Catholics dated Catholics. Few consciously wanted to maintain tribal boundaries. It was just the way it was. As the years went on, however, I became aware that not all such boundaries were of our own making — some were imposed on us by society. For example, I knew that I would not be welcome at some social clubs and that certain fields of commerce were strictly off limits. This offended me, and other Jews I knew, but we didn't go around wringing our hands in anguish. We reluctantly accepted it and got on with making a living for ourselves and our families in the areas where no restrictions existed. It did, however, increase our Jewish consciousness and deepen our religious roots.

Today, of course, things have changed immensely if not completely. Outright restriction is not as common, and not only are Jews made welcome in most facilities as guests but their membership is frequently invited. The practice of the "token Jew" has been left behind by a society that is much more open than the one that existed as recently as twenty or thirty years ago. A positive development has been the advent of clubs with open memberships, such as the Donalda Club in Don Mills, Toronto, a family club with superb golf and tennis facilities to which we have belonged almost since its inception over thirty years ago. The Craigleith Ski Club in Collingwood is another fine example of an excellent open-membership club. There, Isobel is usually first on the hills and the last off, and our sons and grandchildren are particularly active. The Royal Canadian Military Institute never presented a problem for me — as an officer in the armed forces you were presumed to be a gentleman — and it now even realizes that some non-commissioned ranks can be ladies and gentlemen too. Not coincidentally, there has been a huge transformation in the workplace, and nowhere more so than in the senior ranks of financial institutions, corporations, medicine, and universities, which were totally closed to Jews in the past.

But I'm getting ahead of myself; let's return to my youth. Our family circumstances changed dramatically during the Depression, when my easygoing father and uncle lost the family business as well as rental properties that they had inherited. Mortgage foreclosure even forced us to move out of our grandfather's house on Jameson Avenue, and over the course of the next few years we moved almost yearly from rented house to rented house. In these years, my father tried, without out-standing success, to make a living in insurance, and I grew up thinking that moving every year or so and wearing my older brother Bert's hand-me-downs was normal. My younger brother, Bill, felt the same way as he recycled, in modern parlance, my hand-me-downs for their third life, assuming, of course, that they were new when Bert got them — which is highly uncertain. Through all of this, Mother helped keep the family afloat. For extra income, she sold the Book of Knowledge over the phone and later acted as the Toronto representative for a camp in Maine (where I and my siblings spent each summer). Later still, when told by the people in Maine that her services were no longer needed, she start-ed — with sheer determination and no money — our own camp. Named Camp Winebagoe, it was first located in the Rouge River valley on a rented farm and then was moved to the Muskoka district of Ontario. I attended Winebagoe through my teenage years. (It still exists today, under non-family ownership after three generations of Danson dominance; my elder brother, Bert, after a brief stint in my father's insurance office, was to run the camp for decades, with the invaluable assistance of our sister Marilyn and the fantastic support of his wife, Dot.) For me, one of the most prized perks of the family camping enter-prise was that I had the opportunity, every day after school in the win-ter months, to ride the camp horses that were then kept in stables in the city (first at York Mills and Yonge and later along what is now the Bridlepath). Sid Bishop, who operated a riding academy and used our horses in return for their keep, ran these stables. I had a great affection for horses, and when I started thinking that I might have a future in the military, I thought only of the cavalry — which, as it turned out, the Canadian army in the Second World War would replace with tanks and light-armoured units.

At this point, I suppose, one expects to hear the usual story of a poor Jewish boy overcoming all obstacles to excel in school and become a successful doctor, lawyer, business tycoon, or academic. My story is different. From the start, academic work was not my strong suit. I was a curious and apparently bright enough young boy, but when my schol-arship failed to live up to the standards my parents expected they turned to what was then called "progressive education," a popular solution at the time for us problem children. Its guru in Toronto was Dr William Blatz of the University of Toronto's St George School for Child Studies. Blatz terrified me at first. I was certain that he could look right through me, identifying every weakness, every misdeed in my being. After a series of interviews and tests favoured by child psychologists of the day, he confirmed to my devastated but still hopeful parents that I was unlikely to be a Rhodes scholar, or even a serious student for that matter. They were encouraged, however, by Blatz's assurance that I had a quite respectable IQ rating and something they called at the time "gifted" intellectual faculties, which would guarantee me success in the future. My mother had hoped that I would be a lawyer but Blatz assured her that I would be able to hire lawyers. My parents may gain some satisfaction in heaven in the fact that three of my four sons are now successfully practising law.

I often wonder what turn my life would have taken if I had finished high school and successfully pursued a post-secondary education. Certainly, my options were limited without one and I was compelled to direct my energies and talents elsewhere. My first foray into the working world involved selling newspapers at the corner of Queen Street and Sorauren Avenue in Parkdale. Since this was a streetcar stop and my clientele was largely white-collar workers of Conservative political persuasion returning home between 4:00 PM (a slow time) and 6:00, I was generally able to sell out my Tory "Tellys" (the Toronto *Telegram*) in the first fifteen minutes and then spent the remaining one and three-quarter hours flogging the Liberal Toronto *Star*. I myself thought that the *Star* had much better comics, about the only part of a newspaper I considered worth reading other than the sports section, where I followed my beloved Maple Leafs, and the occasional gruesome murder story, a rarity in then "Toronto the Good." I did make eighteen cents a day, which would not have fulfilled Dr Blatz's predictions. Even the choice of location was questionable, for most of my targeted clientele had already purchased their papers downtown to read on the streetcar ride home. It would have made more sense to sell the morning newspapers, the Toronto *Globe* or its rival, the *Mail and Empire*, but that would have meant getting out of bed at 6:00 AM, something I find abhorrent to this day.

I then took a swing at selling *Maclean's* and *Chatelaine* magazines door-to-door. This was tough slugging but I was driven by the goal of selling enough magazines to win the spanking new CCM bicycle complete with hand pump, bell, and carbide light which the local recruiter brought to tantalize us at every sales meeting at the West End YMCA. Later, when we moved from Parkdale to north Toronto, I graduated to the distribution business, the forerunner of today's courier industry. By this time I had acquired a beat-up bicycle from my brother Bert and was able to offer my services, for a fee, delivering bread and cakes for a local mom-and-pop storefront bakery run by a lovely Scottish couple. I worked during school lunch period, from twelve noon to one, and from four to six in the evening, plus all day Saturday, for two dollars a week and all the stale cakes I could eat or take home on Mondays. The bakery, the Broadway Bake Shop, was two doors south of the Broadway Pharmacy on Yonge Street at Broadway. When I learned that the pharmacy needed a delivery boy from five to seven at night, at the premium rate of fifty cents per shift, I acquired a second employer. Since I worked for two stores from five to six, the pressure was great but the rewards handsome. I don't know if the bake shop ever knew I was double dipping, nor did the pharmacy care as long as I did what I was paid for.

In 1937, when I was sixteen, one of my equally delinquent friends told me of a great career opportunity at Columbia Pictures. With a wealth of experience in publication and distribution under my belt, I took advantage of my parents' absence — they were visiting New York at the time, an indication, perhaps, that by now our family's economic fortunes had improved somewhat — to quit school (sixteen was the minimum school-leaving age) and apply to Columbia Pictures. I was accepted as an office boy, responsible for the distribution of posters, the running of errands, and assorted odd jobs, with a salary of $6 for a five-and-a-half-day week. When my parents learned what I had done, they were deeply disappointed — but not furious. They had come to the realization by now that, while I had considerable potential, I was not likely to realize it academically. In any event, I was now able to contribute $1.50 weekly to the family income.

Columbia Pictures of Canada was located on Dundas Square in the downtown area. It was not a producer of anything, but its owners, the

Allen brothers, had distribution rights in Canada for Columbia movies and also owned a chain of movie theatres in Ontario. Jay and his brothers Herb and Jules were benevolent employers and after several months I was summoned to a convocation of the brothers to be told by this august panel that they had decided that I had performed well and was to receive a raise of $1, making my income $7 a week — and this even without a high school degree! I was on my way. Of the Allens, I remember one habit of Jay's (he was known as "J.J.") that amazed me at the time and still does. As a sideline, J.J., the elder of the brothers, imported Alexander Stewarts Cream of Barley, Scotch Whiskey, which was largely consumed by J.J. himself. First thing each morning he trotted off to the men's lavatory with a bottle of Cream of Barley in one hand and a thermos pitcher of water in the other, and he remained there until both were empty. He then went back to his office where he always had a generous booze supply and his secretary kept him supplied with pitchers of water for the balance of the day. I can't recall if, when, and how he got home — though I think he had a chauffeur-driven car, perhaps a Cadillac, Packard, or Pierce-Arrow — but you could be sure that he would be trotting off to the lavatory at nine the next morning with his Cream of Barley in one hand and water thermos in the other.

While Columbia Pictures was my first success, I soon grew eager for greater challenges. Word of my restlessness, to say nothing of my exceptional talents, leaked to Twentieth Century Theatres, located directly above Columbia in the same building. Its president, Nat Taylor, who was at the beginning of an outstanding career in the film industry, offered me as much money as I was making at Columbia but with the added potential of being associated with a rapidly growing organization. This got me back into the area of the publication business on which I had cut my teeth — selling newspapers. It was part of my job to place the newspaper advertisements for the daily column listing each of the Twentieth Century Theatres and the movies they were showing. They were all double-bills, which was taken for granted at the time. Some had air-conditioning, which was always noted in the ads in the summer since many people went to the theatre just to cool off, in spite of the trash that was on the screen. The titles and times of the showings were, of course, critically important; there was no room for error, as I would soon find out.

At that time, Twentieth Century Theatres was essentially a cooperative, which pooled the resources of many individual theatre owners and was led, for a fee, by Nat Taylor. The daily listings were crucial to attendance and box-office receipts, and the owners were not appreciative of my creative use of typefaces such as Newman Outline or Norfolk Bold when these made the notice more difficult to read or the listing ahead or below theirs more prominent. Cultural sensitivity was not their strong suit, yet they tolerated my creative efforts as long as the pictures, times, and air-conditioning specifications were correct. Gradually, I began to give the artistic side of my job more attention, and then the inevitable happened. One day I got the Roxy pictures listed under the Gem heading (short theatre names were essential to reduce the cost of electric marquee signs) and the owners of both theatres landed on me like a ton of bricks — and on Nat Taylor for putting up with me. The owners of the Roxy and the Gem were brothers-in-law, but they hated each other with a passion; they were direct competitors whose theatres were part of the estate of their late father-in-law, and each had a wife who thought that the other sister had acquired the better theatre even though she had married a jerk. Summoned to Nat Taylor's office, I remember virtually sinking through the floor. I'm not sure if he fired me or if I saved him the embarrassment by tendering my resignation, but the result was the same: I was out of a job. Subsequently, Twentieth Century Theatres, even without my talents, grew from success to success and Nat Taylor became a very rich man.

But printers' ink was in my blood and I soon found myself employed by Traders Printing Company marketing direct mail and other printed advertising. I joined the Young Men's Advertising and Sales Club to satisfy my creative urges while expanding my knowledge and contacts in this exciting field. It's true that I didn't exactly corner the market and had to make ends meet with orders for letterheads, envelopes, business cards, labels, and cheap flyers, but I never lost my passion and I was making twelve dollars a week. Somehow Bert Foster of H.B. Foster Printing heard of this bright star on the printing horizon and offered me eighteen dollars a week plus commission. I soon realized that Bert had trouble putting together eighteen dollars a week and that his major customer was his brother-in-law, Albert, who ran a hardware store. Bert printed cheap flyers for Albert's hardware that were distributed door to door by the willing hands available in those Depression years at twenty-five cents an hour, though many of them disappeared down sewers courtesy of less noble distributors.

It was then that a new and challenging opportunity presented itself. War!

Rifleman Danson

Towards the end of 1938, it increasingly appeared to me that war was likely and that I, seventeen years old at the time, would be a participant. My brothers felt the same way, and while I would join the army, they opted for the air force. My parents must have been deeply worried about having their three sons in the military, but they never communicated their anxiety to us. On the contrary, I sensed their pride. After all, as Jews, we were acutely sensitive to the danger posed by Hitler. He had to be stopped.

To get a head start on a military career, I decided to join the militia. My closest friend, Freddy Harris, and I enlisted in the Queen's Own Rifles of Canada in December 1938 but I could not be officially sworn in as a rifleman (the Queen's Own term for private) until my eighteenth birthday, on 8 February 1939. To kids like us, militia service offered lots of excitement, with parades and training every Wednesday plus extra training and lectures on Mondays and sometimes weekends. In addition, there was a week at the military camp in Niagara-on-the-Lake. I remember an interesting character, named Cuthbert, who rose to corporal in our company even though he clearly didn't fit. He was an Englishman, close to sixty years of age, and, at six feet tall, an imposing figure, with an impressive grey handlebar moustache and a wide-brimmed hat that he wore at a rakish angle. I never could figure out what he was doing with us youngsters in the Queen's Own; from his appearance and bearing, he could have been a retired colonel of the Indian army. He tried to enlist for overseas when we were mobilized in 1940 but was immediately rejected. Later, when training in Sussex, New Brunswick, prior to going overseas, we read in the Toronto newspapers that he had dropped dead suddenly in a drugstore on Toronto's

Sherbourne St and that his name wasn't Cuthbert after all; he was from an upper-class British family and his mother was an acquaintance of Lady Aberdeen, wife of the governor general of Canada, who in the end saved him from the noose after he had committed a murder in Quebec's Eastern Townships and been jailed. He had served the longest term of life imprisonment on record before his ultimate release and enlistment in the Queen's Own.

Cuthbert aside, the most interesting thing I remember about my militia years was the royal visit of 1939, when the Queen's Own provided the guard of honour to greet King George VI and Queen Elizabeth at Union Station, Toronto, on May 22nd. Militia regiments were pretty thin in those days but we compensated for our limited numbers and sparse, antiquated First World War equipment with our dedication and enthusiasm. Major Bill Bryant, the officer commanding B Company, was to command the guard, while Edward Dunlop and Charles Dalton were its junior officers, or, as they were properly called, subalterns. (Dunlop was to be awarded the George Medal for his gallantry in saving the lives of many of his soldiers, and, after being blinded in a wartime-training accident in Scotland, was to become a minister in the Ontario government. Dalton was to win a DSO for his leadership on D-Day, and he later became the president of Carling Brewery.) Some thought that this was because they were the best officers, others alleged that it was because they looked the most elegant, and others said that it was because they were the only ones able to afford the full-dress uniforms — or borrow enough parts to make their uniforms complete. Perhaps the truth consisted of a bit of each theory. Sergeant-Major Art Freeman of the Royal Canadian Regiment (RCR), from the minuscule permanent force that was Canada's regular army establishment in 1939, was charged with whipping us into shape. Although I was a relatively green recruit, I was chosen to serve in this "elite" guard. Sad to say, in those days we had a very limited number of full-dress green uniforms, bearskin busbies, and black-leather gaiters. Positions on the guard thus went to those who could be fitted into what was available in the way of uniforms. Another important qualification was to own a decent pair of black boots, since they were not issued in those days and every recruit had to supply his own. Fortunately, I had picked up a pair almost like new from one of the better pawn shops on York Street, the "hock shop" centre of those days where you could buy a full set of First World War medals for the price of a few beers.

One had to see or smell our uniforms to believe them. They had been in mothballs since the time Sir Henry Pellatt took the regiment to England in 1911. Some hardy moths had already done their dirty work — the thread was bare — and many mothers, wives, or girlfriends spent hours stitching and darning them until they were more or less fit to be worn, or worn to be fit. Proudly, we went on our first "green" parade at the old University Avenue Armouries and it was painfully obvious that the years of storage and mildew had caused the uniforms to fade to different shades of green. Fortunately, the regiment was blessed with a distinguished officer, Roger Clarkson, whose family happened to own Parkers Dye Works and who went to work getting the uniforms all one colour and back to us before the arrival of the king and queen.

We trained night after night and on weekends. Sergeant-Major Freeman persisted with incredible patience, and Major Bryant managed to keep his blood pressure below critical levels. Finally, the big day arrived. At this time, normal militia dress was First World War khaki uniforms with "puttees" — leggings designed to test a person's skill as a contortionist and also to develop skills in bandaging casualties or preparing mummies for internment. We were required to wear these khaki uniforms to Union Station, carrying our carefully cleaned, dyed-green uniforms so that they would not be endangered as we travelled on foot or, if we had the seven-cent fare in those years (three cents if you were short enough to qualify for children's fare), by streetcar. On arrival at Union Station, we changed into our "greens" in the Oak Room and formed up outside the station. Through an unforgettable series of precise manoeuvres, which we proceeded to forget, we ended up as a properly sized guard — seven-cent fares on either end tapering to three-cent fares in the centre. We stood for what seemed hours, just in case the royal train arrived early, but through it all we maintained our proud — if a bit self-conscious — posture, basking in the glory of the occasion as thousands of curious and loyal citizens crowded the area and people peering out of every window of the Royal York Hotel examined us with awe. Sergeant-Major Freeman, in contrast, observed us with apprehension.

When their majesties, accompanied by Prime Minister Mackenzie King, emerged from the station, a hush came over the crowd and Major Bryant brought us to attention and gave the command, "Queen's Own Rifles of Canada Guard of Honour — Royal Salute — Present Arms!" The band played the royal anthem and the king inspected our two ranks while the queen and prime minister looked on. We were nervous kids, but proud ones. The royal couple and prime minister then drove off to the other ceremonies that crammed their schedule, and we were marched back into the Oak Room, where we changed into our khakis. This task accomplished, we were rushed up to the Parliament Buildings at Queen's Park to be ready for the arrival of their majesties. Rigidly at attention, anticipating another glimpse of the king and queen, and they of us, we were astonished to find that a mounted escort of the Royal Canadian Dragoons and the Governor General's Horse Guards had placed itself in front of us (backsides facing us); loyally and obediently we presented arms and the horses proceeded to respond rudely to the excitement of the moment. Once the king and queen were safely in the legislature, we marched down University Avenue and then lined the streets outside the Toronto General Hospital. The royal cavalcade, after leaving Queen's Park, drove past the adoring throngs crowding the tree-lined boulevard and we presented arms for the third time that day. The mounted cavalry escort, fortunately, passed at right angles to us and so we were spared any further indignity.

Next we went to St Catharines and Niagara Falls by train, lined more streets, and presented arms time and again as the king and queen travelled from place to place. What a few days! We formed guards and presented arms at numerous locations. The king, who would not have noticed the same faces everywhere he went, was so encouraged by the size of his forces in Canada that he declared war three months later. Perhaps the most moving moment occurred on the Rainbow Bridge, crossing the Niagara River to the United States. We were the last Canadians to present arms as their majesties left our country on the royal train, en route to Washington and a meeting with President Franklin Roosevelt, and like others, I placed a quarter on the track to have it flattened by the weight of the train. That twenty-five-cent piece stayed in my money belt throughout the war and was truly a lucky charm.

It was Sunday, 3 September 1939, when Britain declared war on Germany and Freddy and I expected that the Queen's Own would be mobilized within a few days. I couldn't wait until Monday so I could buy a supply of jockey shorts and socks, certain that the army would not provide us with such clothing in sufficient quantity. But something went wrong at National Defence Headquarters, for the First and Second Canadian Divisions were raised without the Queen's Own. We were devastated but knew that the military brass would have to call on us within a few days or so. When weeks stretched into months, I thought that the war would pass me by and hitchhiked to London, Ontario, to enlist in the RCR, a permanent-force regiment that was headquartered there in Wolseley Barracks. The RCR was part of the First Division and had provided the instructional cadre responsible for basic training in the militia. Major "China" Nielson, who was commanding the regimental depot in London, gently informed me that they were not recruiting reinforcements at that time. I next tried the Royal Canadian Air Force, which gave me the same answer but put me on a waiting list. Not deterred, and unknown to our family and friends, Freddy Harris and I joined a group who were planning to go to the assistance of the Finnish army, then engaged in war with our future Soviet allies. Ten days before we were to sail for Finland, the Finnish-Soviet war ended and only then did I break the news to my horrified parents. I received a warm, patriotic letter from our commander, Lieutenant-Colonel Fraser Hunter, and a ten-dollar cash gratuity.

In June 1940 the Queen's Own finally mobilized as part of the Third Canadian Infantry Division, almost exactly four years before its D-Day assault on the Normandy beach at Bernièrs-sur-Mer, where Freddy Harris was to die. I became B63591 Danson, Rifleman B.J., the 91st soldier to enlist in the regiment in the Second World War. We were then off to Camp Borden, where we were put in tents with eight or ten men in each. It was rather cosy, as we curled up on ground sheets on the flea-ridden sand, but the accommodation and food were better than what some of my tent-mates had known in civilian life during the Depression. In short order I was elevated to the rank of corporal and sent on a small-arms course at Connaught Ranges near Ottawa. There, I was introduced to the Bren gun, a Czechoslovak-designed light-machine gun that was replacing the First World War Lewis gun as the mainstay of the British, and thus Canadian, infantry. It was some time before there was sufficient supply of Bren guns to equip the battalion but they served us well for the rest of the war.

Before our course was completed, we were recalled to Camp Borden because the regiment had been posted overseas. Where, we did not know. There were rumours galore, but our destination turned out to be Newfoundland, a British colony not yet part of Canada and thus qualifying us for the maple-leaf clasp on our not-yet-issued Canadian Volunteer Service Medal. It was the first decoration for most of us; the exceptions were the fairly numerous First World War veterans still young enough, or able to look young enough, to enlist, but few of these lasted through the training prior to D-Day. Our mission was to protect the transatlantic sea-plane base in Botwood and the huge new airbase at Gander, which was the major staging area for flights to the United Kingdom and boasted the world's longest runway (it was also the home of a pig farmer named Joey Smallwood). Eventually, the regiment was moved to Sussex, New Brunswick, where we joined the Régiment de la Chaudière from Quebec and the North Shore New Brunswick Regiment to form the 8th Brigade of the 3rd Canadian Infantry Division and undergo further training. The Royal Rifles of Canada from Quebec City replaced us in Newfoundland. When in England we learned that this regiment was assigned to Hong Kong, we were envious; little did we know then of the fate that was to await these men, along with those of the Winnipeg Grenadiers, when Hong Kong fell to the Japanese on Christmas Day, 1941.

Earlier I explained that one of the best features of my wartime experience was the opportunity it gave me to meet men from all parts of the country and from a wide range of cultural and socio-economic backgrounds. In this mix, I found some unique "characters," more than a few of whom became good friends of mine during the course of training and overseas service.

One of my most fascinating friends was Harry Brown, who had joined the Queen's Own after his most recent career as a bellhop at the King Edward Hotel in Toronto, where he supplemented his meagre tips by some discreet bootlegging and pimping. He always took cash for the booze but frequently accepted payment from his girls in trade. Harry was a wise, thoughtful, and generous friend who was older than most of us. Not particularly good looking, he had only a few good teeth left, but when going on leave he put in his prized set of false teeth. We hardly recognized him; he appeared to have a permanent smile.

Memorable, too, was Harry's close buddy, George Wishart, a chartered accountant from the prestigious firm of Price Waterhouse. George's problem was that he probably enlisted in a semi-drunken state after a highly liquid lunch, but it was a state that he rarely emerged from. He was highly intelligent and, in spite of his alcoholism, highly regarded by his superiors and comrades. His talents were so evident that the army took the risk of sending him for officer training, and he somehow finished the course and was commissioned as a lieutenant. But his change of fortune didn't last long — the booze had too strong a hold on him. He took a fall down a long staircase in an English country home that would have killed him had he been sober. His totally relaxed state saved his life but ended his army career. George died not long after the war while working for an American oil company in the Philippines. It is unlikely that they needed to embalm him. Too bad we didn't know in those days about AA (Alcoholics Anonymous), through which such exceptional talents as his can be saved.

One of the sweetest people in the regiment was David Giffen, an executive from Dominion Securities, a bachelor who, at forty, was at the very top end of the age scale. A quiet-spoken, thoughtful person, respected by all, he reached the rank of company sergeant major and certainly would have been commissioned had he been younger. Too old for infantry battle, he was sent to Italy as an administrator but refused any attempt for a soft spot and a ticket home. He died in Toronto at age ninety-six. I gave the eulogy in the church in which he had been active since the war to an astounded congregation who had no knowledge of his quite remarkable war experience. David never married, a fact that may have contributed to his longevity.

The most pungent characters I knew were two men who volunteered for the little-sought-after job of carting the pails of their latrine produce and that of their comrades to a truck that took it to some far away, leeward location which we never attempted to locate. They were the closest of friends, in their badly stained and greasy fatigue uniforms, probably because no one else would go near them. In the mess hut they sat in splendid isolation, smugly satisfied with a job that took only two or three hours a day. "Shit House" McCord and "Honey Wagon" Hurst — we never knew their first names — played a critical role in wartime, and I often wonder what career paths they followed in peacetime and what stories of their war experiences they told their grandchildren. I am certain, however, that if any of us recognized one of them on the street today, we would greet them with "Hi, Shit House" or "Hi, Honey Wagon." We would be happy to see them even if we wouldn't shake hands.

These were some of the Queen's Own men who, at long last, left for England in July 1941 in a troop convoy from Halifax. We were escorted by several British battleships, cruisers, and a mass of destroyers, including what appeared to be a full horizon of First World War American four-stacker destroyers given to the British in exchange for permanent U.S. bases from Newfoundland to the Caribbean. In spite of rumours of lurking U-boats, it was a rather uneventful crossing, although we were jammed in like sardines. With us were many American civilians bound for Ireland to build air bases, and together we became players in truly the largest floating crap game ever assembled. The worst gambling loss in my whole life occurred when, with all my money exhausted, I threw in a treasured Smith and Wesson revolver won in an earlier game in Sussex. I never saw it again. Disembarking at Greenock, Scotland, we were loaded on trains for Aldershot, the huge British garrison complex built in the Crimean and Boer wars. Aldershot became our first home prior to a series of muddy tent or nissen hut encampments in the south of England. Training was continuous but included generous leave privileges with free-travel warrants to anywhere in England, Scotland, or Wales. You could go to Ireland only if you had close family there.

As soon as we were given leave, Freddy Harris and I went to London, arriving at Waterloo station and taking the Underground to Trafalgar Square. We emerged from "the tube" and gazed in absolute wonder at Nelson's Column, the National Gallery, Admiralty Gate, St Martin's-in-the-Field, and Canada House. We were awe-struck kids standing in the centre of the British Empire, if not the world, as we perceived it. After the usual ritual of having our tin-type photographs taken while feeding the pigeons — to send to our parents — we started to look for accommodation. Down the Strand we found the Savoy and thought this appropriate and deserving after all the spartan military quarters we had endured; however, we soon learned that the Savoy rates were geared more to generals than to two Canadian corporals. The clerk gently directed us across the Strand to the Strand Palace, still pretty heady stuff for us and costing an exorbitant ten shillings and sixpence a night, with breakfast, equivalent then to about two dollars and fifty cents Canadian, close to two days' pay. After some soul searching we decided, "To hell with it, we only live once," an attitude that was to prevail throughout the war.

When on leave, as we could get a free railway pass to any place in Britain, we always signed on for Scotland. Staying in London until our money was almost exhausted, we then checked in at the Overseas League Club to find gratis accommodation in Glasgow, Edinburgh, or Aberdeen homes with warm Scottish hosts and a full range of pubs. On some occasions, Freddy and I would go right to Scotland and actually stay in hotels, which provided more opportunity to stalk the lassies. Once, in Edinburgh, I felt it really unfair to have to go back to Aldershot when my leave expired Saturday midnight, particularly since I had a delightful Aberdonian lass as company. By split-second timing, I could have another night in Edinburgh, catch the last connecting last train in London, and be back in barracks on time. If my timing didn't work, of course, I would be in trouble. Freddy was not about to take the risk and went on ahead — but he didn't have a wee Aberdonian.

After overnighting in London's Russell Hotel, with its bomb-blasted, gauze-covered windows and scrawny breakfast sausages, I rushed to Waterloo station to catch the first Aldershot train in the hope that I could sneak into the barracks unnoticed before mandatory church parade. I caught a cab at Aldershot station in the faint chance that I could make it. The taxi driver pulled to a full stop at our B Company parade square in Mandora Barracks as Sergeant Major "Daddy" Hughes, sometimes called "Frosty" since he was not known to smile, was about to march the company off to the battalion's parade square. I'm not quite sure what "Daddy" said, but it was without a smile and it was clear that I was charged with being absent without leave and was to appear before the commanding officer, Colonel Harry MacKendrick, the next morning.

When that dreaded morning came, I was marched to the orderly room and into the CO's exalted presence, fully expecting to be stripped of my corporal's stripes and downgraded to a proud but chastened rifleman. Colonel MacKendrick roared, "Danson, we don't give you two stripes to roam around Scotland drunk" (which I wasn't, part of the time anyway). "But seeing that it was Scotland, I'm going to let you off this time." I swear that he had a big smile on his face as I was briskly marched out.

A sidelight about church parades. Aldershot was well supplied with Anglican and Roman Catholic churches, but in spite of quite a significant number of Jews in the regiment, it was noticeably lacking in synagogues. Though the more pious Jews stayed away from Christian churches, most of us went along with the Anglicans (the regiment always had an Anglican padre, in our case Captain Jack Clough, to whom we were all deeply devoted, as he was to us); the one Roman Catholic officer, Bob Sawyer, slunk off with his R.C. detachment to Mass. For guidance in church, Freddy, who was also Jewish, and I would depend on two close friends, Earl Stoll and Gerry Rayner, who were nominally Anglican or at least Protestant. Soon, Freddy and I became thoroughly familiar, if slightly uncomfortable, with the Book of Common Prayer, which wasn't really common to us at all. We worked our way through the hymns by dropping a few words not applicable to us such as Jesus Christ, Holy Trinity, or Holy Ghost, which I still can't figure out. We had no difficulty whatsoever with the Lord's Prayer. "Holy, Holy, Holy" was fairly easy and became our favourite processional. "Onward Christian Soldiers" left us with little to sing about but we liked the music and, as the entire regiment attacked it with vocal gusto, we joined enthusiastically with our colleagues from the more junior religions, humming the questionable parts and crossing our fingers. The real challenge was the Apostles' Creed. Somehow we managed an editing miracle that we thought maintained our religious integrity while still allowing us to be just two of the boys. When I go to church parades today at our Regimental Anglican Church, St Paul's Bloor Street in Toronto, I just can't believe how ingenious we were, or how we managed to pull it off, but strange things happen in war.

Marriage

Gerry Rayner and Freddy Harris had been guests of the Bull family in Canons Park, just outside London, who, like many English families, opened their homes to overseas troops. Gerry and Freddy told me of their smashing daughter, Isobel, who was a serious musician and aspiring concert pianist. I thought the situation was worthy of further investigation and called the Bulls' home (EDGware 2911), an initial contact that resulted in lunch in London's West End, many more subsequent lunches, dinners, and, ultimately, breakfast.

On Christmas Eve 1942, Isobel and I were staying at the Lambert Arms, a beautiful old country inn at Aston Rowant in Oxfordshire. We had known each other for about six weeks and found ourselves spending as much time together as army leave would allow. I knew that I was to be sent back to Canada for OCTU, the acronym for the Officer Cadet Training Unit, and the thought of parting was a preoccupation of mine. We were walking the country roads when, somewhat conversationally, I asked her if she would like to marry me. She agreed that she would like it indeed. Isobel was twenty and I was twenty-one, quite marriageable ages at that time. When we broke the news to the Averys, the innkeepers at the Lambert Arms, they treated us like part of their family, no doubt because Isobel's father had made our reservations with Mr Avery, whom he knew. This must also have accounted for our rooms being placed inconveniently on separate floors and at opposite ends of the building.

A special Christmas Eve dinner had been planned for the small group of guests and a few local regulars, but nothing like the feast that the Averys now turned out in our honour. For wartime Britain it was astounding — turkeys and hams, roasts, puddings and wines and ciders that we didn't think still existed; the pre-war wine cellar was saved for such occasions and the local farmers did the rest. We phoned Isobel's parents, who, while they knew little of this young Canadian sergeant (I had been promoted from corporal in early 1942), certainly knew their beautiful, strong-willed, and only daughter and so realized that any appeal to good sense, caution, or patience would be futile. They were aware, however, that I would soon be returning to Canada and this would allow for a respectable engagement and cooling-off period. "Cooling off" was to be the operative term, as we were soon to learn.

I returned to my regiment at Wykehurst Park in Sussex, an estate with an impressive manor house, and, according to the required procedure for non-commissioned ranks, sought my commanding officer's permission to marry — and to do it quickly, before I had to return to Canada. Canadian army regulations required a six months' waiting or cooling-off period after permission had been granted before the marriage could take place. This was the result of too many hasty marriages with unpleasant consequences; indeed, there was a story around the Canadian army of a soldier who, after a rather wild, alcoholic few days on leave in London, awakened one morning to find a strange, tarty looking woman in bed with him. "Who in hell are you?" he asked. "I'm your wife, dearie. Don't you remember?" The cooling-off period was certainly justified to avoid such events, but surely not for cases of pure young love, such as ours. I felt that my commanding officer, now Colonel "Jock" Spragge, who was really "Mr Queen's Own" of the Second World War, would understand my special circumstances and waive the six-month requirement for me. He was not about to do any such thing. Though he was a very much beloved commander, and though he was as concerned about my situation as any parent might be, he had a job to do and he was going to make certain that I was not rushing into marriage "half-cocked," if that is an appropriate term to use in the circumstances. On the contrary, he thought it best for me to go back to Canada, get my commission, and return to England, at which time, if our love was still strong, we could then get married. In any event, he explained, only the brigade commander had the authority to waive the waiting period.

Stunned and deeply dejected, I slunk out of the orderly room in the manor house of Wykehurst Park. I was soon to be shipped off to the appropriately named "Non-effective Transport Depot" (NETD), meaning that I would be in a state of limbo reserved for men who had been taken off the strength of the Canadian army overseas and not yet taken on the strength of the army in Canada. Just after bidding my sad farewells to Isobel, the two of us having given up hope of an early marriage, I learned to my surprise that the adjutant of NETD was an old friend from Oakville, Lieutenant Pat Blackham of the Lorne Scots, who, like so many friends of that period, was later to die in action. As Pat and I renewed our acquaintance, I told him the tragic tale of my non-marriage. Pat had none of the responsibility of Jock Spragge, but he was a sympathetic friend who knew the system. He said that he thought he might be able to arrange a meeting, or more properly an audience, for me with the brigade commander, Brigadier Kenneth Blackader of the Black Watch. He picked up the phone, got through to the staff captain, and set up a meeting for me with the brigadier. The meeting was on. Pat gave me a forty-eight-hour pass and map coordinates for brigade headquarters (but no actual map).

I knew that the brigade headquarters was near the town of Hassocks, north of Brighton, where the Queen's Own had recently been stationed. I was confident that if I got myself to Hassocks on time I would find the brigadier. The greater problem was that we were not on a direct rail line to Brighton. This meant that I would have to take a train up to London, change railway stations, and then get a Brighton line train, all of which would make it virtually impossible to be on time for my audience. Determined to give it my best shot, however, I started hitchhiking in the direction of the Brighton line and was shortly picked up by a Canadian staff car with a lieutenant passenger, to whom, in my enthusiasm, I recited the critical nature and timing of my mission as well as other things that, as it turned out, I shouldn't have. When the officer had taken me as far as he could, I was about to express my thanks when he interrupted me, letting it be known that he was the district intelligence officer and that, in my enthusiasm, I had committed several security breaches. I had told him that Canadian NCOs were being returned to Canada for officer training, that a troopship was sailing in forty-eight hours, and that the future Canadian officers at NETD were being marshalled in the Devil's Punch Bowl near Hindhead. I also pinpointed the 8th Brigade headquarters. I don't recall all the other breaches of security he enumerated as my mind whirled with thoughts of no possible marriage, no commission, and maybe a reduction in rank. But the lieutenant said that he would not report the incident. I don't know who he was, but I have reason to be eternally grateful to him.

I finally landed in Hassocks and found the orderly room of the North Shore Regiment, which, along with La Régiment de la Chaudière and us, the Queen's Own Rifles, comprised the infantry of the 8th Brigade. I spoke with a sympathetic provost sergeant, almost a contradiction in terms, who had a jeep and knew where Brigade HQ was located and offered me a lift. At Brigade HQ, I was quickly ushered into the presence of Brigadier Blackader, an imposing man who intimidated me as a mere sergeant, some ten ranks lower on the scale. He listened to my story but was obviously not to be easily swayed. Meanwhile, brigade business carried on. Staff officers came and went delivering messages and receiving orders while the brigadier continued a civilized conversation with me. After a really quite unbelievable amount of time for a brigadier to give to a sergeant, he observed that I was the most persistent sergeant he had ever encountered. He gave me my permission to marry and properly documented this, noting that I was on embarkation leave, a critical proviso. Smiling broadly and saluting smartly, I rushed to a pay telephone box in the centre of Hassocks to phone London. Isobel answered and was amazed to find me still in England instead of on the high seas dodging German U-boats on my way back to Canada. Explaining my situation, actually *our* situation, I told her to be ready to get married at the closest Registry Office the next morning. I said that I would get the next train for London, reserve a room for our one-night honeymoon at the Cumberland Hotel at Marble Arch, and be at her home as soon as possible.

All of this was somewhat presumptuous since her parents were at the theatre, and I had no assurance that I could get a room at the Cumberland, or, for that matter, in all of London. Most important was the small matter of the registry office. I knew that I had to get a marriage licence and that the British had their own forty-eight-hour cooling-off period after the licence was issued, unless the banns had been read in a church for two or three Sundays running, a condition from which I was disqualified on several counts. There was, however, another exception for which, thanks to Brigadier Blackader, I was clearly qualified: this was for a serviceman on embarkation leave.

I got up to Waterloo Station, took the underground to Marble Arch, and confronted the receptionist at the Cumberland, who said that I was a bloody idiot to think that I could just walk in and demand a room for the next night. I continued my pleading and, with the incredible good luck that had followed me in the past several hours, the manager appeared and intervened. I explained my desperation and showed him my pass for embarkation leave and the brigadier's permission to marry. He was impressed. A room would be mine — or better still, ours! He agreed that we should have a double bed and assured me of the ultimate luxury, a private bathroom. It was then to the Underground for the trip to Isobel's in Canons Park, where I arrived in a spirit of joy and no small passion just as her parents returned from town. They were amazing in their acceptance of this bizarre situation and my father-in-law-to-be was determined to mount a proper wedding feast for his only daughter. Or the best feast he could manage in wartime London with virtually no advance notice. He proceeded to make arrangements at Odinino's in the Hotel Piccadilly for a yet-to-be determined number of people, assuming that we could get the Registry Office into line when it opened for business in the morning.

Family was rounded up and everyone agreed to attend except Isobel's maternal grandfather, a deeply Orthodox Jew, on the grounds that he couldn't travel on the Sabbath and, besides, Jewish marriages could not take place on Saturday. I really don't think he approved of me in any case; I didn't speak Yiddish, which meant to him that I was virtually mute, I didn't wear a yarmulke, and my family belonged to some crackpot Reform Jewish sect quite beyond his comprehension and in a city he never heard of. But he had his principles, which his wife and the whole family lovingly tolerated. Grandma Cohen, the dignified matriarch, practised her religion by her conduct. She saw her granddaughter's marriage as a happy religious and personal occasion that, because of the circumstances of war, could take place only on this particular Sabbath or possibly not at all. She would be there. Grandfather Bull, who really liked weddings, and who, in his eighties, was recovering from his third and contemplating his fourth marriage, had no inhibitions.

Arrangements complete, we went to our respective beds with everyone committed to a ten-thirty wedding the next morning — 6 February 1943 — at Burnt Oak Registry Office in Hendon. Everyone, that is, except the registrar. For the last time I shared a bedroom with my brother-in-law-to-be, John Bull, who in future years was to be lord mayor of Westminster. Next morning, I left the house in time to be at the Registry

Office at nine o'clock so that there would be lots of time to complete the formalities with the registrar and be ready for the arrival of bride, family, and friends at ten-thirty. As it turned out, however, the registrar was not about to be pressed into performing any hasty marriage. I showed him the vital documents and reminded him that the cooling-off period could be waived for a soldier on embarkation leave, which I clearly was. He insisted that embarkation leave was for British servicemen going off to fight the Hun, not for colonials going home to become officers. I don't know if it was the case I made or the attraction of the £2 10s. fee that accounted for his change of heart, but in any event he agreed to backdate the marriage licence by forty-eight hours. I phoned Isobel and the marriage party started to move, converging on the Registry Office at ten-thirty from all parts of London. The party included my best man, Albert Glazer, a family friend from Toronto who, as a flight lieutenant, had just returned from Malta to be invested with a DFC by the king.

Isobel was radiant in her green, fur-trimmed wedding suit. I don't recall a single thing about the perfunctory ceremony except that, instead of "until death do thee part," it ended with "two pounds ten, sergeant." Only then did the registrar allow me to kiss the bride. The lunch at Odinino's was excellent, I guess. Everyone else seemed to be having a wonderful time as the minutes of my leave, and the time allotted for our honeymoon, slipped away. Mr Bull sensed my unease, if not raw panic, although I'm not sure that Isobel didn't kick him under the table. In any case, we were excused and said our joyful and tearful goodbyes. By dead reckoning and with incredible speed, we found our way to the double-bedded room with bath at the Cumberland.

Early on Sunday morning Isobel saw me off at Waterloo Station. It was dawn and she was a beautiful but very sad-looking bride about to take the lonely tube home. As things stood, we were not to see each other again until I returned many months later as a newly minted lieutenant. But that didn't take Pat Blackham and my incredible luck into account. Bound and determined to get Isobel to Canada, I again turned to Pat and he again rose to the occasion, getting me a twenty-four-hour pass, beginning at midnight, which gave me a breathing space of several hours. The most important thing I then had to do was to get Isobel's immigration papers for Canada and at least a place on the waiting list of war brides seeking a berth on a troopship returning to Canada. So back to London and a once more surprised bride. At least I didn't have to worry about a hotel room. I had legal and enjoyable access to the Bull home and all the comforts acquired through the family's ration books and through my mother-in-law's ingratiating herself for the past several years with the local greengrocer, butcher, and fishmonger.

We completed all necessary procedures with Canadian immigration authorities but I still had to get Isobel on a ship so that we could have some time in Canada together before I was commissioned and shipped back to England in time for the invasion of the continent. I also thought it important for Isobel to meet my family, who were in a state ranging from blissful ignorance to terrifying conjecture and raw panic; their sole information about me was derived from months of old letters which still had not clearly indicated the transition from a wide range of English beauties to Isobel totally and irrevocably.

I needed the complete support of the authorities and this could best be assured by setting into action "The Black Network," the excellent group of Queen's Own officers who had been insinuated into key positions in the Canadian army and even in Eisenhower's Allied military headquarters in Grosvenor Square. This unique and unofficial force could accomplish wonders on behalf of the regiment or its members and would stop at nothing short of collaborating with the enemy. The fastest entry into the network was through Canadian Military Headquarters, just off Trafalgar Square on Cockspur Street, where the man to see was Colonel Jack Maclean who was military secretary to General H.D.G. Crerar. On my arrival there, the family nature of the regiment was immediately apparent. Jack had somehow guessed that I had been refused permission for marriage and he was fearful that I had gone off on my own. I filled him in on subsequent events, which gave him some peace of mind, and he assured me that he would do what he could. I suspect that Jack Maclean and Brigadier Blackader had consulted with Jock Spragge who, by then, had given up hope of knocking some sense into me.

It seemed just plain stupid to get back to NETD for midnight when I could spend another precious night with my bride and be up early enough to catch a train that should get me back to camp before morning parade. When I did arrive, everyone was loaded with full kit and clambering into vehicles to get us to the train for the ship at Greenock. We were to guard a large number of prisoners from the Afrika Corps Wehrmacht who would be spending the balance of the war in Canadian prisoner-of-war camps. Had I been half an hour later I would have really missed the boat. As we departed NETD, I caught a glimpse of Pat Blackham shaking his head and with a big smile on his face. It was the last time I would see him.

To Canada and Back

Isobel arrived in New York some six weeks later, towards the end of March on the newly christened *Empress of Scotland*, the former and quickly renamed *Empress of Japan*, which was bringing British airmen to Canada for flight crew training under the Commonwealth Air Training scheme. On special three-day leave from the Officer Cadet Training Unit in Trois-Rivières, Quebec, I met her train in Toronto with my family. Isobel was radiant in her very English tweed suit and a saucy beret that highlighted her sparkling green eyes and peaches-and-cream complexion. She captivated us all — and still does. Our time in Toronto was short, though, because we had to get to Trois-Rivières. Accommodation there was scarce, but I had arranged for a room in the home of Madame Le Brun at 181 rue Bonaventure, where several of my friends and their new wives were staying. The rooms were spacious and joined by double French doors. In order to rent each room separately, Madame Le Brun had the doors removed and replaced with plywood partitions. She had the beds placed with their heads snug to the plywood. Not very private, nor very quiet. Not much sleep either, or any complaints.

I graduated in May 1943 and "Wee Willie Mathers," the commanding officer who to his face was Lieutenant-Colonel Mathers or "Sir," requested (that is, commanded) me to stay on staff as an instructor of cadets aspiring to become officers. We shared part of the camp with the Officer's Selection and Appraisal Unit, which assessed candidates for officers' training. The commanding officer of that unit was Brigadier Milton F. Gregg, a VC winner from the First World War and an incredibly fine person to whom the army would assign units that were not functioning to their potential. Milton, as we called him respectfully and affectionately behind his back, in his quiet unassuming way, brought these units to peak efficiency. He did this by sheer force of character. He chose men (it was only men in those days) whom he thought could perform to his standards and gave them direction and a very light rein; then the chosen ones worked their butts off for him. After the war he became the president of the University of New Brunswick, a federal cabinet minister, and a diplomat. He had a great influence on my life, and we maintained a close association until his death in 1977. I was a pallbearer at his funeral in Fredericton and interment near Sussex. (Before he died, I arranged, as minister of national defence, to name the new armoury in Sussex the Milton F. Gregg Armoury.)

In the early fall of 1943 I was chosen to accompany Brigadier Gregg to his new posting as head of the Battle Drill School near Vernon, British Columbia. The school, nestled in the mountains of the spectacular Okanagan valley, was based on the Coldstream Ranch, the former summer home of an earlier governor general, the Earl of Aberdeen. Its purpose was to train men — selected because of their superior ability — in new military techniques of battle drill, with the emphasis on mobility, concentrated firepower, and group initiative. The course lasted about a month, and in the training we simulated battle conditions with live ammunition and explosives. There were a couple of hundred students at any one time.

My time at Vernon was the happiest of my army career. The instructors were mostly in their early twenties, and many of them, like me, had young brides with them. It was a good time, full of very hard work — and just as hard play. We ate like horses and, when we had the opportunity, drank like fish (using the thirteen-ounce liquor rations of the students, who, by the end of each day, were too tired to drink anything stronger than water). I recall especially a raucous party that resulted in our completely wrecking the interior of a log chalet we had built for an officers' mess, just before an unsuspecting Brigadier Gregg arrived at the building with a party of VIPs. He wasn't amused, but he wasn't too hard on us; he just told us that any future parties would have to be held in a three-sided log structure we had built for demonstrations of how to clear a house of enemy troops — at least it would have only three walls to knock down.

Many of us became very close friends, and in my case the closest was Harlan Keely, who was to die, with the Irish Regiment of Canada, just before the end of the war. Another good friend was Don Holmes, who was to command the RCR in Germany after the war and later become a brigadier-general. He was a "real character" whose bluntness and shenanigans likely prevented him from rising higher than he did; as a senior officer in peacetime, he once called Buckingham Palace from Germany asking to speak to the RCR colonel-in-chief, the Duke of Edinburgh; and, on another occasion, four sheets to the wind, he placed a call to Prime Minister John Diefenbaker in the middle of an Ottawa night. A third friend of mine was Austin Delaney. His father was a well-known trade unionist in British Columbia, and Austin himself was very radical politically. When I once asked him if he was a "Commie," he replied, "Absolutely! Other than Joansie [his wife], the Party is my life." Notwithstanding his politics, Delaney became an intelligence officer at British Second Army headquarters.

Though we loved our days in the Okanagan, we became restless as the months passed: the war was elsewhere and we wanted a piece of the action. The brigadier wanted me to stay, but he understood my motivation. However, he explained that as only an acting captain — I had been promoted to this rank at Vernon — I would be required to revert to my permanent rank of lieutenant. I was aware of this and didn't care; it was more important to be part of The Invasion, as we called it, and to be with my regiment and friends. And so on 6 May 1944, the day of the wedding of a fellow instructor, Tom Hughes, and Beverly French, at the French family's ranch with the apple trees in full blossom, Isobel and I moved on to Camp Borden, Ontario, where we stayed only a short few days before heading to Debert, Nova Scotia, a staging camp for shipment overseas. By now Isobel was pregnant, and the two of us took rooms in the house of a veterinarian in nearby Truro where other officers and their wives (either pregnant or nursing their first-born) were also staying. Each night was spent in passionate farewells.

We learned of D-Day at Debert and of our friends who were casualties in the first wave. My best friend, Freddy Harris, was among them; as a sergeant, he had refused an opportunity for officer training for fear of missing out on D-Day. It may sound strange today, but we were almost heartbroken that our regiments and our buddies, who were more like brothers, were in battle without us. We were, however, soon to join them. In late June or early July, after tearful goodbyes to our wives, we were off to Halifax, where we boarded the *Empress of Scotland,* bound for England. Our war was about to begin.

While at the reinforcement centre in Helmsley, Yorkshire, I spent a short leave in London visiting my in-laws before heading to Southampton to rejoin my regiment in Normandy. In early August, we boarded a small, old vessel used in peacetime as an India troopship. Its crew was still Indian — many of them in turbans. The vessel itself had remarkably spacious quarters for officers and, completing the rather surreal atmosphere, there were even servants. After an uneventful voyage in glorious summer weather, we came to shore at a man-made "Mulberry" harbour, at Arromanches, on the French coast, where trucks were waiting to transport us to our units. I was astonished to see a cousin of mine, Mel Rashkis, on one of the trucks, and I rode with him through a devastated Caen and surrounding countryside to my regiment north of Falaise. The stink of war was heavy in the air. I soon caught up with the Queen's Own and those of my friends who had survived the early battles. It was then that I learned of the death of Gerry Rayner, the second of our four musketeers after Freddy Harris. At Damblainville, I rejoined my old platoon, and shortly afterwards we were ordered to move to Trun, just east of Falaise, to cut off the German retreat.

What happened next marked the end of my war. As I have already explained, I was in my reverse-slope position at Grande Mesnil, near Trun, when I was hit in the head by something with such force, and with such consequent loss of blood from my mouth and nose, that my strength rapidly drained away and I believed my young life was over. I had been in France for just over a week.

Being Hit

Somehow the bleeding stopped and I was reasonably sure I was still alive since this was nothing like heaven. I tried to figure out what had happened to me. Barely able to move my jaw, I was certain that it was broken. But what upset me more was that I could move my tongue and felt what I believed were the jagged ends of smashed teeth. This was particularly disturbing because I had healthy, strong teeth in which I took pride. The war had struck me a cruel blow: at twenty-three, I would have to wear a bridge.

I'm not sure if it was my stretcher-bearer's or my own fingers that reached into my mouth to withdraw a jagged piece of shrapnel about one inch square. It had evidently hit the edge of my helmet and ricocheted into my left temple, down through the back of my eye, severing the optic nerve, distorting the eyeball like a hard-hit tennis ball, detaching the retina, and lodging in the roof of my mouth between the hard and soft palate. The roof was caved in but my teeth were intact. This made me feel that the reverse-slope tactic had worked, for it had allowed me to get as close to the ground as the buttons on my shirt would allow and to lie on an upward slope. A different angle or a second's delay in putting on my helmet might well have seen the shrapnel move in a fatal angle.

Earl Stoll, the only remaining member of our gang of four, came over to me and, close to tears, said goodbye. And goodbye it was, for we were never to see one another again. I found myself tossed on a stretcher and loaded onto a jeep for evacuation. Someone had thoughtfully thrown my battle-dress jacket on first, with the result that I landed on my glasses and broke the right lens, and it was my right eye that I still had intact. The jeep stopped briefly at Battalion Headquarters, a group of farm buildings then in flames, where the acting commanding officer, Major (later Lieutenant-Colonel) Steve Lett, was replacing the legendary Jock Spragge, who had been given the command of the 9th Brigade. We said our farewells and, to the extent that I was able to communicate, I pledged to return. Steve only smiled and waved me on. It was a pledge I was unable to keep.

As the jeep bounced over the country roads, we had reason to fear that the continuing mortar and artillery fire would land squarely on us, but, mercifully, it didn't. On reaching a Polish field-dressing station — a Polish armoured division was providing our tank support — I was handed a paper cup. Assuming that I was to drink the contents, I proceeded to do just that, and as I did the Poles waved their hands for me to stop and made gargling sounds. But by that time it was too late and I brought up the last few days of compo rations and Calvados, retching miserably.

Even under these circumstances, military paper work had to continue. Each casualty was identified with a shipping tag tied to some part of him. Mine had disappeared and my saviours had to complete a new one. The Poles' lack of facility in English and mine in speaking at all, let alone Polish, led to further confusion, so they worked from my dog-tags, which gave rank, name, and religion (regimental numbers were reserved for non-commissioned ranks). As for religion, in the Canadian army you were either Roman Catholic (R.C.), Church of England (C of E), or United Church (U.C.) or lumped in with all lesser religions under "O.D." (Other Denominations). For Jews, the practice of leaving their religion unspecified made sense, protecting them from the possibility of mistreatment — or worse — in the event of their being taken prisoner, though I never heard of any such cases. In any event, my identification as "O.D." confused the Poles, who thought that it meant Muslim, and to confirm this they used all sorts of sign language, which, they felt, illustrated a Muslim at prayer. Somehow, through my own body language, I got the message through that I was Jewish. Then I had the distinct feeling that "Jewish" had a pejorative connotation for the Poles, who hurriedly packed me into another jeep or ambulance for evacuation to a tented British field hospital in the Bayeaux area.

In the confused atmosphere of this busy hospital, I was stripped of all personal effects, maps, equipment, my precious piece of shrapnel, and a filthy pair of jockey shorts that embarrassed me but no one else. Then some angel of mercy arrived with a tray of food consisting primarily of a big slice of overcooked roast beef, which I declined, not because I preferred my beef medium rare, but because there was no way I could chew it. I use the term angel to describe the unflappable nursing sisters, for, in their blue uniforms with gold buttons and flowing white veils, that is exactly what they looked like. In any case, my grunts and sign language got across the message and the angel said that some gruel or soft-boiled eggs would be coming. Before the eggs arrived, one of the medical staff read my shipping label and was horrified to find that I, an officer, had been placed in an other-ranks ward. They swiftly moved me to a smaller, more peaceful ward where the beds actually had white sheets. Again I was offered overdone roast beef and the same routine ensued. Once more my wait for something I could eat was interrupted so I could be moved to another British tented hospital where they had an eye specialist, who apparently didn't make house calls in the area of Bayeaux.

In this new hospital, I swear that I went through exactly the same routine: other-ranks ward, roast beef, officers' ward, more roast beef, yet no gruel or soft-boiled egg arrived. The British doctor, who wanted to remove the pulp that was my left eye but was restrained by Canadian complaints of unnecessary amputations, had me shipped to still another British hospital where there was a Canadian surgical team — if anyone was to take out my eye, it would be Canadians. There, I may have been delirious but I distinctly recall the same sequence being repeated in every detail — wrong ward, overcooked roast beef and all. But, after two or three days of a diet of strong tea, or, as we called it, Sergeant Major's tea, a Canadian medical team arrived at my bedside. The surgeon was Major "Cam" Gray, who before the war had been a star for the University of Toronto Varsity Blues. Having admired Cam's play in Saturday afternoon games at Varsity Stadium, I was thrilled to have him as my doctor.

While I was a pretty groggy kid, I had no idea that I was now listed as DANGEROUSLY ILL AS A RESULT OF WOUNDS in the telegrams my wife was receiving in Toronto. This was the designation that followed similar telegrams listing me as WOUNDED and then SERIOUSLY WOUNDED and that usually preceded the final telegram to one's widow or Silver Star mother. Ignorant of my somewhat grave condition, I brushed aside Gray's concern with my eye and head to draw his attention to another preoccupation of mine. Before rejoining my platoon, the same platoon of which I had been sergeant, I had spent a night in an abandoned German weapon slit with straw covering its bottom. When I reached my unit, and had walked into a field to relieve myself, I noticed a puffy, pus-running sore on a most delicate area. There was no way that I could have directly contracted any venereal disease except from an infected toilet seat; that excuse was an old dodge and commonly discounted, however, and I feared that if I consulted the medical officer I would be immediately labelled a VD suspect and sent rearwards for intensive, and insensitive, testing. There was no way that I was going to expose myself (no pun intended) to the ignominy of being sent out of battle before I had experienced it and particularly under such questionable circumstances. The sore dried up but its presence persisted and I took this first opportunity in safe Canadian hands to get a diagnosis. Gray and his team broke into laughter and dismissed it as a bite. My first injury by the enemy, evidently, had been caused by a German flea, which did not qualify me for a second "wound stripe" or disability pension.

Having removed my primary anxiety, Gray declined to order the removal of my eye, but he did have me dispatched by air, on a Dakota (DC-3) aircraft stacked with stretchers, to England. Whether from relief, hunger, or exhaustion, I lapsed into unconsciousness for the first time and did not recover until I was being borne into a tented casualty-reception and dispatch centre by the airfield at Swindon. Here I found myself in a production line: stretchers resting on pipes sunk in a concrete floor in neat rows, with doctors, nurses, orderlies, and auxiliary service men and women coming along one after the other and bearing cigarettes, tea, newspapers of the same day, shave (thank goodness), toothbrushes, haircuts, bed bath, bed pans (lovingly nicknamed battleships), and urinals (ducks). Then came the dartboard expert, a British doctor who obviously had trained near a pub with a dartboard. Famous among all who were evacuated through Swindon, he would roll up one of your pyjamas legs, stand back with a hypodermic syringe poised in his raised hand, and let it fly with unerring accuracy and painlessly into the calf of your leg. A bulls-eye every time and the new wonder drug penicillin coursed through your system to attack any lingering germs or infection. Even my fleabite succumbed to this magic mould.

Next thing I knew, I was loaded into a Canadian ambulance with two or three stretchers stacked on each side. We were a sick and sad lot, and no one was in worse shape than a badly wounded German officer whose groans testified to his agony. The driver, a lance corporal, accompanied by an ATS (British Auxiliary Territorial Service) girl in the cab, seemed to take every curve in the narrow English roads with a vengeance and slammed the brakes so that we were tossed about unmercifully. Only the restraining straps kept us on our stretchers. We couldn't wait for the journey to end. The corporal, however, was more interested in his ATS girl than in his miserable and cursing passengers, and he ignored our shouts and kicks on the cab. Not only that, but I doubt whether he passed a single pub without stopping for a pint, leaving us helplessly parked outside. I swore that I was going to have him court-martialled.

Courts martial were forgotten, however, when the corporal's sick and battered charges were delivered to the 1st Canadian Neurological Hospital at Basingstoke (otherwise affectionately known as #1 Canadian Nut House). Colonel Kenneth Bottrell, the senior Canadian neurosurgeon, examined me in this haven of cleanliness and order. He said that I was not to eat since I was being X-rayed and prepared for surgery the next morning, but nothing mattered now. My journey was over. I was between clean sheets and in Canadian hands. I could relax and rest among friends. In the morning I was visited by a nursing sister friend, Eve Ackworth, with whom I had become infatuated when she nursed me following a hernia operation in the Toronto Military Hospital in 1940. If the regiment was your immediate family, the Canadian army was like your extended family in those days. I was always running across someone I knew wherever I was. Eve said that she had just heard that I was in the hospital and had come to say goodbye. When I expressed some concern about her premature prognosis, she told me that I was being moved to 22nd Canadian General Hospital at Bramshot because my X-rays indicated that no surgery was required. My eye could be saved. The holes in my head and roof of my mouth were healing, and while I would never again see out of my left eye, medication and rest would likely see me through. At Bramshot I would have the best eye man in the Canadian army. Delighted at this prospect and revelling in my clean-shaven, antiseptic state, I asked for something to eat. I was brought the most beautiful looking golden soft-boiled eggs I had ever seen. I still salivate when I recall them — my first solid food since my last ill-fated compo lunch a million years ago at Grande Mesnil.

Eventually, I found myself ensconced in a lively ward of badly wounded officers in Bramshot. The eye surgeon, Major Elkington of Victoria, British Columbia, was more than just an excellent doctor. He was a fine man for whom I developed a deep respect and affection. By some quirk of military logic, he was on the staff of Basingstoke, which I had just left, and had to travel to Bramshot to attend to me and any other eye-patients there. But he was my very own doctor in that ward, while the others were assembly-line patients visited each day by a team who seemed to have difficulty keeping track of each patient's particular wounds. "Oh, you're the arm case," they would say to some poor chap who had a leg in a cast or was missing a leg altogether. My head was swathed in bandages and they would say, "Oh, you're the lung case," or "leg case" — it would vary from day to day. When I mumbled that I was Major Elkington's eye-patient, they would move on to the next bed to the young Canadian Scottish officer whose lungs were full of blood which had to be drawn off with a large, mean-looking syringe and a very long ugly needle: a painful process for him and a disturbing one for the rest of us. (This officer, Ken Wardroper, turned up in my life many years later as an External Affairs officer and ultimately our high commissioner to Nigeria.)

Elkington's job was to eliminate any infection in my bad eye and keep it from spreading to my good one. Even though I suffered a severe reaction to the penicillin, to the interest of the medical staff who were just learning about this new mould, I continued on it by having it dropped directly into my eye rather than receiving painful shots in tender places. Painful, because some of it, from Connaught Laboratories in Toronto, was pretty rough stuff. But it worked. Thanks to the treatment and my own excellent physical condition — I was then a young man of twenty-three who had just gone through four years of infantry training, most recently as an instructor at the Battle Drill School in British Columbia where I ran up and down mountains — I was on the mend.

It was while I was at Bramshot that I learned of the death of Earl Stoll. All deaths in war are tragic, but Earl's was especially so — and unnecessary. He had been hit at Boulogne by a shell fragment that tore into his thigh, causing him to bleed profusely and lose consciousness. Later, when he woke up, he found himself in a captured German field hospital; unfortunately, in his delirious state, he didn't realize it was captured, and when night fell he tried to make his escape — only to trip on the guy wire supporting a tent. He was found in the morning of 20 September, having bled to death.

I was lucky. Yet maybe something more than luck was involved. My mother, a deeply religious woman, attributed my survival to "the will of God," the same God who decided that so many of my friends, including my three closest, should die, and the same God who reigned over the dead German soldier for whom I had said a silent prayer as I stood over his grotesquely bloated stinking corpse in the hot August sun in a Normandy wheat field just a few days earlier. His emptied wallet laid by him, with family pictures scattered on the ground, and a mass of flies buzzed around each exposed orifice — eyes, ears, nostrils, and mouth. But, in spite of this, and in spite of everything else we went through, neither I nor any of my comrades were cynical about religion. Indeed, when I once canvassed my platoon to see who wanted a Bible, I found that every single man carried his army-issue Bible in his top left pocket, over his heart, me included. And they did not go unread, nor was prayer a stranger to us. In my own case, I remember that, when told of Earl Stoll's death, I fell to my knees, not a Jewish practice, in the hospital chapel reciting some religious mantra from my childhood as tears streamed down my cheeks. Perhaps we didn't understand God, but we lived with his constant presence, a lifeline to sanity amidst the insanity of war.

Regardless of the reasons for my survival — luck, God, or whatever — survive I did. In December I would be back in Canada with my English war bride and our first son, who had been born in October while I was in hospital. I was returning home a much different person from the young man — a boy, really — who had enlisted with such enthusiasm some five years ago; my youth now seemed so remote as to be part of another age. And the country I was returning to had changed as well. It, and I, would experience even more startling changes in the years ahead.

Chapter Two
Plastics and Politics,
1944–68

I returned to Canada in December 1944 on the newly outfitted hospital ship *Letitia,* which followed a southerly route close to the Azores and Bermuda — enabling us to enjoy the sunshine and to avoid the main shipping lanes and thus the principal U-boat concentrations — before heading north to Halifax. Hospital ships were supposedly immune from enemy attack according to the Geneva Convention but there had been either mistakes or a reported disregard for the rules on occasion. To avoid any confusion, our ship was painted a gleaming white with huge red crosses on the sides and funnels that were floodlit at night. In addition, there were no blackout provisions and so many lights were strung around that the ship resembled a Christmas tree. The objective was to avoid uncertainty in the mind or eyes of any U-boat captain lurking in our way. After years of rigid blackout procedures in England, we had an uneasy feeling, and the off chance that we were being tracked by German submarines, even if they were only "peeping Hermans," did nothing to allay our anxiety. Our uneasiness, however, was eventually overcome by plentiful food and tender loving care by an excellent medical staff, care that included carrying or wheeling us (or at least those who could be moved) up to the deck to bask in the sun. No one was openly concerned about their newly acquired wounds, many of which were amputations.

In Halifax we were loaded into hospital trains for dispatch to our homes (or the hospitals closest to them) across Canada. I was going to my parents' home on Wells Hill Avenue in Toronto, which became something of a transit depot. Isobel and our new baby son, Ken, had been living there since I had returned overseas. My older brother, Bert, was still in England with his war bride, Dot (coincidentally, Isobel's cousin), but they also would be knocking at the door seeking accommodation as soon as the war ended.

The Toronto contingent of the hospital trains arrived in the city in the midst of the heaviest snowstorm in recent memory. Just getting to our house from Union Station was a hazardous adventure. It took days to get traffic back to normal and my kit with all my clothes except those I was wearing did not catch up with me for almost a week, an inconvenience mitigated by the need to stay home in bed with my young bride. While it was not necessary for me to spend any lengthy time in hospital, after some four months of it in England, I did need to visit Christie Street Hospital on a regular basis as an outpatient, and sometimes Chorley Park Hospital (the former lieutenant governor's residence in Rosedale) as well. Fortunately, the Christie Street Hospital, a former factory that had been converted into a veterans' hospital after the First World War, was not far from home. At the same time, I faced a long period of recuperation during which I was required to rest during the day. The only employer I could find who would accommodate such an arrangement was my father.

Insurance Agent

After my father's small chain of clothing stores had gone bankrupt in the Depression, he began a career in the insurance business, working as an agent for Travellers Insurance Company. By the time I returned from the war, he had started his own independent insurance agency, in partnership with his friend Ted Hobson. I went to work for this company, a job I could handle because I had access to a large leather couch in my father's office where I could sleep for one or two hours after lunch, as my recuperation required. My salary was thirty-five dollars a week, the same as I had received as a lieutenant, which I found perfectly adequate. The bonus was a car, a brand new Dodge, which was among the first civilian cars produced after the war. It was an unbelievable luxury after army trucks, tracked Bren-gun carriers, Jeeps, bicycles, motorbikes, and other modes of infantry transportation, most of which was on our feet.

I had not intended to work in the insurance business. As I have already explained, before returning overseas in 1944, Harlan Keely, an officer in the Irish Regiment of Canada, and I had been instructors at the Battle Drill School in Vernon, and we had intended to go into business in the Okanagan valley after the war. Harlan's death in Holland towards the end of the war, however, ended these plans. Back in Toronto in 1945, I still longed for British Columbia, but my options were limited by my need for recuperation. Nevertheless, had Harlan lived, I'm sure that we would have made it to the Okanagan, shaky health or not. I often wonder how my life would have turned out if the universe had unfolded that way.

In any event, my health improved and I became disenchanted with the insurance business. Indeed, I had never been enchanted with it. It was not an exciting process, however necessary, and I found myself seeing big dollar signs attached to people; you looked at them in terms of what they were worth to you, rather than what they meant to you. Furthermore, while everyone was a potential client, few felt a compelling need for your product: an insurance agent, particularly a life-insurance agent, was someone most people wanted to avoid. And, as if all this was not bad enough, non-life, or casualty, insurance — the main part of my father's business — was a cumbersome, old-fashioned process of printing an insurance policy and then adding riders, or endorsements, little pieces of paper stuck to the main policy which largely consisted of exemptions, things that were not insured or limitations on those that were. Most clients didn't bother to read all this small print and, if they did, were thoroughly confused by it. In a word, the industry seemed Dickensian, not part of the modern world at all. All the same, I thought that I might be able to tolerate a career in insurance if there was some sign of progress. Computers were still in the future but IBM punch cards were a step in the right direction. I called on some of the leading and most respected men in the business to try and get a feeling for where the industry was heading. I was received courteously, but with some bewilderment and condescension. These captains of the insurance business thought that everything was just fine the way it was and wondered why anyone would want to improve a perfectly satisfactory process. I decided that this wasn't a business I wanted to be engaged in for the rest of my life.

One of our firm's Toronto clients, Maple Leaf Plastics, a small company of about seventy-five employees located initially on Bloor at Christie Pits and later in Scarborough, was in the fascinating new plastics-moulding business, making a variety of plastic products from dishes and toys to auto accessories. I had known the firm's two owners from my early days in the film business. In 1950 one of the owners, Gus Solway, died suddenly in his mid-thirties, and I was invited to take on his role as sales manager, at a starting salary of around $5,000. I knew absolutely nothing about plastics but was eager to leave insurance behind me. I was also convinced that plastics was the business of the future; the people in the industry were young, enthusiastic, and inquisitive, with a driving sense of purpose and heady optimism about the prospects for this growing and rapidly changing sector. And so I jumped at the opportunity. In short order I realized that, while I wasn't a particularly technical person, I could develop the technical knowledge necessary to hold my own with those around me. Yet in time a certain amount of frustration set in, for I began to appreciate that my opportunities would remain limited while I was working for someone else. For this reason, and also because I wanted eventually to be financially independent enough to be able to pursue my interest in politics, I decided to go out on my own in 1953. I had just reached the $10,000 income level, not bad in those days, but Isobel and I talked it over and decided that we could survive on $100 a week until I got established. How long that would take, I had no idea.

Anyway, I left Maple Leaf and Barnett J. Danson and Associates came into being. It was an impressive name but one would have to look hard for the associates. The company in fact consisted of one person, me: I even typed my own letters. My office was located in a dingy room over a wine store at Queen and Victoria streets, in the heart of downtown Toronto but out of the city's high-rent area. In those days, wine was cheap plonk sherry drunk mostly by "winos," who were not bashful about approaching me for the price of a streetcar fare, purportedly necessary for them to get a job. I fully expected to run into one of my old army buddies this way, but apparently all were more gainfully employed.

On the day I had left Maple Leaf, I visited my friend and lawyer, Arthur Minden, who was delighted with my decision and gave me full encouragement, saying that I should take my time and not worry about immediate expenses — he would take care of that. This extraordinary break lifted a large weight off my shoulders. Arthur told me that he would arrange for the Royal Bank at Bay and Lombard streets to have $1,000 in an account in my name the next morning, with his guarantee. That was about two months' living expenses for us. But Arthur went further. He promised that, when I got through the $1,000, there would be another $1,000 ... and another and another. I never used more than the first $1,000, but, as I moved ahead, Arthur kept asking me if I could grow faster with more capital. Though I was reluctant to borrow money, at one stage I felt that if I had the necessary back-up cash I could break out of what was now a small manufacturing operation — with one salesman other than me — by increasing our production and hiring some of the best engineering and marketing people in the plastics industry. Arthur quickly guaranteed another $50,000. By the time he died at much too early an age, he had instructed his heirs to continue his guarantee to me as long as I needed it. I have never forgotten his incredible generosity.

At a later phase in the company's development, another friend, the budding property developer Walter Zwig, came to my rescue when the bank manager was on my back, payroll had to be met, suppliers paid, and, Isobel suggested, the children fed. Anyone who has built a small business from scratch will most likely have gone through the same experience at some stage. In any case, Walter tided me over at a critical time, when he himself needed every dollar of credit available for his burgeoning operation. I shall ever be thankful to him. A sidelight, but an interesting one, concerns still another benefactor, C.L. Burton, the owner of the Robert Simpson Company, which was one of the two dominant retail chains in the country, the other being Eaton's. It was a time before credit cards and most young couples had a small line of credit — $200 to $500, depending on their credit-worthiness — with one or both of these companies. I was stretched to the limit and the kids still needed shoes, as well as bread, when I read C.L. Burton's autobiography, *A Sense of Urgency*, chronicling his spectacularly successful entrepreneurial career. In addition to encouraging me in my own modest venture, this book inspired me to write to Mr Burton himself to explain my problem in paying off the $200 or so I owed Simpsons. This really great man answered my letter immediately, wishing me luck and advising me that he had instructed his people to give me a breather on payments for a limited period, after which he was certain I would be a huge success. I never met C.L. personally, but I have recited this experience to Mary Alice Stuart, his granddaughter and a good friend of ours.

Danson Corporation

My "associates" and I started representing a small but very good manufacturer of plastic scrap grinders (used in the recycling of imperfect parts, and essential to the injection-moulding of thermoplastics) in Framingham, Massachusetts, and a small company in Windsor, Ontario, which built fine, costly steel tooling for the moulding of plastics but was not capable of marketing its skills. I had faith in these companies and helped to build them to a significant size. They became my main source of income — my goal was to sell one grinder a week netting me $100 each, thus meeting the family budget — which was supplemented by growing sales of custom-built tooling for plastics moulding. At the outset, we acted as agents for others, with an expanding stable of suppliers from the United States, the United Kingdom, and Germany. Most were recognized as leaders in their field and others were attempting to establish themselves as such. We then began building production and processing machinery under licensing agreements with American companies, but as the company grew — first to a few people and ultimately to about fifty — we developed an integrated sales and manufacturing operation, making the plastics-extrusion equipment that processes plastic materials and produces products such as pipe, sheet, and film that are so common today but that then were in their infancy. We also moved as we grew, from the tiny downtown office to a good-sized plant in Scarborough. The business prospered beyond my wildest dreams, grossing about $6 million annually by the late 1960s. Our operation was not large by modern-day standards but was then quite a respectable size and made us the leaders in our field.

We gained a reputation for high performance and excellent working and personal relationships throughout the industry. U.S. and European companies that wanted to make their mark in Canada generally came to us first. One of the most successful of these was an Italian firm, Metalmeccanica of Milan, headed by Commandatore Marco Giani, an experienced pioneer in the Italian plastics industry which itself was in the forefront of plastics development. A friend in the British plastics industry, John Baldry, a bachelor who ended up marrying Giani's attractive, bright, and extremely competent secretary, Maria-Giovanna Moretti, brought Giani and me together. John became distributor for Metalmeccanica in the United Kingdom and Danson Corporation, as the company was now known, played the same role for Canada and the United States. I developed a close friendship with Giani; he was the fairest and most reliable person with whom I did business — at a minimum he honoured every commitment he made and more frequently exceeded them. He had no children and treated Baldry and me and our key personnel like nephews. His real nephew, Franco Giani, was like his son and ultimately inherited the business. My personal relationships with Baldry and the Gianis continue to this day.

Marco Giani was a dignified European businessman whose office was akin to an art gallery with classical Italian paintings. He had an innovative mind and style. He didn't flinch when we told him that his machines, which were highly regarded in Europe, would have to be extensively modified to compete in the North American market. Our engineers, working with his engineering chief Dario Pizzi and with his manufacturing arm under the Paravaccinis, father and son, became a smooth operating team in spite of language difficulties. With blueprints, slide rules (where have they gone?), hand gestures, wine, a lot of laughs on both sides, and a solid knowledge of our business and markets, we succeeded in producing machines that were fully competitive, in terms of both performance and price, with anything in North America. Extremely important was standardization of vital components such as motors, hydraulics, and control mechanisms to make them compatible with products in Canada and the United States. Our relationship with Metalmeccanica was a great and profitable relationship that took us to Italy several times each year.

Selling Italian plastic-moulding machines in Canada was relatively easy for us since we were well established in the industry from coast to coast. We sold what we built ourselves or the highest-quality production and processing equipment built elsewhere. This included the largest injection-moulding machines available, which were key to our becoming the principal supplier to General Motors of Canada as that company built its first in-house plastics operation. The fact that we were within an hour's drive of GM's Oshawa, Ontario, plant, had highly skilled personnel, and could help them develop the capability to be competent and ultimately self-sufficient in the plastics field consolidated our position with this giant of the automotive business. Following General Motors' lead, other companies — particularly suppliers to the automotive industry — soon were counted among our clients.

Our relationship with GM was one of the main elements in our rapid expansion; the credit here goes to a growing marketing and engineering team that our competitors couldn't match. Peter Stephen and Ted Koch were the leaders of our injection-moulding team and Jack Reid, my senior partner, headed the extrusion team. Our ability to exploit the American market with Metalmeccanica was another major factor in our success. As relative unknowns to most of the U.S. plastics industry, we associated with the established distributors whom we knew well and who knew us. Quality and price alone were not enough to convince Americans to buy a foreign-made machine from a Canadian company. We established warehouses in New Jersey and Michigan and chartered a U.S. company in Cleveland, Ohio, and we were determined to eliminate delays for parts and service, not uncommon with foreign suppliers. No customer anywhere had to wait more than twenty-four hours for a serviceman to be in their plant. U.S. customs was another matter. The United States is a huge market and a very small niche in it was big business compared to Canada, but when a U.S. supplier lost out to us they pulled out all stops. Americans, unlike Canadians, call on their congressman when they need help. Soon we found our servicemen being stopped at the border for carrying tools or blueprints that, it was alleged, were taking jobs from Americans. Our U.S. competitors never had a leg to stand on but the Customs people had word from a congressman's office to make life difficult for us. This, of course, we could never prove but the pattern was consistent.

The most costly and glaring example was when, to meet delivery schedules, we chartered an Alitalia DC-8 cargo aircraft to bring a shipment of machines directly from Milan to New York's Idlewild Airport for delivery to our Hoboken, New Jersey, warehouse and then to waiting customers across the United States. This was an expensive way to ship heavy machinery but it was necessary to keep up with the growing demand. When the plane was scheduled to arrive, we were all prepared to move quickly but the authorities at Idlewild pleaded ignorance. The plane had landed but there was no information on what had happened to the cargo. Twelve anxious days elapsed before our machines were located in a field at Idlewild thoroughly soaked and rusting: they were lightly crated and protected for air shipment as opposed to the rugged packing and saltwater proofing required for sea transport. There was no effective recourse. Alitalia had delivered their cargo and we were faced with the hopeless task of attempting reimbursement from government "authorities." It was an expensive lesson and my first experience of what we now call "non-tariff barriers."

One of the great strengths of Danson Corporation was my executive assistant, Jo Cummings. Of course she wasn't called that at the time — just secretary. Jo was one of those meticulously trained and skilled English "girls" for whom I have a predilection, my wife being another. She was invaluable to me and a delight to work with. I often felt that she should be president and chief executive officer, or at least executive vice-president, leaving us entrepreneurial types to do what we did best and expand the business while she kept Danson Corporation and us on an even keel. In fact, I floated this idea with my colleagues, who thought it outrageous.

Speaking of my colleagues, to attract and motivate talented people, I made it a practice to offer to sell them shares in the company after a reasonable period in which each of us could determine if this should be a permanent arrangement. It was not a free ride, however. They had to pay cash up front to ensure that they had the same commitment to the firm that I had. It might have meant putting a second or third mortgage on their house, or borrowing from family, but it gave them a sense of ownership. And, besides, the price was right. Shares that we transferred at book value were virtually doubling in value each year. It was a good deal for all and worked well — we were a superb team. There is a sad postscript, however. When I entered the federal cabinet in 1974, I needed to distance myself from the company. The usual option in such circumstances was to put one's assets into a blind trust, but, since in my mind this was not a feasible arrangement for running a business, I sold my 67.5 percent share of the operation to my associates, with payments scheduled so that they could pay me out of profits over a period of several years. It didn't work out quite as we had planned. While they continued to expand the business, they extended a generous line of credit to secure a substantial chunk of business that was just too attractive to turn down. Unfortunately, the customer went broke under highly questionable circumstances and Danson Corporation was put into bankruptcy. It had taken twenty years of blood, sweat, and tears to build the company and three years to break it — which happened before I was fully paid out. Nevertheless, most of the key people built new businesses out of the ashes of Danson Corporation and, to the best of my knowledge, are all doing quite well.

But all this was in the future. In the 1950s and 1960s, the company was on a roll and both Isobel and I were busy to say the least. Besides my work in Toronto, I made frequent business trips abroad, to Germany, Britain, Italy, and, occasionally, France. I also became active in various industry organizations, such as the technically oriented Society of Plastics Engineers and the management-oriented Society of the Plastics Industry, which were important vehicles for valuable interchange of ideas on quality and technical standards as well as markets. I also became the first chairman of the Society of the Plastics Industry of Canada while simultaneously serving on the board of its American counterpart, based in New York. Meanwhile, at home, Isobel was in charge, managing a household almost single-handed while her husband was preoccupied with business. And there was a lot to manage. By the mid-1950s our family had grown to six: our son John was born in 1946, two years after our first-born, Ken, and two more sons, Peter and Tim, followed in 1951 and 1954 respectively.

To accommodate this growing brood, we changed homes a few times, living first in a bungalow on St Germain, in the Avenue Road and Lawrence area, from 1945 to 1949, then in Rosedale from 1950 to 1955, and finally in a magnificent and historic farmhouse on Old Colony Road (later Harrison Road) in the Bayview and York Mills area of North York. The last house had been built in 1828 by William Harrison, one of the pioneer farmers in the region and an associate of William Lyon Mackenzie, who died in the Rebellion of 1837. Buying this grand old place had not been part of our original plan; we had sold the Rosedale house at what was then a healthy profit of $5,000 to raise much needed cash for my business, with the intention of renting suitable living quarters where we could. Then, however, Isobel found the Old Colony Road farmhouse and its one and a half acres of land, all for the bargain price of $30,000. So, rather than inject a good chunk of equity into the business, we went $6,000 into debt and moved to Old Colony Road. Fortunately, by this time the business was going well and the bank manager was off my back, for the moment anyway. The Old Colony Road farmhouse was a great home for our four very active sons and us for the next twenty years. We furnished it with early Canadian furniture and were constantly patching it up when its age began to show.

The boys each had their morning paper routes and were expected to save their earnings towards some objective such as a bicycle, new skates, or skis and still have enough left over towards their half-share of their first year's university tuition. The paper routes had to be morning ones to allow for sports in the afternoons. That was tough for them on cold, dark winter mornings and tougher for Isobel who had to take them in tow while I was on my way to or from London, Milan, Gananoque, or Georgetown — or fast asleep at home. The boys not only survived, they quickly learned the value of money and how to manage it, gaining a sense of responsibility in the process; three of them are now fine lawyers and one an equally fine educator. After travelling the world and attending universities in Canada and abroad, all of them settled in Toronto and had great families of their own, providing us with ten wonderful grandchildren, six of whom are the girls we could never produce in spite of prodigious effort. That's not counting four great daughters-in-law, one of whom is a lawyer, one an educator, one a doctor, and one a fantastic homemaker.

During the late 1950s and early 1960s, in the midst of all my business and family responsibilities, I somehow found the time to help establish a new synagogue. From the time of my youth, I had been associated with Holy Blossom Temple in Toronto, a Reform synagogue where, as I've already recounted, my grandparents were among the earliest members, my mother was an active figure, and all the Danson children received their religious education. Over the course of the 1950s, however, I became increasingly restive at Holy Blossom, feeling that it had become too large and impersonal and was losing its sense of spirituality under its then leadership. I wasn't alone in this view, and in 1957 a few of us came together to found a new Reform synagogue. The first meeting of the steering committee was held in October of that year, and the next month we held our first lay service in the basement of the First Unitarian Church at St Clair and Avenue Road. Michael Gelber, a Torontonian living in New York, and a rabbinical student, developed a highly innovative ritual that we adapted with enthusiasm. Michael commuted to Toronto every second week until we were able to afford a full-time ordained Reform rabbi. This was a critical phase in our development. Soon afterwards, a building committee and board set to work, with a fundraising goal of $300,000 — $50,000 for land on which to build a new synagogue, and $250,000 for the synagogue itself. Formal services under the leadership of rabbis — first Andre Ungar, then Louis Cashdan — continued at the Unitarian church from 1958 through 1963; the first bar mitzvah, on 3 September 1958, was that of my eldest son, Ken. Finally, in June 1963, our new synagogue, Temple Emanu-El, located at the end of my own street of Old Colony Road, was officially consecrated. It was an elegantly understated acoustical and architectural gem, designed by Irving Grossman, a Toronto architect of considerable talent who died much too young. From the beginning, our temple, as part of the Canadian Council of Reform Congregations and of the Union of American Hebrew Congregations, stressed a less conventional form of worship and developed innovative rituals that required a high degree of individual involvement and an intimacy among members of the congregation. To this end, we aimed to keep the congregation small, about two hundred families. All in all, I think we succeeded in creating the kind of religious environment we hoped for. Arthur Bielfeld came to

Emanu-El as rabbi in 1969 and has provided exceptional leadership since then. He will be retiring soon, leaving the congregation and the institution much richer in so many ways.

Political Combat

My interest in politics had begun to germinate during the war, when I reached the conclusion that, if you fought for your country, you had a right to play a part in shaping its future, as well as a responsibility to do so. This meant involvement in the political process, which, in my case, had to start with the selection of a political party. My family was nominally Conservative and I thought that was where I would end up. Indeed, I remember a conversation with my mother that took place in our home in Parkdale, so I could not have been more than eleven at the time. How the question of politics arose I can't recall, particularly since it was during one of my sex-education sessions where my mother used a pet white rat, or rather two pet white rats, for identification of differing genitalia, something I had already learned in the streets but to which I nevertheless listened with feigned innocence and great interest. This was before sex and politics were common public issues, or discussed with children. In any event, between penis and vagina my mother made a very uncharacteristic statement. She said that she and my father, like their parents, were Conservative and she either hoped or expected (I can't remember which) that I would be Conservative too: a most unusual observation to a ten or eleven year old and from parents who showed no active interest in politics and who would normally encourage me to make up my own mind. This admonition did not have as much effect on my future as did the information on the sex life of pet white rats.

As a young soldier overseas, I recall writing to George Drew, the then Conservative premier of Ontario, to sound him out on political issues. His vague, non-committal response left me bewildered. I then turned to the Co-operative Commonwealth Federation, or CCF (forerunner of the New Democratic Party), which, along with the cooperative movement in general, appealed to my social conscience. I wrote to Father Moses Coady of St Francis Xavier University in Nova Scotia, founder of the Antigonish cooperative movement, and his reply, unlike Drew's, impressed me greatly. Ironically, considering my eventual commitment, I just couldn't find it in me to consider the Liberals, mainly because, like all young red-blooded Canadian soldiers, I had no use for Mackenzie King's opposition to conscription, which we felt was the only fair and efficient way to run a decent war.

On my return from overseas, I started my canvass of the parties. First, I turned to the young Conservatives, encouraged by the later Tory backroom powerhouse, Eddie (Fast Eddie) Goodman, since I thought that's where I would end up and Eddie couldn't believe that any rational person would do otherwise. He feels exactly the same today. Next I approached the CCF, which, I soon concluded, was comprised of bright, dedicated people who had little concept about what makes an industrial economy tick and what motivates the people who make it work. I was (and am) comfortable in the company of democratic socialists, but I could no more make my political home in their party than I could with the Conservatives. Finally, despite my misgivings, I considered the Liberals. Mackenzie King notwithstanding, I certainly admired the Liberal cabinet of the time, which, with men such as C.D. Howe, Angus Macdonald, Chubby Power, Brooke Claxton, Douglas Abbott, Paul Martin, and Louis St Laurent, was as great a group as had ever been assembled. It had performed near-miracles in managing the country's war effort, and now, in peacetime, seemed as formidable as ever, even to a dyed-in-the-wool King-hater like me. And so I gradually sought out rank-and-file Liberals, particularly young Liberals such as Vernon Singer, Welland Woodruff, Keith Davey, and Joe Potts, who made me welcome and comfortable; these were people whose values I shared. I also liked the fact that, for Liberals, Quebec was an integral part of their party rather than a weak appendage, as it was in the others.

But still I hesitated. How could I ever join the party of Mackenzie King? I continued to dither until Milton Gregg, then president of the University of New Brunswick and my revered former commanding officer, accepted King's invitation to join the cabinet in 1947. Milton's background had also been Conservative, but not fanatically so. Like most Victoria Cross winners, he was quiet, self-effacing, and unwarlike, a decent human being — indeed, one of the most decent men I have ever encountered. If Milton could become a Liberal, the party was certainly good enough for me, and I joined.

During the next twenty years, from the late 1940s to the late 1960s, I immersed myself in Liberal politics, serving in riding organizations and working in election campaigns at both the federal and provincial levels. In the federal campaign of 1949, I was co-campaign manager for Jack Smith, handling the south end of the riding of York North. I found the experience exhilarating, particularly since Smith won by a comfortable margin. There is one story about the campaign that bears retelling. Our southern committee rooms were over one of the first laundromats I can remember, at Fairlawn and Avenue Road. We had a big window over the entrance to the store and we thought that it would be a good idea to stage a parade ending up in front of the campaign office with a mass rally of Liberals and anyone else who would come. Smith, a man with a big heart and just as big a waistline, agreed that it was a great idea and he would give a stirring speech from the window above the laundromat entrance — that is, he felt this way until he looked the site over and realized that, as the crowd would be looking up at him, they would also be looking at the big sign of the laundromat under the window where he was to appear. It read in large letters, "The Tub O'Suds." The rally never took place.

I also became active in a variety of Liberal organizations, including the Liberal Businessman's Club (of which I was president for a time) and the Toronto and Yorks Liberal Association. Among the high points were trips to Ottawa every one or two years for meetings of the federal party's advisory council, for which one qualified by being able to afford the trip to Ottawa and a hotel room. Leadership conventions, both provincial and federal, the crucibles of the political experience, were also highlights not to be missed. The first I attended was especially memorable, for not only was it the one that elected Louis St Laurent as Mackenzie King's successor, but on this occasion I had a personal encounter — if a fleeting one — with my nemesis, the retiring prime minister, whom by now I had grudgingly forgiven, much to his gratification, I'm sure.

The convention, held in 1948, was meeting in the Cow Palace on the Ottawa Exhibition Grounds, and I was sitting with Isobel close to the aisle as the prime minister and cabinet entered, just a couple of feet from me. They were, as I've said, an impressive, even intimidating lot, and I, like everyone, was standing and cheering. One of the cabinet ministers in the procession was my old brigadier, Milton Gregg, then minister of labour. As the cabinet walked past majestically, Gregg noticed Isobel and me and tapped the prime minister on the shoulder. "Prime Minister," he said, "I want you to meet someone." Introducing me, he commented that the two of us had a common characteristic — a distinguished nose — and he then told King of how during the war, while we were training officers at the Battle Drill School in Vernon, he had caught me doing an impersonation of him in the mess, complete with droning speaking style. I hadn't known that Gregg was there — he and his wife, Dorothy, had entered the room from a door behind me — and he watched it all, laughing along with his wife and the others. I thought at the time it was a good performance, but little did I know that the audience's reaction was mainly because of the Greggs' entry behind me. King, looking understandably distracted while adoring Liberals looked on in wonderment, listened to the story politely and then the procession continued. It was my first brush with power, and even though I still had serious reservations about King, I admit to having been more than a little impressed. And, of course, I was delighted as always to see the much beloved Milton. Parenthetically, I might note that my last encounter with King would be when he was lowered into the sacred ground beside his parents in Toronto's Mount Pleasant Cemetery. The full cabinet was there, including Milton Gregg, having accompanied their late leader by train from Ottawa. They were all in black tailcoats, striped trousers, and silk top hats. Somehow the Conservative George Hees and I found ourselves together with the dignitaries at the graveside.

I left the 1948 convention feeling energized, very taken with the dignified Louis St Laurent and eager to do battle for the Liberal cause. Provincially, of course, there was little to be excited about, for Ontario Liberals continued to languish in the political wilderness, where, thanks to the follies of an earlier leader, Mitch Hepburn, they had been consigned in 1945 and where they would remain until the mid-1980s. But, even in this forbidding terrain, we were nothing if not feisty, plugging away election after election, choosing leader after leader to take us to the promised land, and nominating scores of candidates who, more often than not, were engaged in kamikaze missions. Perhaps our greatest near triumph in those early years occurred in November 1950, when we persuaded Harry Cassidy, the highly respected dean of the School of Social Work at the University of Toronto, and a signatory of the socialist Regina Manifesto, the founding document of the CCF, that he was truly a Liberal — or, if that was stretching the truth too much, that he could win the provincial Liberal leadership and subsequent election and then be in a position to implement his ideas as leader of a Liberal government. At the time, the great farmer-orator Farquhar Oliver was stepping down as Liberal leader in Ontario after yet another electoral defeat. Leslie Frost, the apparently unbeatable Conservative premier from Lindsay, was at the height of his power and popularity. The heir apparent to Oliver was a previously little known lawyer from Pickering, Walter Thomson.

As a matter of fact, I initially supported Thomson, as did my friends Vernon Singer and Welland Woodruff, but as I became exposed to Thomson's tactics, values, and virtual lack of principle, I could stomach him no longer. I joined a group of "Young Turks" — including Keith Davey (later a national director of the Liberal Party, and a senator), future Ontario Supreme Court justices Joe Potts and David Anderson, Jim Service, a future mayor of North York, Archie Whitelaw, a future president of the Ontario Liberal Party, and future senators Dan Lang and Dick Stanbury — to try to save the day. We were determined that Walter Thomson not become our leader and looked for alternatives whom we could support without reservation, or at least too many reservations. We were not much more than kids and the rank and file of the party, who were amused by our naive youthful enthusiasm, didn't take us too seriously. Certainly not as seriously as we took ourselves. After canvassing just about anyone who had their name in the papers and we thought should be Liberals, someone suggested Harry Cassidy, and he didn't say absolutely no under any circumstances. Nor did he say yes. We persevered.

Gradually, the disenchantment with Thomson became more widespread and we appeared to be the only group with any hope of coming up with an alternative. The days were ticking off in the countdown to the convention date and Harry, in spite of the wiser advice of his more mature friends and colleagues, could not turn down the blandishments of the Young Turks. I was going to say young Liberals, but I don't think that was too important to Harry. Actually, I think that he listened to us in spite of the fact that we were Liberals; he just couldn't resist such honest enthusiasm. Just less than forty-eight hours before the vote he gave us the go ahead and we were off like jackrabbits. *No* signs, *no* buttons, *no* literature, and no real organization. And not five cents in our treasury. Just commitment, enthusiasm, energy, and boundless optimism. We made signs of cardboard, we recruited people, and we mimeographed naive literature. And best of all, because we had neither time nor money for buttons, we got hold of some brown Kraft shipping tags and overnight printed them with red Liberal letters reading "Tag on to Harry Cassidy," and hundreds of delegates did. At the convention, which was held in the ballroom of Toronto's Royal York Hotel, we denied Walter Thomson a first-ballot victory in spite of his pervasive organization and seemingly unlimited funds. When it was time for the final ballot, there was tension on all sides and the room was alive with chanting for Cassidy. The vote was held, as was our collective breath during the count. Thomson won narrowly and then went on to one of the worst Liberal defeats in history. Harry Cassidy heaved a hefty sigh of relief, as did his wife. We went back to our studies or jobs and the never-ending struggle to elect Liberals.

At this point, I wish to say a little more about Keith Davey. Keith, a key Liberal Party insider and election strategist from the early 1960s on, is the oldest of my political friends and, with the exception of his wife, Dorothy, the best. I can't recall when we first met but neither can I recall any meaningful political work beyond the riding level where he wasn't a key player. We were among the most active of the young Liberals in the post-war years, cooking up audacious schemes to clobber Tories and carry the true faith of liberalism to the people. For Keith especially, the be-all and end-all of life was winning elections — not that he won them all, of course. Although he didn't ever run to lose, he really believed that he could win any and every election he engaged in. And "engage" is a good word for Keith and elections. He was absolutely and totally and personally engaged — like a general in battle. But he never attempted to play the role of monarch or president. He left that to Pearson and

Trudeau, two leaders whom he carried to victory many times. His most notable triumphs came in 1963, when Pearson's Liberals ousted the Conservative government of John Diefenbaker; 1968, when Trudeau swept to power on a wave of "Trudeaumania"; 1974, when Trudeau regained the majority he had lost in 1972; and 1980, when Trudeau, after his defeat the preceding year at the hands of Joe Clark's Conservatives, stormed back into office. Keith's influence, in short, was immense; he was the sort of man who is vital to making our party system function. After him, they threw away the mould.

As a political activist, I discovered that my political instincts were fairly good. Always listening carefully to what taxi drivers, gas-pump operators, and barbers had to say — these people, then as now, are the most reliable barometers of public opinion — I predicted the St Laurent sweep of 1949 (winning a bet with Eddie Goodman in the process, the money going to the purchase of my first alarm-clock radio) and was equally certain that we were going to do badly in the federal election of 1957, which we did. I did not, however, predict the magnitude of the Liberals' defeat in 1958, and indeed I was shaken by the results. Like many other Liberals, I was prepared to concede Lester Pearson's limitations as an orator and leader of the opposition, but also like them, I had the greatest respect for him as a man, as a great Canadian, and as an international statesman. As for his nemesis, John Diefenbaker, I wasn't impressed with him at all in the 1957 and 1958 campaigns — he struck me as a charlatan — and over the next few years, as his government stumbled through crisis after crisis, I had no reason to change my opinion, though I did come to have a better appreciation of his capacity for political theatre. More will be said of Diefenbaker in the next chapter, when I turn to my arrival in the House of Commons as a freshly minted MP in 1968.

My first attempt at running for elected office occurred in October 1967, when I ran for the provincial Liberal Party in my home constituency of York Mills. The incumbent was a very fine and popular Conservative, Dalton Bales, a minister in the cabinet of John Robarts, one of the long continuous line of Tory premiers who appeared to have a permanent lock on the job. Most thought that my candidacy was doomed, but ever-hopeful Liberals were happy to have a live, warm candidate and I was naive enough to believe that I could be a giant killer. (Everyone knew that only a Liberal could play such a role, for, while our chances were slim, the NDP's were virtually nil in York Mills.) At a meeting with the Liberal riding executive, I was immensely impressed by an attractive, vivacious woman who displayed exceptional political smarts in a thoroughly refined but highly pragmatic way. She was Dorothy Petrie, now Mrs Keith Davey. I rarely made an important political decision without consulting Keith, and, when I asked his advice on a campaign manager, he recommended Dorothy Petrie without any hesitation. Dorothy went on to make her mark in the highest levels of the Liberal Party and managed the 1974 federal election campaign for Ontario, which resulted in a majority Liberal government. She did this with the same charm, intelligence, sensitivity, and inner toughness that have marked her every effort and gained the respect and affection of all, but especially Keith Davey. Meeting her was the luckiest break in my entire political career and the beginning of a warm, ongoing friendship.

I was unopposed at the Liberal nomination meeting. Indeed, Liberals were happy that they had someone — anyone — to run in this traditionally Tory riding against a highly respected cabinet minister in the Big Blue Machine of John Robarts. The nomination meeting was my first opportunity to mesmerize the voters and the press with my brilliant plans for the province on just about every provincial issue, as well as a few federal and international ones. The morning papers the next day, I was confident, would herald the entry of a new bright comet on the Canadian political solar scene. I had taken great pains in drafting this memorable speech and, conscious of time constraints, managed to whittle it down to about an hour and a half. After all, history was not made in a day. Dorothy, the cool, consummate campaign manager, properly asked to see my speech. Flattered, I presented this meticulous draft to her and awaited her murmurs of praise as she scanned it. I was impressed with her speed-reading, not realizing that she was counting the pages and converting them into minutes and quarter hours. Her repetition of "My God," I thought, indicated the great impact of the ideas that flowed from its pages. After a short time, her jaw dropped in wonder and her hands lowered the papers to her knees. I waited expectantly for her comments. "Barney ...You can't do this!" she said, her soft warm eyes turning to cold steel. I was shattered, but not deterred, for I had some peculiar idea that voters would welcome a politician of great breadth with fresh ideas. What I didn't quite realize was that they had to be present and awake while I expounded my ideas. After much coaxing, threats, and possible violence from my campaign committee, I proposed to cut back the speech to an even hour, which was still not acceptable to them. As a compromise, we agreed that I would release the entire written text to the press and delete massive parts in my speech, thus keeping it to a half-hour. This would also leave time for our revered leader, Bob Nixon, to extol the virtues of this new addition to the public life of our party, province, and nation, not to mention the world.

Finally, the big night arrived. After my introduction as the next MPP for York Mills, followed by a long, warm, and enthusiastic applause (after all, most of the audience were family and blindly loyal Liberals and friends), I launched into my historic address. Just as it seemed I was warming up, I noticed many in the audience muttering to one another. Obvious remarks on my brilliant dissertation. This encouraged me to include some of the portions that had been red-pencilled for deletion. Before too long, it appeared to me, the occasional person was so moved that he or she made an emotional departure. When my closest friend and doctor, along with his family, made for the exit, I decided to tell a few hilarious jokes to lighten the mood created by the speech's heavy content, but the audience that was left was obviously more interested in my ideas. In God's good time, I concluded with a passionate commitment to serve York Mills, Ontario, Canada, and mankind with all the strength and dedication at my command. The audience was so entranced that they could hardly bring themselves to applaud. They did, however, manage to get to their feet, heading for the doors. As I stepped down from the platform, Dorothy's eyes were glaring. "You spoke for forty-five minutes!" she exclaimed. "Quiet," I said, "You'll wake up my father." Fortunately, we all remained friends, but Dorothy and Keith Davey will never let me forget my maiden speech. And Bob Nixon is too polite ever to refer to it.

I knocked on doors throughout York Mills and attended as many all-candidates meetings as we could organize and have Dalton Bales agree to attend. His strategy, to the extent that he needed one at all, was to keep my profile as low as possible, the opposite of my strategy. And he wasn't enthusiastic about giving me the exposure all-candidates meetings would provide. As the campaign progressed, we could sense momentum building and actually thought that I might possibly win. Any candidate who doesn't believe he or she can win is doomed from the start. In the end, the election-night results showed that we had doubled the Liberal vote while cutting Dalton's majority by half from the previous election. It had all been the result of the almost picture-perfect campaign run by Dorothy, the indefatigable door knocking and coffee partying by Isobel, and the unflinching support of my family and friends. Still, while the operation was a great success, the patient died. Dorothy was in tears as the returns came in. I wasn't particularly happy either, though I took some solace from the gains we had made and from the knowledge that I not only had gained great experience but had also established myself as a credible political figure within the party and the community. I had learned some lessons too.

Trudeaumania and Me

Turn the clock ahead one year. In federal politics, Pearson's quiet, unassuming manner commanded respect from all parties and the public in general but he had a difficult time in the political arena; after the catastrophe of 1958, he won two elections, in 1963 and 1965, but in neither case achieved a majority. Conservative leader Robert Stanfield had many of the same strengths and weaknesses, and so did Bob Nixon in provincial politics. They were without enemies, with the exception of John Diefenbaker in Stanfield's case, and they elevated the political process and brought credit to those who engage in it. Besides being unpretentious and self-deprecating, they all had a basic modesty, a low-key sense of humour (although Nixon could be raucous at times), and an ability to laugh at themselves. All of them also exuded integrity.

With regard to Pearson, many felt that he could not survive a fourth election and those of us who had great affection for him wanted him spared defeat after a very outstanding career. I wrote to him in March 1966 expressing my view that he should consider retiring from office at a high point in his career but assuring him that, whatever his decision, he would retain my support and that of the party. His response of April 25th was as surprisingly frank as it was revealing. Noting that "we are opposed by a man who considers the House of Commons as a criminal court where he is the prosecutor and must always act so as to get back into power at all costs," and that Diefenbaker's "bitter and malicious and personal attacks" had recently dragged down the government "to his own level," Pearson expressed his willingness to step down if that would be in the best interests of the country:

> I agree with you that "something is terribly wrong" in Parliament and in politics. If a new leadership in our Party would help put it right, I would be glad to co-operate immediately to bring that about. I assure you that I have no desire to remain in politics unless I think that by so remaining I am contributing something to my country. Personally, nothing would please me more than to return to a more private and easier life.
>
> However, the personal irritation, which I have mentioned, at being associated with Mr. Diefenbaker as jointly responsible for the deterioration of the situation would not affect my decision to leave political life if there were not other considerations as well. There are such considerations, especially the strengthening of unity inside our Party and, far more important, inside the country, between English-speaking and French-speaking Canadians. I hope that I am not being egotistical in saying that, were I to retire from politics at this particular time, it would have a harmful effect on this over-riding issue.
>
> There are indeed first-class men of a younger generation in our Party who will soon be able to take over. You may be assured that I will not stand in their way for a day, if and when the party feels that a change is required in the national interest.

A year and a half later, in December 1967, Pearson tendered his resignation as leader of the Liberal Party and thus as prime minister, to take effect once a new leader was chosen by the party. Senator John Nichol, president of the party, announced a leadership convention for 6 April 1968, to be held in Ottawa's Civic Centre, a step up from the old Cow Palace of Mackenzie King's day. The battle for succession was on. There was no shortage of talent in the Liberal cabinet, and a number of ministers soon threw their hats into the ring: Mitchell Sharp, Paul Martin, Robert Winters, Joe Green, John Turner, and Paul Hellyer — all well-established names. Another contender was Eric Kierans, a respected ex-minister from Quebec who intrigued many. And then there was this new upstart, the justice minister from Quebec, Pierre Elliott Trudeau, who was interesting, apparently sexy, and a bit off the wall, or so many of us thought. The son of a wealthy businessman, and even in his late forties a bachelor to whom beautiful women were powerfully drawn, Trudeau had been a law professor at the University of Montreal before entering federal politics in 1965 as one of the "Three Wise Men" from Quebec, the others being his close friends Gérard Pelletier and Jean Marchand. He had an impressive background: he had served in the Privy Council Office in 1950-51, had been one of the leading intellectuals involved in the opposition to the former Duplessis regime (editing the left-leaning, anti-Duplessis *Cité Libre*), and, by 1968, was a highly respected minister of justice. But for a while he wasn't able to make up his mind whether or not to run; he wanted Jean Marchand to run instead, but Jean wanted him to do so. He was virtually unknown to the rank and file of the party, let alone the country. Not to be taken seriously.

Paul Hellyer, the minister of transport, was a person I had known from the 1949 campaign that had confirmed St Laurent as prime minister and that had resulted in Paul's own election in the Toronto riding of Davenport. He was young (forty-five), experienced in cabinet, and had a reputation for originality and integrity. Many of us who had been Young Liberals together backed him as the first declared candidate in the race, and I became the chairman of his campaign in the Toronto area. He worked hard and had a loyal group of supporters, including Keith Davey, Dorothy Petrie, Joe Potts, Bob Andras, and Marcel Prud'homme, the latter two being MPs. At first, Hellyer seemed to be the frontrunner, but then Trudeau came into the race. Those who had come to know him in Parliament (such as Donald Macdonald and Bob

Stanbury) had immense respect for him and enthusiasm for his candidacy. He attracted the younger, progressive element in the party and many important ministers and former ministers. One of these was Finance Minister Mitchell Sharp, who, after sensing the political winds, decided that he couldn't win, withdrew his candidacy, and announced his support of Trudeau.

Like most Liberals outside Parliament, I did not know Trudeau, and when I encountered him at leadership meetings across the country, I felt that I was none the wiser. His style and intellectual capacity certainly made him extremely attractive to many; indeed, his personal charm made the term "charisma" part of the Canadian vocabulary for the first time. His backers just had to stand him in front of an audience and most were won over, even when what he had to say was vague, trite, or abstract beyond belief. It was frustrating for a Hellyer supporter to see his candidate, who exuded stability, experience, and personal integrity, upstaged by this upstart. I just couldn't understand what all the fuss was about. Nevertheless, while Hellyer opposed Trudeau strongly on philosophy and issues, he once answered my question as to what Trudeau was really like with a warm smile and a single word, "charming."

At the convention itself, Trudeau stole the show with his speech to the delegates. When he started speaking, stillness descended on the audience; the atmosphere was electric. His first words were not ones we expected. There was no preliminary "My fellow Liberals" or "Mr Chairman"; rather, he talked about the riots at the Democratic convention in Chicago, the turmoil in modern society, the need for Canada to become a "just society." Instead of a ringing appeal to the delegates to support him so he could lead the party to victory, he offered a dissertation on those things he considered important. The sense one had was that if you agreed with him that was fine but if you didn't that was fine too. The focus was not on details, on political minutiae, but on the larger picture. It was not just highly thoughtful but visionary. As he concluded, there was an explosion of excitement and not a few tears. Trudeau signs seemed to spring out of nowhere and filled the hall. Personally, I was deeply moved, even overwhelmed. While I was intensely loyal to Hellyer, I knew that if he were forced off the ballot, my support would go to Trudeau. As it happened, Hellyer dropped out after the second ballot and threw his support to Bob Winters. Though I had great respect for Winters, I thought that Trudeau was more likely to excite the party and the electorate and take us in a direction with which I could more closely identify. When I put on a Trudeau button, Paul was furious with me but my mind was made up. On the third ballot, there were three candidates, Trudeau, Winters, and John Turner (whose loyal, construction-helmeted crew stuck with him to the end). I voted for Trudeau and he won, garnering 249 more votes than the second-place candidate, Winters. We had our new leader, and what a leader he was. I never had any doubt that I had made the right choice.

At all leadership conventions, the competition is intense and emotions run high. One develops an intense loyalty to a candidate and to see him or her defeated and hurt is not a happy experience. In my case in 1968, it was not easy to let Hellyer down by not respecting his choice for the final ballot. The feelings I had at the time were expressed in a memorandum, which I wrote after the convention and which was later published by the respected columnists Doug Fisher and Harry Crowe in the Toronto *Telegram*. I can do no better now than quote it in full:

> After almost four months of devoting almost every waking hour to "your man," after neglecting your business, and your family, after nights and weekends of meetings, phone calls and travel, after a week of pre-convention organization with three or four hours sleep a night, "your man" has dropped from the ballot.
>
> Tired, overwrought, emotionally drained, you must make a choice for another man. You hadn't thought that a likely prospect. You weren't certain "your man" would win, but you were sure he'd be on the final ballot.
>
> Even then you had a secret second choice, but the ball game had changed.
>
> The names were different than you and the pollsters expected.
>
> The partisans of remaining candidates were swooping down like enthusiastic vultures trying to get you to carry their man's signs or wear their man's badges.

Tensions had reached a critical pitch. The atmosphere was that of a pressure vessel. The stakes were high. The people on "your man's" team who had become the closest friends in recent weeks were in disarray.

"Your man" had chosen an alliance you couldn't buy. A man you respected mightily, but who was not your choice.

Integrity, skill, intellectual capacity, experience, philosophy, and age — all factors in your choice, but a great chunk of fundamental instinct became the overriding influence.

Your choice is made. The former enemy. The pressures from all sides continue. They follow you to the voting booth where you are somehow unexplainably surprised to find "your man's" name missing.

Punching the ballot becomes a great emotional effort. You almost freeze — but punch it you do, almost with a feeling of sticking a pin into "your man" in his moment of agony.

The count is announced. The man you voted for is the winner and you're satisfied and relieved. Satisfied because in spite of the pressure, you were voting for your own choice in all sincerity, fully conscious of the seriousness and responsibility of your ballot. Relieved it was over.

You can't join in the cheers and the celebrations even though you know your choice was a wise one.

You round up your family from the stands and board a waiting bus for your hotel to collapse in exhaustion. Your family understands. Their sympathy shows in their eyes and they are quietly proud. They know the agony and disappointment you have experienced, but you are proud because it was agony and you understood the pressures and voted from your gut.

With the convention over, Liberals had to decide whether or not to call an early election. We were all dead tired. There were deep wounds in the party between supporters of different candidates, and we had exhausted our fundraising capability. Senator Dick Stanbury, the president of the Ontario branch of the Liberal Party of Canada, was part of a small group who were to advise Trudeau on an election call. In spite of all the difficulties, we recognized that there was tremendous interest in Trudeau and that the momentum from the convention was growing across the country. It was as if the people couldn't wait to validate the convention choice. My instinct was that we should go soon. And we did. The election was set for June 25th.

By this time, I had developed a profile in the Toronto region because of my candidacy in the recent provincial election and my role in the leadership campaign. I was approached to run. It was an attractive proposition. Certainly, the excitement of my recent political activity and the now largely unquestioned appeal of Pierre Trudeau, whom I had still to meet one on one, whetted my appetite. I had, however, set some important pre-conditions to running federally. I had known many fine men who, when they were defeated or retired, came to the painful realization that they had paid a high price for their time in politics, not only for themselves but also for their families. Often, middle-aged men (as in the military, it was only men in those days, with the impressive exception of Grace MacInnis of the NDP) had left promising careers to enter politics and spent the most productive years of their lives away from home. Their wives saw all too little of them and never received the companionship and love they deserved while their husbands were absorbed in the fascinating, fulfilling, and ego-satisfying life of politics. Then, after their political careers were over, they returned to children whom they hardly knew and who had missed the regular presence and influence of a father. They also found themselves in a difficult financial position. While federal politics paid a living wage, no one made enough to save and, at that time, pensions were minuscule. And so, in middle age, these men had missed their career opportunities and were often in desperate financial shape, sometimes as a result of yet unpaid campaign expenses. I was not prepared to see my life unfold this way, nor was I prepared to inflict such a fate upon my wife and sons.

The first pre-condition for my entry into politics was that our sons would be reasonably grown up and established in their post-secondary education; this would make them less dependent on my presence and would enable my wife to share the political life with me. The second pre-condition was that I would be sufficiently independent financially to cushion the return to private life. The second condition was met by the late 1960s. The first could be waived when I ran provincially in 1967, for provincial legislative sessions were much shorter and I would be able to remain close to both my family and my business. Federal politics, however, were another matter. In 1968 Tim, our youngest, was just sixteen and still in high school. He needed a father at home. But, in the end, I decided to run; the temptation and timing were just too great to resist. My decision initially caused Tim some difficulty, but, with great determination, he came through it with flying colours — and helped to relieve his father's guilt in the process.

My first choice for a riding was my original constituency of York North, where the incumbent Liberal member, John Addison, had announced that he would not run again and where I had cut my electoral teeth during Jack Smith's federal campaign in 1949. It was an enormous riding located to the north of metropolitan Toronto, spreading east and west and encompassing Vaughan and Markham townships plus the municipality of Richmond Hill and including the towns of Woodbridge and Markham and the village of Unionville. It was also diverse, consisting of small towns, some new suburban development, and extensive farming communities. Politically, it was a swing seat that Liberals held except when there was a strong sweep against us across the country. I tested the political waters among the key Liberals in York North and was confident of enough support to win the nomination. Dorothy Petrie, my fantastic campaign manager in the 1967 provincial contest, agreed to play the same role again.

On nomination night in the town of Thornhill, I had one opponent, Mart Kenney, a well-known orchestra leader. I won the nomination and the friendship of Kenney, who, with his wife, the great singer Norma Locke, supported me in the election (his grandson Jason Kenney is now a stalwart Canadian Alliance MP). My nomination speech was short, personal, and oriented to York North: I wasn't about to subject the delegates to earnest reflections on the remarkable future they and Canada would enjoy when I was elected. The following excerpt conveys the excitement that surrounded Trudeau at the time:

We have a country and people of which others expect great things.

We have a country with boundless resources and a people with boundless potential. This is no time to choose a government or leader of the status quo, or of safety and good management alone.

This is a time when we must have good management, it is true, but we need and deserve a great deal more. That's why we can be proud as Liberals of our choice of Pierre Elliott Trudeau as our leader. That is why Canadians are fortunate to have man of insight, intellect and responsibility who will give our nation renewed pride and thrust. A man who truly leads and opens new vistas, but realizes that governing is the art of the possible, rather than just dreams, visions and promises.

Prime Minister Trudeau can and will form a majority government with skill.

He will take us from the era of Mr. Pearson's "New Politics" to the era of the "Just Society." A society of hope, of growth, of reason, of sensitivity and compassion.

He will give renewed pride and hope to our French speaking compatriots and he will keep this country whole.

He will decimate the NDP who, aside from their rock based socialists, are, as Mr. St. Laurent described them, "Liberals in a Hurry," who can now return to their true political home.

Most importantly he has captured the hopes and aspirations of our youth, many of whom have been disillusioned with the way we have been handling things — and I can't say I blame them in many respects. This youth, a million of whom will be voting for their first

time in a federal election, are restless. They are bright
and informed and ambitious as no generation before
them has been. They identify with Prime Minister
Trudeau and he identifies with them.

Mr. Trudeau is a man of great stature. He has work-
able plans, the courage and touch of stubbornness necessary to implement them. And he has surrounded
himself with a cabinet of advisors that gives balance
and confidence.

I am convinced that he is destined to be amongst
our greatest of Prime Ministers and a statesman of
world stature, in a world sadly bereft of great leaders.

We as Canadians and Liberals can be proud to be
part of this era. I personally want to be part of what is
to be the most progressive and exciting government in
our history.

With the campaign on, and Trudeaumania sweeping the country,
we could smell victory in the air right from the start. There was nary
a snag, but one amusing moment comes to mind. At a rally in
Markham where Trudeau was the main attraction, he introduced me
first as Bernie Dawson and then as Bernie Danson. When he got the
last name right, after gentle nudging and other game tries, I gave him
my card. Trudeau then declared, "Whether his name be Bernie or
Barney Danson, he's a good man and we want him in Ottawa." (In
later years, this became a small joke between us. Many times in caucus
and cabinet, he would light-heartedly call me Bernie Dawson.)
On election day, I received almost 10,000 more votes than my
Conservative opponent, Gordon Hurlburt, a North York councillor
and, as it happened, a cottage neighbour and friend (26,045 to
16,499); Jack Grant of the NDP placed third, with 779 votes. Overall
in the country, Liberals won an impressive majority, with 154 seats to
the Conservatives' 72, the NDP's 22, and the Créditistes' 14. Thirteen
Liberal newcomers were elected in the Toronto area alone, including,
besides me, Alastair Gillespie, Martin O'Connell, Robert Kaplan and
John Roberts — all future cabinet ministers.

A day or two before the election, Gordon Hurlburt had called me, saying, though not in so many words, that the contest was all but over, that he didn't have a chance. "This Trudeau thing," he said, is "just too big." This took me by surprise: I was confident, but I certainly didn't think that my victory was assured. I was ready, as I would always be in elections, to fight for every vote until the last minute, never relaxing until the returns came in and my victory was made official. But Hurlburt was right. Trudeau's appeal was too much for him, just as it was for so many others. The end result was that something I had long thought about — and strived for — was now a reality. I was bound for Ottawa.

Chapter Three
Member of Parliament
for York North,
1968–70

My first night in Ottawa as a newly elected MP was not particularly restful. I stayed at the Chateau Laurier, and if I got any sleep at all it was over by five or six in the morning. I walked the short distance to Parliament Hill and later, when I took my seat in the Commons chamber and looked around at the elegant carvings and stained glass windows, it was with a feeling of some awe. It was a place of history and I was part of it, not just a spectator in the galleries as I had been so many times before.

In speaking with colleagues in later years, I learned that just about each one had an almost identical experience on entering the Commons as an MP for the first time. And, although we became quite at ease in our surroundings rather quickly, we always approached and entered the parliamentary precinct with a sense of privilege and respect. Even after we left politics, and others had taken our places, we remained deeply attached to the stones and mortar, to say nothing of the institution itself. Going back is like visiting an old school or regiment. You were an integral part of it. You are still a member of the club, although others are carrying the banner. Somehow, it's partly yours and no one can ever take that from you.

Early Days

During my first term as an MP I initially lived in a garret on the top floor of the Chateau Laurier — likely used by the servants of guests in the Chateau's early days — and then in apartments and in a rented house in New Edinburgh. At one point I shared a duplex with fellow Liberal MPs Hugh Faulkner and Jim Jerome. Isobel frequently stayed with me in Ottawa, making the drive from Toronto with Diana Gillespie, wife of my fellow MP and good friend Alastair. I myself returned to Toronto on weekends. These visits gave me a chance both to see Isobel, Tim, and whichever of the other sons might have been home from university at the time, and to handle constituency business and attend various events and functions in the riding.

The hours were long — about eighty a week, when weekends in the riding were included, with each day beginning at about eight and ending around eleven — but I didn't mind. It was a fascinating time for me, with every day full of new experiences and new challenges, and it was made all the more gratifying by the good friendships I quickly formed among my colleagues. The Liberal class of 1968, all of us riding on Trudeau's coattails, was an impressive group, including such talented new recruits as Hugh Faulkner, Judd Buchanan, Alastair Gillespie, John Roberts, Pat Mahoney, Martin O'Connell, Jack "Bud" Cullen (my seatmate), Ray Perrault (the former Liberal leader in British Columbia), and Bob Kaplan, all of whom achieved cabinet rank, and Jim Jerome, who became Speaker of the House. With 155 members, the caucus was also large, spilling over onto the opposition side of the House. The Liberals sitting there were called "the rump," an endearing term for a group who often asserted their presence noisily, out of all proportion to their numbers. I wasn't with the rump — it started with the "G's," backbenchers being seated alphabetically — but "D" for "Danson" put me about as far from the speaker's chair as one could get, given that the cabinet seats took a big chunk of the middle; in fact, if I had been any farther from the speaker, I would have been sitting in the Rideau Canal. At such a distance from the speaker it was never easy getting his eye, but that didn't stop me and those around me from trying. I remember one occasion when my seatmate, Bud Cullen, rose to his feet repeatedly in unsuccessful attempts to ask a question. After several valiant but unsuccessful attempts to help him out, I rose on a point of privilege — which requires the speaker to let you speak — and asked permission to introduce to the House my colleague, "Jumping Jack" Cullen. The speaker refused my request but eventually gave Bud the floor. We were a closely knit group and many of us keep in close touch to this day. The person to whom I was closest was Alastair Gillespie. A Rhodes scholar, low-key but imposing, a man of unquestioned integrity and great and widely recognized ability, he was to precede me into the cabinet by two years, and, after serving with distinction in three different portfolios, was to go down to defeat along with me and all other Toronto-area ministers in the election of May 1979.

Besides the Liberal neophytes, there was a formidable line-up of heavy hitters. This group included, apart from the prime minister himself, Charles "Bud" Drury, a modest, taciturn, and thorough loner, much admired by Trudeau and all of those who knew him. Jean Chrétien was another dominant figure, affable, warm-hearted, and sharp as a whip, with political instincts comparable to those of Harry Truman. Then there was Don Jamieson, an irrepressible Newfoundlander who had a quick wit and a fund of "Newfie" stories (he was also a superb speaker and rarely used a note); Allan MacEachen, the "laird of Cape Breton," a politically brilliant if eccentric character about whom more will be said; John Turner, a true political star backed up by a substantial team of supporters across the country, with the looks and charm of a movie star but considerable substance and ambition as well; and Donald Macdonald, "The Thumper," extraordinarily competent, always dependable, and a formidable competitor who could well have become prime minister if Trudeau had not rethought his resignation in 1979. Finally, there were major players from an earlier generation, notably Mitchell Sharp, reliable, unflappable, and rich in knowledge, who often acted as a brake on the rest of us when his considerable experience and instincts told him we were being too brash; and Paul Martin, government leader in the Senate, the father of federal Medicare and one of the most distinguished figures in Canadian parliamentary history, a man who could spot a political minefield before any of us even smelled danger.

On the opposition benches there were giants too. Robert Stanfield comes first to mind. A former premier of Nova Scotia who became leader of the federal Conservative Party in 1967, Stanfield failed to take his party to victory but was an effective, if self-effacing, leader of the opposition, a man of great substance and integrity whose laconic speaking style could never match Trudeau's eloquence. When Stanfield gave up the Tory leadership in 1976, Trudeau encouraged me to approach him to see whether he would be interested in taking on a new role. He could have, Trudeau told me, any prestigious appointment he wished — senator, lieutenant governor of Nova Scotia, high commissioner to Britain and possibly Governor General — but Stanfield responded to my overture by saying that he just wanted to be a private person again. I think as well of the larger-than-life, irrepressible Réal Caouette who led his band of Créditistes through many a crisis and ultimately into oblivion, for the party was nothing without Caouette himself. And not to be forgotten are a band of New Democrats: NDP leader Tommy Douglas, the pioneer of Medicare in Saskatchewan, one of the few politicians to make a successful transition from provincial to federal politics, perhaps the finest orator in the House and certainly one of the funniest, held in respect and affection by all, none more than me; David Lewis, Douglas's comrade-in-arms, known for his rapier-like intelligence and debating skill; Stanley Knowles, the conscience of the House of Commons, who loved the House so much that we all were certain he hated any thought of summer recess or any other break that shut it down (in fact, it was joked that his seat in the Commons was glued to his bottom); and the spunky Grace MacInnis from British Columbia, the daughter of J.S. Woodsworth, founder of the CCF, the only female MP when I arrived on the scene.

The reader might notice in the above names a special affinity for New Democrats. I plead guilty. Indeed, if I could be excused for jumping ahead in the narrative, I might also mention two other New Democrats who impressed me greatly during my political career. One was Ed Broadbent, leader of the NDP from 1975 to 1989, who had the respect of everyone in the House; he was tough and aggressive but never demeaned either himself or others. The other was Bob Rae. Elected as an MP in 1978, near the end of my time in Ottawa, he was a brilliant finance critic and a superb federal parliamentarian. His move to Ontario politics, first to lead the provincial NDP in 1982 and then to become premier in 1990, was a step up the political ladder, but I think it was a great loss to the federal NDP and Parliament. Had he been a Liberal, which he could easily have been, I'm convinced that he might have become prime minister of Canada.

But let's return to the House of 1968. Two MPs who mightily impressed me, and others, were Jed Baldwin of Peace River, Alberta, the Conservative house leader, and Gordon Fairweather, a respected veteran from Rothesay, New Brunswick. Jed was a fairly soft-spoken man with a delightful light touch and sense of humour. Gordon, more dour than Jed, shared many values I consider Liberal. I guess he would rate as a "Red Tory." He radiated integrity and decency combined with an elevated set of principles which were a hallmark of his political career. Jed was delightful and decent, while Gordon was decent with considerable depth. Of course, there were many others with these qualities on both sides of the House, including most, if not all, Liberals.

The former leader of the Conservative Party, John Diefenbaker, was in a category by himself. Undoubtedly one of the most colourful and in some ways remarkable, even outrageous men ever to serve in Canadian public life, "Dief" was above all a House of Commons man. He loved the place. It was his stage and he helped make the drama. A ferocious competitor, and partisan to the core, he was also one of the most unforgiving people in the House of Commons. He could neither forgive nor forget the people who deposed him as Conservative leader. To him, Dalton Camp was a four-letter word, something lower than a Judas Iscariot. As for Stanfield, who had replaced him as leader, though he was the only current hope of unseating the Grit enemy, Dief would never pass up an opportunity to upstage or humiliate him. It was this aspect of his character that, above all others, convinced me that Diefenbaker was a small man. I never served in the House of Commons when he was prime minister but what I saw of him confirmed his reputation as petty, mean, and vindictive. These were not qualities foreign to Canadian prime ministers but Dief was the only one who combined all three with such vengeance. To my mind, his treatment of Stanfield, one of the finest men ever to sit in Parliament, was shameful.

Having said all this about Dief, I must admit that I personally had a warm, cordial relationship with him, but I was always wary. I knew that one slip and he would be after me for the rest of his life — and mine. To my knowledge, I was the only Liberal with whom Dief would "pair," the parliamentary jargon for agreeing with an opposition member to abstain from voting in his absence. Now, at this stage of Dief's life, he would leave the Parliament Buildings right after Question Period, his favourite act, which gave him the opportunity he relished to inflict damage on the government. One day, however, a key vote arose and the prime minister wanted us all in our seats and voting. It was important not just to win the vote but also to do so decisively and visibly. Every minister had to be seen and to be recorded as supporting the government bill; pairs were off, even with the Dief. Well, you didn't just break a pair if you wanted to keep your reputation or have any hope of ever again being able to find a pair. And to have broken a pair with Dief would have been tantamount to political suicide. He would plague you until your last day on this earth. Anyway, when I heard of the prime minister's direction to us, I tried to reach Dief but he had left his office and his secretary had strict instructions not to give out his home number and not to bother him. She was impervious to my plight and, I am sure, was trained to treat any Liberal as the devil incarnate. I was close to desperate but she would not phone her boss. However, intentionally or unintentionally, she let slip that Sean O'Sullivan was the only person from whom Diefenbaker would accept a phone call. Sean was the young MP from Hamilton who earlier had been Dief's executive assistant and in later years would leave politics for the priesthood, only to die tragically young after a long and painful battle with leukaemia. I located Sean, who was attending a parliamentary committee meeting, and explained my dilemma. He promised to get "The Chief" on the phone and persuade him to agree to forego the pair.

I never did hear back from Sean, whose eye I unsuccessfully tried to get across the floor of the House as we assembled for the vote. Dief was not there and the sky did not come tumbling down as I stood to register my vote. I never did hear any more about it and Sean was uncharacteristically evasive when I tried to find out how Dief reacted. I can only speculate that he told Sean that everything would be all right but not to give me the satisfaction of knowing so. He just left me to stew.

Diefenbaker and I carried on a jokingly taunting sparring match in Question Period from time to time. When I had made my jab, he would rise at his seat to get the speaker's eye. Permission to proceed was always granted to Dief as a former prime minister but he never hesitated in

Paternal grandfather and name-sake Barnett Danson (d.1919), "one of the four grandparents I never knew."

My father, "J.B."

My mother's engagement photograph, 1914.

My parents at Camp
Winebagoe, Muskoka, 1943.

The author at age six; portrait by S. Soboloff, 1927.
"As I sat for this portrait,
Soboloff was working on a
portrait of Sir Henry Pellatt
– also of the Queen's Own –
at the same time."

Top: With my high school fraternity, the Delta Sigma Mu, 1939. I'm on the far left, back row. My good friend Freddy Harris, in the first row, far left, was killed on D-Day. Bob Raphael, middle row second from right, also served with us in the Queen's Own. All served in WWII.

Right: Two young Canuks' first leave in London in Trafalger Square, 1941. On the left me, 1921–. On the right Freddy Harris, 1921– 6 June 1944

EARL STOLL   GERRY RAYNER   FREDDIE HARRIS   BARNEY DANSON
ALDERSHOT ENGLAND SEPT. 1941   4 Corporals of The Q.O.R.
KILLED IN ACTION (DOW)   KILLED IN ACTION   KILLED IN ACTION   WOUNDED IN ACTION
AS LIEUT. SEPT 44   JULY 44 AS LIEUT   D-DAY 6 JUN 44 AS Sgt.   AUG 44 AS LIEUT.

From left: Earl Stoll, Gerry Rayner, Freddy Harris, and I as corporals in Aldershot, England, 1941. I was the only one to survive.

Sgt. Danson, February 1942, Aldershot, England, with high tech transporter.

With Isobel, on our first meeting, Surbiton, Surrey, October 1942.

The day Isobel and I became engaged, 24 December 1942, Aston Rowant, near Oxford. I am wearing "civvies" belonging to Isobel's cousin "Sony" Cohen, who was in tanks in North Africa with General Montgomery's 8th Army at the time.

On graduation as a 2nd lieutenant (a one-pip wonder), with Isobel, May 1943.

With our first son, Ken, on return from overseas, December 1944.

With family at Camp Winebagoe, circa 1956. Back: John, me, and Ken.
Front: Isobel, Tim, and Peter.

In our orchard, Old Colony Road, Toronto, 1967.

The family, 1976. From left: John, me, John's wife Elaine, Ken, Isobel, Peter, and Tim.

Brigadier the Hon. Milton F. Gregg VC, a great human being and an immense influence on my life.

With Pierre Trudeau at an election rally in Markham,
June 1968.

Sharing a laugh with two political giants, John Diefenbaker and Tommy
Douglas, the best orators and debaters in the House of Commons – and
the funniest too.

On my passionate elephant in Kandy, Ceylon (Sri Lanka), 1971.

Commonwealth Conference, Singapore, 1971.

At the Kremlin, 1971. From left: Trudeau, me, Victor Sukhodryev, interpreter, Premier Alexei Kosygin, and Foreign Minister Andrei Gromyko.

With Pierre and Margaret Trudeau at Samarkand, Uzbekistan, USSR,
1971.

A happy Barney, election night, 1974.

order to await the speaker's ruling. He was by now showing what was thought at the time (though no longer) to be the effects of Parkinson's disease, which never slowed him down but caused his jowls to shake and his head and hands to twitch slightly. Yet none of this detracted from his commanding presence and the drama he created just by rising in the House. "The honourable member is said by some to be quite a wit," he once thundered in reference to me. Pausing for effect and to hear the chuckles rising in the House, he then added, "I must tell you Mr. Speaker, they're only half right." He stood momentarily to hear the laughter and join if not lead it, and slowly resumed his seat with his shoulders heaving and jowls trembling as he enjoyed his joke and savoured the reaction of the House. I'm not certain just how many times he repeated this particular intervention but he relished it, as did I, on each occasion. It was certainly better to be on the receiving end of this put-down than of those he reserved for others who had tried to take him on. One went something like; "I don't debate with midgets." Another: "If you want to hunt elephants, don't use a peashooter."

One could go on indefinitely with Diefenbaker stories but I now wish to turn back to the Commons itself. The highlight of each parliamentary day was Question Period: the time when the opposition leaders and backbenchers and sometimes government backbenchers asked questions of the prime minister or the members of the cabinet. It was, and is, a highly partisan exchange, with each side trying to "one-up" the other, all of it accompanied by loud and sometimes rude interjections by supporters and adversaries. Desk thumping from the government benches or groans from the opposition almost always accompanied the minister's or questioner's comments no matter how innocuous or inane. The more partisan or biting the comment, the greater the tumult, as we thumped our desks, shouted and howled like school kids. One Tory MP — who was no shrinking violet himself — told me how intimidating it was for an opposition member to be faced every day with a huge mass of vociferous Liberals, all poised to jump over anyone who dared to attack the government. Question Period remains boisterous today, but, because of television, it is a mild affair compared to the freewheeling, irreverent performances of my day, polite applause often displacing desk thumping. It still serves, however, to keep the government on its toes, and woe betide the minister who is not thoroughly briefed and current in his or her portfolio. It is also vital in giving opposition leaders a public profile against which their performance and competence can be judged.

The highlight of each week was Wednesday morning caucus when each party met separately and privately to discuss and argue matters of policy, political tactics, and strategy. Each minister was accountable to caucus and the exchanges were frank. At the end of the discussion the prime minister, who never intervened but certainly took in every word and nuance, would analyse what had been said, note any considerations that had been missed, and offer his conclusions about the direction he felt we should take. These concluding remarks were invariably brilliant, so much so that the entire caucus frequently gave him a standing ovation. Occasionally, of course, even Trudeau could not quell the uncertainty that some felt regarding a given measure or course of action. On these occasions, the matter would usually be shelved for further consideration. Every now and then, however, Allan MacEachen, the laird of Cape Breton and its banker of first resort, would give a barn-burning, inspirational speech that brought caucus on side. It was not a frequent occurrence but when he let loose, either in caucus or in the Commons, it was a formidable performance that often saved the government and won the day.

In the long intervals between these spectacular performances, Allan, a dour Scot, meditated in the isolation of his thoughts. He had few, if any, close friends, but no enemies and many admirers, although I must say that the Treasury was always at risk when he had a project that benefited Nova Scotia; certainly all opposition was demolished if the beneficiary was Cape Breton Island. In my experience, apart from Jean Marchand and Gérard Pelletier, no one commanded Trudeau's respect more than Allan MacEachen and another senior minister, Bud Drury.

I understand that Allan's greatest performance occurred after my time in Ottawa, in December 1979, when Joe Clark's government fell in an historical demonstration of parliamentary ineptitude. Trudeau had announced his decision to resign and there was disagreement in the caucus whether an attempt should be made to persuade him to carry on. Then the silent Scot rose to make a passionate call for support of Trudeau, which left the caucus speechless. Divisions overcome, all

Liberals joined in a unanimous outpouring of affection and loyalty for Trudeau that he found irresistible. The rest is history. After the 1980 election, in which the Liberals were returned to power after the short-lived interregnum of Clark's Conservatives, Trudeau rewarded MacEachen with the post of secretary of state for external affairs, the one portfolio he filled with a notable lack of distinction — if, of course, you forget his stint in Finance. Following an audience with Allan, foreign leaders must have thought that Canadians were a strange, silent people indeed. In such meetings Allan was often completely silent, which caused great embarrassment until the host or a guest or some life-giving staffer came to the rescue.

My first two years were a continuous learning experience. At the riding level I was determined to respond quickly and thoroughly to my constituents' concerns and I also made a point of meeting regularly and frequently with them; not only was I in my constituency office virtually every weekend but I held community meetings in the riding several times each year. While in Ottawa, I briefed the people I represented both with mailings and with a regular "Ottawa Report" that was published in local weekly newspapers. In Parliament I found most of the work endlessly interesting. This was particularly true of parliamentary committees. I served on two committees, the Committee on Natural Resources and Public Works and the Committee on Finance, Trade and Economic Affairs, or, as it was commonly known, the Finance Committee. The second was the more important of the two by far. Most of the Liberals who served on this committee ultimately ended up as cabinet ministers, the list including Alastair Gillespie, Pat Mahoney, Herb Gray, Martin O'Connell, John Roberts, and Robert Kaplan. Our first assignment was a study of interest rates and inflation, and the people who appeared before us were among the leading economists in North America, one being John Kenneth Galbraith, a personal icon of mine. This experience was worth several years' study of economics and provided invaluable training for what came next.

Tax Reform: The Benson White Paper

Finance Minister Edgar Benson let go a political thunderclap when he introduced his White Paper on tax reform in November 1969. This was a complex proposal based largely on the philosophy of the recent Carter commission which held that, in simple terms, "a buck was a buck": that is, the government should treat each dollar earned as the equivalent of any other dollar and no exceptions should be made or expense deductions given. The White Paper envisaged a more equitable tax system, but powerful interests and small businesses reacted with shock and anger — not, ostensibly, over the issue of equity, but because, they argued, the paper's proposals were largely theoretical and impractical. The fact that it would endanger some of their "sacred cows" — such as deductibility of expenses — was not raised openly. Over the course of about a year the Finance Committee, which sat mainly in Ottawa but also conducted hearings across the country, met with an array of individuals and interest groups, most of them hostile to the government's plans. In fact, no interest group, of which I am aware, failed to appear before us with their special pleading and, in many cases, they had legitimate arguments. One organization that is still significant and active today, the Canadian Federation of Independent Business, was founded by John Bulloch with the specific purpose of fighting, and, ideally, sinking the White Paper, a task that Bulloch pursued with vigour.

Bulloch became a catalyst for broadly based, countrywide semi-hysteria in the ranks of small business, from "mom and pop" smoke shops to some quite substantial independent and often family enterprises. When Bulloch called the first protest meeting in the Canadian Room of the Royal York Hotel in Toronto, I decided to go in order to hear what the grass-roots were thinking and to meet this upstart whose merchant-tailor father incidentally had measured me for my first officer's uniform in the Second World War. Feeling the pulse was part of my job as a member of the Finance Committee, but I had no idea at this time of how high the public blood pressure was — and how quickly it was continuing to rise.

The Canadian Room was jammed and the hotel staff kept bringing more chairs in to accommodate the unexpectedly large audience. It was almost scary as Bulloch, a new and fresh face on the scene, worked the crowd like a southern Baptist preacher. Some years later Bulloch would confide to me that he, too, had found it a bit scary but he got caught up in the fervour. The crowd was a tinderbox of emotion waiting to be ignited, and ignite them he did. I'm surprised that they didn't end up burning Edgar Benson in effigy — or in person if they could have gotten their hands on him — and I was no less concerned that some of this anger might result in physical violence directed at me. I was certainly disabused of my original intention of discussing the White Paper calmly and thoughtfully. The message was clear. This was to be a no-holds-barred war, even if non-lethal. (Interestingly, years later I was asked to be the guest speaker at the dinner celebrating the twenty-fifth anniversary of Bulloch's Canadian Federation of Independent Business!)

Defending the White Paper made life politically and personally difficult. Going home to Toronto on weekends was hell. No social gathering was safe as one person or a group of people cornered me to put forward their case or to express their sometimes extreme positions, which often spilled over into personal abuse. Walking down the street, particularly Bay Street, was an obstacle course. People would cross the street to my side to berate me or cross to the other side to avoid me. And I wasn't alone. Diana Gillespie, Alastair's feisty wife, nailed a sign on the door of their ski chalet reading "Welcome. As long as you don't mention the White Paper." There was no respite. The hostility was continuous and pervasive.

Initially the White Paper was considered an integrated package: if one element was changed, the document would begin to unravel. Ultimately, however, the government was forced to compromise. If I recall correctly, our committee made over one hundred recommendations, some three-quarters of which were accepted by "Ben" Benson and the government. By November 1971 legislation had been introduced that departed in a number of ways large and small from the White Paper though a few of the latter's provisions, such as the introduction of a capital gains tax, the abolition of estate taxes, and stricter rules governing business expenses, survived. Some may say that the White Paper was gutted in the interests of appeasing the powerful and that a rare opportunity to promote a more equal distribution of wealth through the tax system was squandered in the process. I don't agree. In my view the White Paper, while noble in its objectives, was wrong-headed in some areas, difficult or impossible to understand, let alone implement, in others, and, in general, full of political land mines and perhaps some booby-traps. No government could implement it unaltered and live to tell the tale. In any case, the purpose of any white paper is to explain the intention of government and the method of achieving it, while thoroughly ventilating the matter by public representation and discussion. The Benson White Paper did exactly that. The Finance Committee's hearings on the subject were an expression of democracy, one that took over a year of my life and ten years off it.

Legislation for a New Era

On other fronts the Trudeau government introduced a number of important measures in its first couple of years. One was Minister of Justice John Turner's landmark omnibus bill of amendments to the Criminal Code that, among other improvements, broadened the grounds for divorce and removed homosexuality from the Criminal Code ("the state," as Trudeau said, "has no business in the bedrooms of the nation"). Another was the Official Languages Act which, at long last, set Canada on the road to being able to provide its French-speaking citizens with government services in their own language, where numbers warranted. I supported the government's legislative program without serious personal reservations and, despite some opposition in my own riding, was particularly enthusiastic about the Official Languages Act. I firmly believed that the government's official-bilingualism initiative was a matter of simple justice and vital to the future of the country. I also felt then, as I still do now, that Canadians had taken a rare opportunity which would enrich the country mightily — the presence of two official languages — and turned it into a problem. As it turns out, in our increasingly international economy and multicultural society, facility in both languages gives those so gifted a distinct advantage and is an added plus for those with a third language at home. Yet in Canada we all too often let extremists and single-issue advocates spook us.

In September 1968, not long after I had taken my seat, I introduced a private member's bill dealing with Remembrance Day. With the notable exception of a bill introduced by the then backbencher Jean Chrétien to change the name of Trans Canada Airlines to Air Canada, a change that took effect in 1965, private member's bills rarely become law. Indeed, most never even reach the floor for debate. There is such a plethora of these bills that the few that do get debated are chosen by lottery — the luck of the draw. They do, however, allow a private member on the "backbenches" to float an idea and, since they are all printed, to provoke comment. Occasionally the public, media, or parliamentary interest in a private member's bill prompts the government to follow through on it in legislative terms. That didn't happen with my bill, but there was certainly no lack of comment about it.

In the early years after the Second World War, a large element of our population had either served in the armed forces during that conflict or had family members who had. As a result, for a great number of Canadians at the time, the war was a vital part of their lives and the celebration of the First World War Armistice on November 11th as Remembrance Day was an intensely personal experience. However, as time went on and people passed on, Remembrance Day, except for the Royal Canadian Legion and other veteran's organizations, became just another statutory holiday for people who didn't give its meaning much, if any, thought; even the schools, churches, and synagogues gave it less and less emphasis. This was the background to my private member's bill.

The bill had two elements. The first was that Remembrance Day, when not falling on a weekend, be publicly celebrated on the Saturday or Sunday (depending on religious persuasion) prior to November 11th so that it would be not just a holiday but a day of real spiritual significance. This idea was controversial but, strangely enough, had the support of many veterans groups — the Legion branches were divided about fifty/fifty, as far as I could determine. The second element of the bill, which was far more controversial, proposed that *all* veterans of the Second World War participate in Remembrance Day observances. This was prompted by my belief that we were not celebrating war but remembering those who died in wars. It also reflected my knowledge as a soldier that not all Germans were Nazis nor were all Italians fascists and all Japanese imperialists; many, like our own men, did not enlist for ideological reasons at all. For large numbers on both sides, their country was at war and they either chose or were forced to enlist and defend it. There was still another consideration. I felt that our remembrance of war should encompass all those who lost their lives as a result of it and be relevant to all of our citizens, including those of German, Italian, and Japanese origin. More particularly, I felt it unfair that the children of these immigrants — most of whom had been born in Canada and certainly all of whom were being raised as Canadians — should be made to feel on Remembrance Day as something less than fully Canadian. This was surely not a wise way to build a country as diverse as ours. As I felt then and still feel now, it is certainly important to remember the past, but the mark of a mature society is the ability, while not forgiving former enemies for the crimes of war and those that led to it, to stop hating. One must never forget, and it is not always possible to forgive, but there must be a time to stop hating before that hatred devours us. To the extent we can put the past behind us, we should. It was in this spirit that my bill proposed to open Remembrance Day observances to our former adversaries.

No action had been taken on my bill by the time Parliament was prorogued but I introduced the bill again on 7 November 1969. Shortly afterwards I was in the House one day when I was told that Colonel Sydney Lambert, the senior Protestant chaplain in the Canadian army in my time and a respected veteran of the First World War, was on the phone and wanted to speak to me. When I answered, he promptly tore into my bill and me with such vehemence that I was left shaking. I responded to Lambert by saying that I didn't agree but that, if such a distinguished Canadian as he — one for whom all soldiers had such profound admiration — felt so strongly about the bill, I would withdraw it immediately. Which is what I did. Looking back at it now, I believe that the bill was a sensible one. It didn't have a chance of becoming law, but if there had been clear enthusiasm for its underlying principles, it would have been worthy of further action. However, with significant opposition from some 50 percent of veterans and with the vehement opposition of a respected icon like Colonel Lambert, I thought it prudent to put the measure aside, at least for the moment.

An Arctic Tour

I once had told Jean Chrétien, then minister of Indian affairs and northern development, that I had always wanted to visit the Arctic, an area of
some fascination for me. One day during Question Period he came over
to me and asked if I was still interested in doing this. I said, "Absolutely!"
and he said, "OK, be at the airport at 5 o'clock." There were two government parties going to the Arctic to celebrate the centennial of the
Northwest Territories and to attend the first Arctic Winter Games. The
prime minister, his staff, and John Munro, minister of national health
and welfare, were to visit the central and eastern regions, Chrétien and
I were to visit the west, and the two groups were to meet in Yellowknife.

I raced back to my apartment, phoned Isobel to tell her that I would
not be home that weekend, threw some clothes in a suitcase, and raced
to the airport, where I was assured by John Rae, Chrétien's executive
assistant, that they had adequate Arctic gear for me. We then boarded a
plane bound for Inuvik. I had not known Chrétien very well personally
before this time, but the two of us now established a warm and lasting
relationship. I was especially struck by how much he loved his portfolio
and by the positive chemistry he had established with native people;
there was obviously a great rapport between them.

I developed a deep attachment to the Arctic, captivated both by the
stark yet beautiful environment and by the Inuit people, with their soft,
gentle personalities, their quiet intelligence, and their dry sense of
humour. I also loved the rugged simplicity of their art, reflecting the
genius of largely self-trained artists and of the harsh world in which they
tenaciously survived. In fact, Isobel and I had been collectors of
Eskimo/Inuit art since the late 1950s, a pursuit that started with our purchase of an excellent carving for eighteen dollars at the Canadian
Handicraft Guild shop on Peel St in Montreal. A carver named Moses —
there were several named Moses, each of them identified by a number —
was one whose work we particularly wanted to own. On reaching
Yellowknife, I asked Stu Hodgson, the commissioner of the Northwest
Territories, if he knew where our Moses might be. Stu replied that he
knew exactly where he was and could take me to him. Moses was well

established in the local jail, where he had spent a good part of his life, having dispatched each of his three wives with a bullet in the centre of her forehead. And so I met this shy, soft-spoken, and extremely talented artist in the new and modern jail that served the entire Territories. Apparently Moses was a gentle person until he got drunk when he went berserk. Afterwards he had no memory whatsoever of what he had done and was once again his shy, quiet self. Besides being horrified by Moses's crimes, I failed to understand how he continued to attract wives. I was also puzzled by his drinking habits, since the Inuit at that time, unlike other aboriginal groups, had not generally been afflicted with the worst habits of whites. That would come later. I remember wondering how the Inuit as a whole could be protected from these elements of white "civilization."

Moses's work was grabbed up as soon as it was produced and he had nothing, except a few small trinkets, to show me. Stu Hodgson promised that he would buy a good carving from Moses for me as soon as possible. He was as good as his word, which is standard practice for Stu, and I collected a beautiful bird by Moses on a subsequent Arctic trip. When we got it home and matched the artist's hieroglyphics and numbers with those on another carving we had acquired years earlier, we found that we had owned a Moses all the time. But having *two* Moses carvings is great.

After the Arctic Games Chrétien was to make a visit to the remote settlement of Old Crow in the Yukon. This involved a flight of about one hour and required landing on a frozen river. On arrival there we were taken to the community hall where the entire population of Old Crow was assembled along with their neighbours from within dog-sled and ski-doo commuting distance. Also there was Eric Nielsen, the veteran Tory MP for the Yukon. We were salivating in anticipation of a promised meal of moose-nose soup and roasted caribou. The seating arrangement was unique to say the least. Chrétien was seated at the centre of a head-table set up on a stage flanked by the rest of the official party. When the food was brought in, the local community, our hosts, sat on the floor before us, watching us eat what they knew was a very special treat. It wasn't to be just ordinary moose and caribou fare, however — that, in their view, would not be equal to this historic occasion; instead, they had used their scant resources to fly in roasts of beef from Edmonton at considerable cost. We hid our disappointment and chewed our very well-done Edmonton fare. Our hosts sat silently, engrossed by the spectacle and very proud. It was an event that no doubt was well remembered in Old Crow years afterwards.

Returning from this trip we stopped in Saskatoon, where Chrétien was to address a large meeting of Saskatchewan native groups. He was warmly received — the natives liked him and he liked them — but that didn't stop one after another band chief and organization head from stepping up to the microphone and berating him for every sin, real and imagined, committed by the federal government, the Department of Indian Affairs, and Chrétien himself since the arrival of Jacques Cartier in 1534. Chrétien, adopting his easy-going manner — as opposed to the highly partisan and combative side of his character that today is often on display in the Commons — responded to the substantive criticisms and deflected the others.

Back in Ottawa a few weeks later, I ran into a group of the same native leaders in the lobby of the Chateau Laurier and invited them to the Colonel By lounge for some refreshment. The conversation was free and frank and all warm and complimentary to Jean Chrétien. After the second, or maybe it was the third, beer I asked how they reconciled their speeches in Saskatoon with the obvious affection and respect they had for him, to which they replied, "We were speaking in a room full of our supporters. That was just Indian politics." They were kind enough not to add, "just like yours." In my dealings with aboriginals and Metis I always found that, while they could quickly spot a "phoney" or hypocrite, if they felt you were sincere and open they trusted you and your relationship with them was both cordial and constructive. One of the proudest moments of my political life was when, as minister of urban affairs with responsibility for off-reserve housing, I was presented with a plaque recognizing me as an honorary life member of the Ontario Métis and Non-Status Indian Association in a ceremony at White River, Ontario.

Parliamentary Secretary

The post of parliamentary secretary — meaning an elected assistant to a cabinet minister — is considered a learning ground for promising MPs or a reward for those who have served well. Prior to 1970, parliamentary secretaries held their positions until they reached ministerial rank or, of course, until they left Parliament by defeat or retirement or their party was relegated to the opposition. Trudeau, however, introduced a new system. Wanting to replace some of the current parliamentary secretaries, so as to give new members a chance to demonstrate their skills, and just as anxious to avoid embarrassing individuals by singling them out for either promotion or demotion, he decided in September 1970 to replace all existing parliamentary secretaries with fresh appointees for a two-year term. This became the regular practice and was accepted in the future but it was awkward for the first group of parliamentary secretaries replaced, particularly those who had served many years in the role. Before the first new batch was appointed, there were rumours that Alastair Gillespie, Pat Mahoney, and I were likely candidates. Yet no one was certain of appointment or of the cabinet portfolio to which they would be assigned until it was announced by the Prime Minister's Office. To my great surprise and joy, not only was I made a parliamentary secretary but also I caught the brass ring as parliamentary secretary to Prime Minister Trudeau himself, replacing the legendary Jimmie Walker. Jimmie had had a distinguished career as MP for York Centre, a Toronto-area riding, before becoming Liberal Whip in the Commons in the Pearson era, a demanding job that required him to make deals with the Créditistes and occasionally the NDP to keep the minority Liberal government afloat in the House. The stress drove him to a heart attack after which he was rewarded by being made parliamentary secretary to Trudeau, a post that Trudeau himself had filled with Pearson before becoming justice minister in 1967.

Parliamentary secretaries do not have any legislative responsibilities. Their minister largely determines the extent of their role and there is a wide variation in the extent to which ministers involve their parliamentary secretaries. They routinely represent their ministers in debate on private members bills and may answer for him or her in Question Period, in their absence, although this is now most often done by another designated minister or, on occasion, the prime minister himself. Good ministers involve their parliamentary secretaries in all or most of their departmental meetings, some giving them responsibility for specific areas of their portfolio responsibilities. In addition, parliamentary secretaries act as the lead government supporter on parliamentary committees, while also delivering speeches and performing representational duties on their ministers' behalf. It is an excellent method of developing and recognizing talent when properly utilized by ministers. Regrettably, some ministers waste the opportunity, often because they are unwilling to share any of the power or limelight with others, sometimes because of simple disinterest, and not infrequently because they don't like or have confidence in the parliamentary secretary assigned to them.

In my case, there was no department in which to become involved but I couldn't have asked for a more fascinating and thoughtful boss. Trudeau included me in a wide variety of his meetings and virtually all his travels and I acted as unofficial liaison with caucus. Being the only parliamentarian on his staff, I had a special role in the regular meetings of his staff, chaired by his principle secretary at the time, Marc Lalonde. There was a lot of backroom talent in the Prime Minister's Office (PMO), including such luminaries as Ivan Head, Joyce Fairbairn, and Colin Kenny (the latter two now senators), and in the Privy Council Office (PCO), the bureaucratic arm of the prime minister, headed at the time by the legendary Gordon Robertson, the most senior civil servant in the land. I was expected to provide the parliamentary/political view on many issues.

I found the close association with Trudeau an incredibly exhilarating experience. He was never "palsy-walsy" but almost always warm and respectful. He had moments when you knew or should have known to keep your distance: when he was physically exhausted or had one of his not infrequent head colds, which often happened at the same time, and of course when he was obviously preoccupied with the kind of matters that preoccupy a prime minister. These were not the strictly partisan preoccupations that absorbed some prime ministers like Diefenbaker or Mulroney. That was not Trudeau's suit; he all too frequently had little patience with these kinds of issues. His ability to concentrate on matters of policy, however, was prodigious.

The October Crisis

My first trip as parliamentary secretary to the prime minister was to be to the Soviet Union, and was scheduled for October 1970, but it was postponed when the FLQ crisis erupted. This story is so well known that I need not tell it in detail here. Suffice to say that the atmosphere in Ottawa, and particularly on the Hill, was bunker-like. There were armed military personnel at all critical points in the city, and because a British diplomat, James Cross, had been kidnapped in Montreal — an event followed by the kidnap and murder of Quebec cabinet minister Pierre Laporte — each minister and each embassy was assigned guards on a twenty-four-hour basis. Parliament Hill was virtually an armed camp and the PMO and PCO were the primary control centres where developments and threats had to be assessed and counter-actions decided upon. Marc Lalonde, as the prime minister's principal secretary, and Jean Marchand, the senior Quebec minister, played key roles, as did Gordon Robertson, the secretary to the cabinet. Though I was the prime minister's parliamentary secretary, I was not in the "inner loop" of decision makers who plotted the government's response, but I was a close observer of the action. Trudeau never looked more preoccupied than he did in those tense days.

Our fear at the time was more a result of what we did not know rather than of what we did. Canada had not been faced with such a crisis before and our security apparatus had been caught off guard. We simply were not accustomed to the level of intelligence and security common in other countries. We had to grow up in a hurry. Meanwhile, hysteria increasingly prevailed at the senior levels of the provincial government in Quebec, particularly after Laporte's murder. When Premier Robert Bourassa called the prime minister for help, including military guards for him and his ministers, we provided it. We were obliged to do so under the National Defence Act, although the extent and nature of the response was ultimately the call of the chief of the defence staff. Later, as tension escalated in Quebec, especially in Montreal, it became apparent that emergency measures were needed. Bourassa and the mayor of Montreal, Jean Drapeau, asked for the imposition of the War Measures Act, the only legislation on the books that would allow an all-out military and police response to the crisis. The federal government hesitated briefly. The War Measures Act was Draconian legislation that could well be abused by the police and military, who would use their powers to the fullest extent that the act allowed. That was their job in the absence of any less sweeping legislation, and they were not about to expose themselves to the risk of failure and the criticism that would entail. Ultimately, however, Ottawa acceded to the request of Bourassa and Drapeau; any other response, as Trudeau later argued, would have been irresponsible. In the event, some four hundred suspects were arrested and jailed without charge, as the law allowed; virtually all of them were soon released for lack of evidence.

Clearly the politicians and the police had overreacted. But that is with twenty/twenty hindsight. In the PMO, where the buck stops, rapid and decisive action was called for. A strong police and military presence in Montreal calmed the public's fears and within a couple of weeks the police had caught the kidnappers and secured Cross's release. Some may debate whether this result had anything to do with the War Measures Act, but the fact is that the October Crisis ended with the disintegration of the FLQ and the complete cessation of the terrorist activity that had afflicted Quebec intermittently since the 1960s. An overwhelming majority of Canadians, including those in Quebec, strongly supported the government's action and, by the end of 1970, the War Measures Act had been replaced with the Emergency Powers Act to enable the government to respond to future domestic crises in a more measured and graduated fashion. I believed then, as I do now, that this was an essential piece of legislation which allows a response appropriate to the threat and gives government the necessary powers to deal with any escalating crisis.

Never again do I want to repeat the experience of the Pierre Laporte funeral. The prime minister's entourage, of which I was part, was ferried by armed forces helicopters from Ottawa to Montreal where it was met and encircled by soldiers with their submachine guns at the ready, facing outward in the event that anyone chose us, and particularly the prime minister, as targets. We were taken in a heavily guarded convoy to Notre Dame Basilica in Place d'Armes in the heart of Old Montreal. The crowd was massive and troops provided an armed cordon as we entered the church. Sharpshooters were visible on the roof of each adjacent building and armed police were strategically but discreetly placed within the church. Montreal was like an armed camp; it all seemed unreal. I shall never forget the tension that engulfed the entire congregation as the Sûreté du Quebec pallbearers marched in unison down the main aisle with Laporte's casket, draped with the Fleur-de-lis, borne on their shoulders. Each step resounded with an eerie clarity that sent tremors down every spine. Few in the crowded church were personal friends of Laporte but all knew that he, and this moment in the FLQ drama, was a part of our nation's history.

The next time I would be in Notre Dame Basilica was thirty years later, for Pierre Trudeau's own funeral. Like my experience in 1970, it was an occasion I shall never forget.

Chapter Four
Parliamentary Secretary
to the Prime Minister,
1970–72

With the postponement of the Soviet Union trip as a result of the FLQ crisis, my first trip abroad as the prime minister's parliamentary secretary took place early the following year. The Commonwealth Conference was being held in Singapore in January 1971, and the prime minister decided to use the occasion as an opportunity to visit other, mostly Commonwealth, countries in the region. It was a twenty-eight-day tour that would take us to Pakistan, India, Indonesia, Ceylon (now Sri Lanka), and (an unscheduled visit) Iran.

The Singapore conference was a pivotal one in the history of the Commonwealth, for its member states were then bitterly divided over the decision of Britain's recently elected Conservative government of Edward Heath to honour an agreement — entered into originally by the Macmillan government but then suspended by Harold Wilson's Labour Party — providing for arm sales to the apartheid regime of South Africa. The British policy, formally known as the Simonstown Agreement (Simonstown being a major South African naval base), had infuriated the countries of black Africa to such an extent that many threatened to leave the Commonwealth if it were not reversed, an example that would possibly be followed by Asian and Caribbean states. In late 1970 Trudeau dispatched his principal foreign-policy adviser, the immensely well-informed Ivan Head, to Africa for consultations with two African leaders, Julius Nyerere of Tanzania and Kenneth Kaunda of Zambia, who had long been the main African spokesmen on the South African issue. Knowing the prime minister's strong feelings on the matter and the urgency of the situation, Head, who always had Trudeau's complete confidence, had the authority to speak for the government of Canada. In Africa, he received from Nyerere a "Declaration of Principles" that committed the Commonwealth to repudiation of the Simonstown Agreement. Nyerere let it be known that neither he nor Kaunda would attend the Singapore conference if Canada did not agree in advance to support the declaration. Head, after some hesitation, said that Canada would support it, a decision that was later ratified by Trudeau. The task would now be to keep the British on side, no easy feat. When Heath, visiting Ottawa shortly afterwards, was shown the African declaration and told of Canada's decision to support it, he was enraged. Britain was now the country threatening to leave the Commonwealth. Such was the tense backdrop to the Singapore conference.

We travelled by Armed Forces Boeing 707 transport aircraft with a large contingent of diplomatic and trade advisers, about thirty media personnel, and the ever-present RCMP security officers. Besides myself, Trudeau's personal staff consisted of Ivan Head, Tim Porteous, executive assistant to the prime minister and later president of the Canada Council, Marshall Crowe, deputy secretary to the cabinet, and Peter Roberts, press secretary and later our ambassador to Moscow. We were seated in a special compartment called the capsule that was inserted behind the cockpit, and other officials joined us there for briefings and discussions. There were two dining tables, each with four seats, which we used as worktables to accommodate the mass of papers and extensive briefing books covering each of the countries to be visited and the Commonwealth Conference itself. These papers and books contained an immense amount of material on assorted topics — the conference agenda, protocol, biographies of heads of government, others we would meet, and Canada's relationships with each country. Two bunks lined the side of the aircraft behind our work area; one was for the prime minister, and the other he offered to me, as the next senior person politically on board the aircraft. This was a big improvement on curling up on a seat or today's economy travel.

We stopped for refuelling at our NATO base in Lahr, Germany. I had noticed in my briefing book that the base commander was a Colonel (later Brigadier-General) Gordon Sellars, with whom I had served during the war. I was at the prime minister's side as he was introduced to each of the senior officers, and when we came to Colonel Sellars, I said jokingly, "Prime Minister, he's a lousy soldier." Sellars, who hadn't expected me, turned scarlet. Then, however, he realized who the culprit was and our brief reunion commenced.

Pakistan

Four thousand miles and eighteen hours later, we landed for our first official visit in Islamabad, the new capital of Pakistan, adjacent to the old city of Rawalpindi, a former British military garrison city and centre for the northwest frontier. Martial law had been declared in Pakistan in 1968, but just prior to our arrival, in December 1970, free elections had been held for a constituent assembly which had the task of devising, in six weeks, a new constitution. Not an easy job for a nation divided into two parts, West Pakistan and East Pakistan (now Bangladesh), separated by some 1,400 miles of somewhat hostile Indian territory. East Pakistan had the larger population but was small in size and impoverished. West Pakistan, much bigger in size, had more economic resources by far and was the seat of government. Zulfikar Ali Bhutto, leader of the People's Party, had won a significant majority of seats in West Pakistan, but in East Pakistan the Awami League had prevailed. When we were there, it was said that Bhutto would lead a coalition which would include representatives from both sections; after our departure, however, General Yahya Khan, chief of the general staff and president under the prevailing martial law, refused to accept the election results, and this decision led to a flurry of developments. East Pakistan rose in rebellion, India declared war on Pakistan, Bhutto replaced Khan as president of West Pakistan, and in December 1971 East Pakistan became the independent state of Bangladesh. I wasn't surprised that President Khan's bullheadedness had provoked a war, for during our visit he had struck me as a ruthless operator. I remember him saying at a luncheon in Islamabad that his government was not democratic; it wasn't even a military government. Instead, he thundered, banging his fist on the table for emphasis, Pakistan's government was martial law!

Much of our official discussions in Islamabad centred on Canada's aid programs in Pakistan — a subject of great interest to the Pakistanis and us — and the other Pakistani preoccupation at the time, India's nuclear capability. Pakistan had just bought two CANDU nuclear reactors for Karachi, but it had had to sign a nuclear-safeguard agreement basically committing itself to only peaceful use of the technology. India had purchased a smaller test reactor before the nuclear-safeguard agreements were in place and thus faced no such restrictions. The Pakistanis, knowing that we were going to India next, wanted us to get a firm commitment from Indira Gandhi, the then prime minister, that India would never use its reactor for military purposes. Trudeau assured the Pakistanis that we would raise the matter with her, although none of us could have confidence in the result.

An official government dinner, given by the governor of the state of Sind, was held in Karachi, the first capital of the new Pakistan after its secession from India. While there, we stayed at the official residence of the governor, built in the days of the British Raj. The dinner took place in the garden of the residence under brightly decorated canvas marquees. Prime Minister-apparent Bhutto was to be seated next to me. He had expected to sit next to Trudeau, which I would have thought appropriate: it was Bhutto with whom Trudeau would have to deal in the future. The current martial-law regime had no love for the wealthy but left-wing Bhutto and demanded the observance of strict protocol, since the process of establishing Bhutto as prime minister had not yet been completed. As we waited for dinner to be served, there seemed to be undue delay and much whispering among the government ministers. Bhutto had disappeared. He was not about to sit with the parliamentary secretary and insisted on sitting next to Trudeau or he wouldn't return. Someone prevailed upon him not to create an embarrassing incident — though the matter was of no concern to us — and he ultimately took his place on my left. Nearby was a Mr Haqe, the minister of commerce from East Pakistan, a cultivated and senior businessman from Dacca, who was my counterpart. It was the custom for our hosts in each country to assign a minister to this role to act as my personal host. Haqe, who was to lead the Pakistan delegation to Singapore, had a civil relationship with Bhutto. The other ministers in close proximity apparently did not.

During the course of the dinner, Bhutto implied to each of the rather elderly Pakistani men near us around the table just what their fate would be when he took office. It wasn't kid-glove politics. Indeed, I was told that Bhutto's "war cry" during the massive political rallies of those days was to the effect that he, once in power, would impale his political enemies anally — a threat that exemplified the politics of the subcontinent. At the emotional climax of these highly charged meetings, Bhutto would shriek "Up their ass," or something equally expressive and endearing. So his little, less than gentle, reminders were not taken lightly and I swear that each one of his Pakistani listeners turned white.

Haqe suggested that it would be helpful if Trudeau and Bhutto had an opportunity to meet in the informal and congenial atmosphere of a private home with a small group of younger academics, politicians, and business people. He had apparently raised this with an approving Bhutto and asked if I would take it up with Trudeau, which I did and he agreed. It is possible that this proposal was part of the negotiation that brought Bhutto to the dinner table. We arrived at the designated home and were introduced to about fifteen or twenty Pakistani men and women who all spoke as if they had just returned from Oxford or Cambridge, which in all likelihood they had. I believe that Ivan Head, Tim Porteous, Peter Roberts, and High Commissioner John Small were with us. A very attractive, generously endowed young woman from Lahore was seated beside Trudeau, as was not uncommon (and which never drew any complaint from him). The conversation was spirited and then Bhutto arrived and began his monologue. In his favour, he could not be accused of false modesty. He pontificated and name-dropped for at least half an hour, hoping to impress Trudeau as much as he apparently impressed himself. From our viewpoint, it was an opportunity to size up this rather unattractive, self-centred man. (His personal deficiencies were not, however, any reason to murder him by hanging, as would happen at the hands of his successors in 1979.) We also came face to face with the nature of politics in ostensibly "democratic" nations with cultures and traditions markedly different from ours.

Before leaving Karachi for India, we made the obligatory pilgrimage to the tomb of Mohammed Ali Jina, the founding leader of Pakistan. It was a large, elaborate structure on a high hill that overlooked all of

Karachi and could be seen from anywhere in the city. This appeared to be designed as Pakistan's alternative to India's Taj Mahal, but nothing, as I will recount, could match the Taj. The official departure ceremonies were complicated by the fact that British Prime Minister Heath, also on his way to Singapore, had arrived an hour or so before we left. This meant that President Khan and his officials had to meet Heath and his party, escort them to the governor's mansion so they could get settled, and rush back to the airport to see us off. The guard of honour, brass band, and diplomatic corps just stayed in place at the airport, as did the cabinet ministers who did not have to be with Heath. It went smoothly, however, and they didn't even get our national anthems mixed up, although the Pakistani version of "O Canada" was such that we wouldn't have known the difference.

India

Before landing in New Delhi for the beginning of our official visit, we stopped at Agra, site of the Taj Mahal, and were welcomed by the Indian high commissioner to Canada, Ashok Bhadkamkar, who had preceded us on this trip. I had seen so many tourist pictures of the Taj that the prospect of a visit to it did not cause me much excitement. Until I saw it. One of the ten wonders of the world, the Taj is an architectural, engineering, and aesthetic masterpiece, set in exquisitely designed and manicured gardens on the banks of the Yamuna River. It was built from 1632 to 1654 by the Mogul emperor Jahan Mahal as a tomb for his wife, who lies in the precise centre of the Taj so that she and the emperor would be facing one another when he was interred in a matching tomb. The latter was to be constructed on the other side of the river and was to be in black marble to contrast with the luminescent white marble of the original. As it happened, however, the emperor died before this second tomb could be built, and thus he is buried in a tomb beside his wife. This second tomb is the only element of the Taj that is not perfectly symmetrical. Everything else is precise. The four minarets are not only in exact juxtaposition to one another, but each is tilted at a slight, virtually imperceptible angle away from the main structure so as to fall away from the Taj in the event of an earthquake. Such attention to detail is almost unnoticed to the untrained eye. The Sanskrit on each arched entrance is larger in the upper portions than in the sides and those parts close to the bottom so that the viewer would sense that all are the same size when viewed from the ground. What almost spoiled the visit was the noisy crowd of spectators, souvenir vendors, and TV camera crews. I murmured to the prime minister that this was too good to spoil and should be viewed alone and in silence, and he nodded in agreement. It was dark by the time we left.

We had been told that the most beautiful view of the Taj is at dawn, when the structure seems to be rising through the mist from the river. The late Ron Collister, a TV journalist in the press party, and I decided to see this for ourselves. Since we were scheduled to leave Agra early the next morning, we needed to wake up at 5:30 to see the Taj and be ready for take-off with the rest of the prime minister's entourage. We found a sleepy cab driver, bartered successfully for a round-trip fare, and left in the dark. As light broke gently through the mist, the dome of the mosque's white marble glistened as it appeared to emerge from the river. One could not help but gasp. We viewed the main structure, the gardens, and minarets from every angle and each glimpse had a different impact on us. I can't remember if we were there for one or three hours. We knew that we had to watch the time, but we could have spent a day or more gazing at what I believe must be the most beautiful and intriguing structure in the whole world.

We joined the main party at the hotel for the trip to the airport. Because our next stop, Varanasi, was too small to accommodate our 707, we were to fly there in an Indian air force Avro aircraft. En route to the airport, we were to stop at an important temple, and as we approached it we noticed a number of obviously Western tourists being held back from our entourage by the local police. On getting closer, we recognized several Canadian lawyer-friends who were in India to attend a Commonwealth Bar Association conference. Trudeau had the driver stop the car while we greeted Jack Godfrey (later senator), Alan Linden (later Mr Justice Linden and head of the Law Reform Commission of Canada), Ontario Chief Justice William Gale and others. When I saw Jack and Mary Godfrey subsequently in Singapore, they told me that the police guard had explained to them that they had to be held back because the prime minister of Canada was arriving. Jack said that he was a friend of the prime minister, but the guard made it clear that he was not falling for this line, only to change his tune when he saw the warm greeting that Godfrey received from the prime minister (after all, Jack was the chief fundraiser for the Liberal Party).

On arrival at our hotel in Varanasi, we were greeted by a large student protest. Apparently, they had heard that there was discrimination against Indians in Canada. That was in 1971 and the students seem to have been confused by stories of the plight of our aboriginal Indians. Against all RCMP and Indian advice, Trudeau invited the leaders of the demonstration into the hotel to hear their concerns. They were not used to such consideration and were initially agitated, but, in a style that was typical for him when he was dealing with students, he treated them with respect, without a hint of condescension, and charmed them over. I don't know if any of them immigrated to Canada and voted Liberal as a result, but most of us observed this impressive exchange with admiration.

Varanasi, formerly known as Benares, is one of the holiest of Hindu cities, known for its "ghats," where the sacred process of cremation takes place and ashes are cast into the Ganges River. After viewing a non-stop succession of cremations — hardly light entertainment — we cruised the river on a somewhat rickety ferry boat, hoping that it wouldn't capsize if one moved too quickly to one side. Many equally or even more flimsy craft were docked along the shore, filled with American, European, and, as I learned, Canadian students, or more properly, former students, who were mostly stoned on the easily available and inexpensive marijuana and other drugs. Gingerly but happily disembarking from our ferry we began to visit still more Indian temples and before returning to our hotel we stopped at the local Jesuit school where the prime minister had received hospitality during his much earlier visits to India as a young man tramping through Asia. Although invited to join him, Ivan Head and I remained in the car, feeling that we would be intruding on a personal reunion. It became a long wait when Trudeau decided to attend Mass, as he almost always did whenever he had the opportunity, no matter how remote the location.

We finally reached our hotel for dinner, hot and sweaty and informally dressed (this was Trudeau's style, which we all happily adopted). Three white-garbed Canadian priests from the school sat opposite us at the long table and, while Trudeau was engaged in conversation with one, all the while flanked by an attractive Indian woman, I engaged the others. In my riding of York North, Father Lionel Stanford was rector of Regis College, a Jesuit seminary, and we had become good friends. He had told me of his brother Maurice ("Moe"), who had been a missionary in India for over twenty-five years and whose letters Lionel often read to me. I asked my dinner companions if they had ever heard of him. "That's him talking to Mr Trudeau," one replied. The facial resemblance was obvious, but the voice was an incredible duplicate of Father Lionel's. It was one of those almost unbelievable coincidences that tempt you to say it's a small world, which of course it isn't, making the coincidence all the more remarkable. Father "Moe" reminded me that the Stanfords and Trudeaus were neighbours in the Outremont district of Montreal. Both Stanfords have since died, Moe in India and Lionel in Israel.

The next day we visited an Indian village where two small Canadian aid programs were about to transform the lives of its inhabitants by building a new elementary school and a tube well with pump, to provide fresh water to a village where disease was endemic. Trudeau was to officiate at the inauguration of both. The most dramatic moment was when he threw the switch that started the electric pump, which caused the water to flow. To the villagers, it was a miracle to have fresh potable water. To us, it was a miracle that the switch actually worked, which isn't always the case, particularly when the media cameras are rolling to record the event for Canadian newspapers and televisions. Neil Overend of the Canadian International Development Agency was delighted, but his joy evaporated the next day when he learned from his Canadian headquarters that the newspapers' front pages showed only Pierre Trudeau on a local camel, which was a small sidelight of the visit. The impression at home was that Trudeau was having a great time at public expense riding camels around the world in hot climates while Canadians were freezing. This is one of the hazards of politics, however; no one is much interested in tube wells or the punishing schedules

121

with little sleep that are typical of these trips, commonly called junkets. Camels are romantic — and not only, apparently, to other camels. On the other hand, I have never heard of a politician confronting a camera he didn't like.

Soon we were on our way in an automobile convoy to the airport and our Indian air force plane, which was to take us back to Agra to pick up our 707. I was riding with our high commissioner, Jim George, when the convoy stopped and Indian High Commissioner Bhadkamkar opened the door and told me I was to get into the prime minister's car. He was with the local governor in a plush limousine filled with garlands, which are presented at virtually every stop as a symbol of welcome, and he looked askance as the high commissioner almost pushed me towards and into his car. Neither he nor I understood what was happening. Perceiving this, the high commissioner said, "Look, do as I say. It's an Indian thing." We thought that it was some local form of protocol and went along with it, as if we had any option. The car took off at high speed, through villages and along dirt roads, scattering people, animals, and carts in our way until we found the airport, screeching to a stop at the ramp of our aircraft. With the engine turning over, we were rapidly boarded and the plane took off the minute the rest of our entourage arrived. It was only then that the high commissioner told us that there had been student riots in the region, with cars overturned, buses burned, and nine people killed. There is no reason to believe that we were the target of the riots, but as high-profile foreigners we were fair game. Our Indian hosts were taking no chances. It was unsettling for us to learn afterwards that, had we been attacked, the other vehicles in the convoy were to take off into the fields to distract the attackers and give us a greater opportunity for escape.

Our Indian aircraft landed at Agra and taxied directly to our 707, which was to take us to New Delhi for the formal and official visit with Mrs Gandhi and her ministers. It was normal procedure in India for the host, or hostess in this case, to place a garland of flowers around your neck as a greeting. I suggested to the prime minister that he reverse the role and place a garland on Mrs Gandhi. We seemed to have accumulated a cabin-full on our visits to Varanasi and Agra. Checking this procedure with Bhadkamkar in the event that it might be offensive, we were assured that it would not be. When we landed in New Delhi before we were properly attired for a state visit — our usual practice on boarding our aircraft was to change into informal, even sloppy clothes — we rushed to dress as we taxied to the official welcoming site with its saluting base, military guard of honour, brass band, and diplomatic corps. The plane came to a full stop right in front of Mrs Gandhi, who could observe Trudeau through a window as he rapidly pulled his trousers over his jockey shorts. Fully, but hurriedly, dressed, he bounded down the runway and, to Mrs Gandhi's surprise and delight, garlanded her. After being introduced to the receiving line of ministers, high commissioners, ambassadors, and officials, and warmly welcomed by our own high commissioner to India, Jim George, and his wife, Caroline, Trudeau mounted the saluting base as the military band played the national anthems of both countries. The Indians did a highly credible job with "O Canada," while we found their anthem enchanting, almost like a love song. Having become something of a connoisseur of national anthems after so many foreign visits, I rate the Indian among the three that have impressed me the most, the other two being the French "Marseillaise," which is spine-tingling, and that of the former USSR and now Russia, which is melodious and stirring. Nevertheless, there is nothing quite so moving as hearing your own national anthem, when you are in a foreign country. The farther from home you are and the longer you have been away, the more emotional is the impact. Even hard-bitten politicians have been known to shed a tear. (What upsets me about "O Canada" is the slow pace at which it is frequently played, making it sound like a dirge. At a faster tempo and when properly played, it is as stirring as any national anthem and always evokes an emotional response.)

Mrs Gandhi escorted Trudeau to the former British viceroy's palace, now the president's palace. Known as the Rashtrapati Bhavan, it was vast, larger than Buckingham Palace we were told, and if walking to your assigned quarters is any indication, I can well believe it, although I have not yet stayed at Buckingham Palace. We were each escorted by an Indian army cavalry officer resplendent in dress blues with chinking chain epaulets and spurs and sporting a waxed, curled moustache. The scene was more British than anything I have seen in Britain. My quarters were huge and magnificently furnished with a fully stocked bar and a large ebony desk fit for a viceroy. The clothes closet would have made a proper room in itself, but the bathroom was the most impressive feature: a massive marble tub in which one could easily drown, and a sink and counter that were like an altar, making you want to pray each time you washed. The water closet, or toilet, was set in its own room and was like a throne. The great difficulty was that it took twice as long to bathe or wash and dress, since you had to cover so much ground. Without a high degree of organization, you could wear yourself out if you had to nip back and forth between your clothes and ablution facilities to fetch a tie, a dress shirt, a pair of socks, or any other item. The quarters were designed for use by people who had many servants to help them, not uncommon in a nation of abundant and cheap labour. Indeed, servants were constantly available, sitting outside the door to the suite and ready to respond instantly to any demand, command, or wish. But that was not our style and was even a cause of embarrassment for me.

Breakfast was served in one's room and in my case beside open dormer windows overlooking the manicured gardens of the palace. Fortunately, our stay was short or I might never have found it possible to acclimatize to the real world again. I would have been terribly upset not to have the turbaned cavalry detachment with lances ride by my open window at breakfast — something out of the movie *The Lives of the Bengal Lancers*. With breakfast over, the equerry arrived in full dress to escort me to the next assembly area, since it would have been impossible to find my own way through the maze of corridors and rooms. The formal, official meetings took place in the Blue Room of the palace in a very stilted environment. It was here that the prime minister raised the question — diplomatic lingo for making his pitch — of the nuclear safeguards that concerned the Pakistanis and us even more so. He tried to get Mrs Gandhi to commit herself and India to only peaceful and non-explosive use of the nuclear material. However, Mrs Ghandi was a very vague woman and always seemed preoccupied, which was understandable for the leader of such a large and complex country where miserable poverty and almost indescribable wealth existed side by side and where violence was a common feature of political life. This would be the case in 1984 when Mrs Gandhi was assassinated by her own guards. She responded to Mr Trudeau's urging for nuclear safeguards comparable to those that bound Pakistan, her uneasy neighbour, with apparent understanding but little more. As we departed for our next engagement, I asked the prime minister if he thought we had her commitment. He shook his head or shrugged his shoulders, I'm not sure which, but clearly an expression of some exasperation. Some years later, we were in the House of Commons when word came that India had exploded a nuclear device. I said to Trudeau, "It looks as if she hadn't given us a commitment." He responded in much the same way as he had in New Delhi and with words such as "I guess not."

India's population in 1971 was over 550 million, an increase of 200 million in twenty years. Mrs Gandhi was much concerned about this population explosion and frustrated because she could not establish effective birth-control programs in the face of cultural taboos. She discussed each method of contraception in some detail and explained why they were ineffective. Lack of education was the principal problem, but even where birth-control methods were known, she claimed that men considered it a poor reflection on their masculinity if they were not regularly producing babies. I suggested, not totally facetiously, that long evenings without much else to do might be a contributing factor, and perhaps it would be wise to put a television set in each village or district. I understand that this, in fact, has largely taken place, but I would guess that it is more the result of the natural spread of technology rather than of a family-planning program. Whether it has had any effect on population growth I would not know, but it is unlikely since the population has since passed one billion. Perhaps some of the movies may even have stimulated reproductive activity.

Prime Minister Heath and his party caught up with us in New Delhi, which meant that Mrs Gandhi had two other Commonwealth prime ministers to contend with at one time. This did not seem to phase her one bit. After all, she had long experience in Commonwealth politics and was the daughter of Jawaharlal Nehru, which made this sort of situation almost commonplace for her. Her foreign minister, Sardar Swaran Singh, was a competent and respected statesman who carried a good portion of the load, but there was no question of who was boss, no matter how apparently distracted she was. She arranged a dinner and concert, featuring Indian music and dance, for her two prime ministerial guests and their parties. By this time, we had seen a lot of Indian dance and, while intriguing at first, a little went a long way. This evening, however, a brother and a sister, aged seventeen and nineteen, if I recall correctly, performed with such exquisite perfection that no other Indian dance I had seen could even closely compare. A young male dancer who was really quite fantastic also performed. We learned only later that these were the greatest dancers in India of that day. We were fortunate indeed, but that wasn't all. The great sitar player Ravi Shankar also performed, accompanied by a drummer who used his hands on two small tom-tom-like instruments. The music was slow and seemingly repetitive in the beginning but wove a web of rhythms that became captivating. Then the rhythm quickened and the drums beat louder and faster and drew the audience into an intimate relationship with the performers and their music. With the emotions growing quite feverish as the music reached a climax, it was almost a sexual experience that, when finished, left the exhausted audience in awed silence. Soon the silence was followed by spontaneous, enthusiastic, and sustained applause, quite unlike any sexual experience of which I am aware.

It was good being with the Heath party again, for, notwithstanding the disagreement between Britain and Canada over the issue of South Africa, we had developed a close relationship over many meetings. Heath's parliamentary private secretary, as the British call the equivalent of our parliamentary secretary, was Timothy Kitson, now Sir Timothy. He represented a Yorkshire constituency near Leeds which I had first come to know during the war when I was stationed briefly near Helmsley, home of the Black Swan pub, more lovingly called the "Dirty Duck" by the troops. It was always a great reunion when we met. Of course, all was not sweetness and light at this time. At the dinner following the concert I just mentioned, the British and Canadian delegations forcefully put forward their respective views on the subject of South Africa. Neither gave an inch.

Before leaving India, Mrs Gandhi gave a colourful buffet luncheon in Mr Trudeau's honour in the magnificent gardens of the Rashtrapati Bhavan, attended by senior members of the Indian government, the diplomatic corps, and the military. To the present day, the Indian army carries on much of the tradition and ceremony from the days of the British Raj. On this occasion, turbaned, medal-bedecked, lance-bearing guards, in majestic scarlet tunics, white trousers, and knee-high, brilliantly polished boots, were an impressive presence. Generals, admirals, and air marshals were there in abundance. We Canadians, including Justice Minister John Turner and his wife, Geills, in India for the Commonwealth Bar Association conference, were delighted with this unique display of pageantry. After prime ministers Gandhi and Trudeau proposed their obligatory toasts to one another and their countries, we devoted our attention to the lavish buffet, carefully designed to accommodate Hindu and Muslim dietary codes. I couldn't help but wonder how many Indian villages could have been fed with just the leftovers. Through all of this, Mrs Gandhi remained a distracted woman, perhaps because of an upcoming election (which has also been known to distract Canadian prime ministers). It was uncertain whether she would leave the country at this time to head her country's delegation to the Singapore conference. She finally decided to remain in India and the delegation was led by Foreign Minister Sardar Swaran Singh.

After an exhausting few days in this fascinating, but in so many ways depressing, country, we said our farewells. Mrs Gandhi was waiting to accompany Trudeau to the airport, but he was behind schedule. This was not an infrequent occurrence with the prime minister, particularly if he had one of his heavy head colds, which made him less than amiable company. For me, it was one of the requirements of my job to stay with our host or hostess until the prime minister arrived and thus I had the rare opportunity of spending private time with many of the leading world figures of the day. It was sometimes an awkward experience since small talk is not the forte of presidents and prime ministers, though we often spoke in a relaxed way of our private lives and families. With Mrs Gandhi, however, who said little even in her most gregarious moments, it was painful (Allan MacEachen would have been much more at home in this situation). It wasn't her job to entertain me, and so it was with relief that we welcomed the tardy Trudeau. One never has to worry about the plane taking off without you when travelling with the prime minister. To full pomp and ceremony, we took off for Singapore, our principal destination and reason for the trip in the first place.

Singapore and the Commonwealth Conference

We were met by John Hadwen, our high commissioner to Kuala Lumpur, Malaysia, and his wife, Shirley (John was also accredited to Singapore, where our permanent representative was our trade commissioner, John Blackwood). Lee Kuan Yew, the prime minister of Singapore, was our host and chairman of the conference, but he could not possibly meet each of the heads of government before the conference. Instead, a senior Singapore official was scheduled to meet with Trudeau; however, the prime minister was exhausted after a fitful sleep on the plane and wouldn't have any part of it. It was probably just as well, for, given his fatigue, I doubt whether relationships between countries would have been enhanced if such a meeting had occurred.

Getting to know Lee Kuan Yew as the conference progressed convinced me that no one could act on his behalf. Singapore was very much an authoritarian one-man show, although one could not help but be impressed with him and with what he had accomplished for his country. That, of course, is the excuse that has been used to justify many dictatorships in the past but Singapore was something short of a police state. It was a modern, prosperous city-state that had its priorities right. Housing, hospitals, and schools were at the highest level, just behind commerce, which was flourishing, as Singapore was becoming one of the world's leading economic centres. The virtual miracle achieved by Lee was the integration of the three principal ethnic groups — Chinese, Malaysians, and Indians.

Thirty-one countries were represented at the conference, which was properly called the Commonwealth Heads of Government Meeting. Not all these countries were represented by their president or prime minister. Many had elections to contend with and others were afraid to leave their countries for fear of rivals taking power in their absence. Actually, this was the case with Milton Obote, president of Uganda, who was deposed by Idi Amin during the conference and dared not return home. Archbishop Makarios of Cyprus, who assumed the modest title of "His Beatitude," stayed for only part of the conference. As delegations were seated alphabetically in a huge circle, we sat next to the Cypriot delegation, which was taken over by the foreign minister, Spyros Kyprianou, who was to succeed

Makarios as prime minister following "His Beatitude's" death in 1977. On our other side was the Botswana delegation, led by the country's impressive and cultivated head of state, Sir Seretse Khama.

Trudeau knew most of these men and women from the last conference in London and other occasions, but they were mostly just familiar names to me and I was anxious to observe them in action. Many failed to come across as personalities at all: perhaps they were wisely silent, absorbing the words of others, or perhaps they did not comprehend what was being said. I couldn't get any kind of reading on Uganda's Milton Obote, who was likely preoccupied by events in his own country. I did have occasion to meet Obote some ten years later in Kampala and still could not get a reading on him, but that story is to follow. Zambia's Kenneth Kaunda was an interesting, soft-spoken man, either very sensitive, highly emotional, or self-conscious, who had the distracting habit of breaking down and crying during his speeches. Julius Nyerere of Tanzania was the most impressive of the African leaders. He enjoyed the immense respect of all the others, particularly Trudeau, and his address to the conference brought tears to many eyes. Lee Kuan Yew was superb as our Singapore host. His opening speech was a tour de force. Obviously having a good feel for the issues and a sense of the occasion, he gave a soliloquy on living in freedom in a nation that had been invaded and occupied by the Japanese, and described how he "had to bow down low three times in humiliation." This made an impression that had never left him.

Canada stood high among these sister nations of the Commonwealth, as it still does. The late Arnold Smith, a Canadian diplomat of great distinction, served as the Commonwealth's first secretary general from 1965 to 1975. His skill in managing this conference was impressive and the esteem in which he was held by all Commonwealth members was evident. Trudeau, for his part, had captured attention at the previous Commonwealth conference held in London and in Singapore he continued to fascinate, intriguing everyone and attracting attention wherever he went. The visibility he had halfway around the world was quite incredible. I doubt if any other Canadian prime minister has been so well recognized and the subject of so much interest abroad.

Following Lee Kuan Yew's inspiring welcoming address, the conference got off to a long-drawn-out start as each delegation felt obliged to deliver lengthy prepared statements which tested the patience of everyone except the speaker of the moment. Trudeau half-facetiously made the suggestion that we dispense with time-consuming, often banal, and self-serving statements designed for home consumption and file a transcript of each with the secretary general. This did not deter many but I don't recall Trudeau making an opening statement. Indeed, I think it may have been his filing suggestion that was his opening statement. It was not his style or inclination to speak for the sake of speaking. As a result, at meeting after meeting, Ivan Head would draft thoughtful papers for him to deliver and he generally glanced at them and put them aside, often with a comment that they were too long. Each of us put in our two cents' worth, or more properly, took out our two cents' worth, but to no avail. He wasn't a man to be pushed and it seemed the harder we tried the more intransigent he became.

Other delegations were as anxious to hear him as we were. As the days dragged on, anticipation built. I think that on this occasion he remained silent for so long, not because he had nothing to contribute, but rather because he wanted to hear the opinions of others before he made a definitive statement, much as he would do in cabinet. When he finally did speak, the usual background murmurs and chair shuffling, as well as the coughing and nose blowing, stopped. All eyes and ears hung on his every word. It was apparent that Trudeau exercised the same attraction on the international stage as he did at home in his heyday — and at the time of his death. His personal appeal was magnetic. He was also greatly admired as a leader capable of bridging differences between seemingly entrenched positions. And this is exactly what he did at Singapore.

Proceedings had barely begun when black leaders abused Heath, or more properly Britain, unmercifully. The atmosphere grew more poisonous by the hour, so much so that a breakdown of the conference seemed possible. Trudeau, however, played a critical role in maintaining dialogue between the opposing sides over the eight days of the conference, both by his reasoned, conciliatory statements to the delegates in the plenary sessions and by his interventions in private meetings, where both he and his staff commanded the respect of Britain and the developing countries alike. Ultimately, Heath, encouraged by his foreign minister, Sir Alec Douglas-Home, softened his stand, and the conference agreed to a communiqué that pledged the Commonwealth to oppose racism and yet recognized the right of each state to pursue its own interests — a slippery way of saying that each nation had the right to define racism in its own way. The critical passage read: "We recognize racial prejudice as a dangerous sickness threatening the healthy development of the human race and racial discrimination as an unmitigated evil of society. Each of us will vigorously combat this evil within our own nation. No country will afford to regimes which practise racial discrimination assistance which in its own judgement directly contributes to the pursuit or consolidation of this evil policy."

The words "in its own judgement" allowed the logjam to be broken and the Commonwealth to remain intact. A number of people had been instrumental in averting the crisis but Trudeau's special role was recognized by Lee Kuan Yew when, in his closing remarks to the conference, he praised Trudeau for his "outstanding contribution." He added: "Mr. Trudeau, of Caucasian stock, prime minister of a country with the highest per capita income of any Commonwealth country, had felt that the stature of man himself would be diminished if Commonwealth countries were to treat their fellow humans the way white South Africans were doing."

On a Sunday break in the conference, Trudeau scheduled a day trip to Borneo. I decided to take a pass on this since I wanted a quiet day in Singapore, which ended with a steam bath and massage provided by a very attractive, petite, mini-skirted Oriental girl in the hotel sauna. I had made it back to our floor when Trudeau returned from his trip. Obviously exhausted and burned to a crisp, he asked what I had been doing and I told him I just had a great massage by the cutest little Asian girl. He asked where and how much, borrowed the two dollars (Singapore), and jumped on the next elevator. He never paid me back.

Indonesia

After Singapore, our next official visit was to Indonesia, the only one scheduled to a non-Commonwealth country. Landing in Jakarta minutes before sundown — our flight had been delayed because the conference had lasted longer than anticipated — we were welcomed by President Thojib Suharto, our ambassador, Tom Delworth, and his wife, Pamela Osler, who had once been a next-door neighbour of ours in Toronto. Then we were whisked to our guest quarters and given only a few minutes to change into black tie for a state dinner. We were already behind schedule and the guests were awaiting our arrival. I was told that Mrs Suharto personally checked out our accommodation and ran her fingers over the furniture to make certain there was no dust. She couldn't have foreseen my problem, however. I had purchased a new dress shirt in Singapore since I had used up my supply and didn't have time to have them laundered. As I unwrapped the shirt I discovered that it was without buttons and required studs, which I did not have because I always considered them a nuisance, particularly when travelling. The minutes were flashing by and I hit upon a solution. I carried a quantity of Canadian flag lapel pins in my pocket to give to children as souvenirs. With some dexterity I was able to put my shirt together with my maple-leaf studs and turn up out of breath at the dinner. The Indonesian ministers' wives in traditional national dress were intrigued by my Canadian flag studs, which I courteously distributed as my shirt came apart. An evening of Indonesian food, music, and dance followed and I was well ventilated.

Indonesia was not only a recipient of Canadian aid but represented a significant trading opportunity because of its large population and potential oil wealth. To do business in the country, however, Canadian companies had to learn how to operate under difficult and perplexing conditions. Suharto was in total control. His ministers and their wives seemed in fear of him; the waiters served him on their knees. Just about every official we came in contact with was from the military and they, on direction from Suharto, ran the country. In fact, while security was obvious in all countries, it was oppressive in Indonesia. It was the only way Suharto could exercise the rigid control on which he insisted. There were also ethnic tensions. Though Indonesia had long been part of the Dutch colonial empire, there did not appear to be any lingering Dutch influence although some Dutch-based companies were still active in the country. The Indonesians, however, deeply resented the Dutch. They also resented, but tolerated, the large Chinese community, which made up the bulk of the merchant class. There had been serious anti-Chinese riots in the past, some culminating in slaughter, but the Chinese had hung on and maintained their separate culture. This included legal gambling (an important part of their culture) for Chinese only. Indonesians were strictly forbidden to participate by their government. One evening after the usual official functions, the Indonesian ambassador to Canada, Admiral Bandaro, took us to see one of their gambling establishments and, while they welcomed us, they wouldn't allow the admiral inside the door.

With hindsight and in light of subsequent developments in Indonesia — the corruption of the Suharto regime, the slaughter in East Timor, the Bre-X scandal — one might say that Indonesia was a country that should have been of little interest to Canada, but the fact is that the country's huge geographic size and massive population of over 125 million made it too important to ignore. Our relationship with Indonesia, however, always carried risk and was marked by great caution on our part — though perhaps not enough.

Ceylon

Our next stop was Ceylon, as Sri Lanka was then known. We were right on time, flying in our 707 from Jakarta, but received word that the prime minister, Mrs Sirimavo Bandaranaike, whom we had met in Singapore, was detained. We were asked to circle until she got to the airport to greet us, a request that seemed a bit unusual but we understood that important matters of state sometimes interfere with such formalities. What we didn't realize is that the Ceylonese sense of time wasn't the same as ours. Meetings, dinners, and tours were always well behind schedule but this didn't seem to bother or embarrass anyone. There was no rush. The circling at low level gave us an opportunity to see the entire country, surely one of the most beautiful in the world, an island shaped like a pearl set off the southern tip of India in the blue waters of the Indian Ocean, with a ring of white sand beaches. We circled several times before we got word that Mrs Bandaranaike was at the Bandaranaike International Airport, named after her husband whom she had succeeded as prime minister after his assassination in 1959.

The Ceylonese welcome, when we finally landed, was relaxed, as was everything in Ceylon. In Singapore I had told Mrs Bandaranaike that I was looking forward to purchasing for Isobel some of the semi-precious stones for which her country was noted. "You should buy them in Singapore. You'll get a much better price in Singapore and you can trust the dealers." A surprising statement from the prime minister of Ceylon! As it happened, I didn't have the time to do much shopping in Singapore — other than buying three custom-made summer suits at $40 each, two of which I still wear — and so I put myself at the mercy of the Colombo dealers. Fortunately, I did very well indeed, because I had met Mrs Bandaranaike's late husband's nephew, Felix Bandaranaike, the minister of finance and of just about everything else, and his wife in Singapore and they took me to the Gem Museum, the best source in Colombo and owned by a member of the opposition party. Felix made certain I got both quality and value. This was before credit cards were common currency but they took my cheque, which pleased me mightily since I thought it would take months before it cleared my bank in Toronto. Regrettably, then as now, the banks were capable of lightning efficiency when it served their purpose and the cheque cleared in days.

Mrs Bandaranaike installed us in her official residence (she lived in her own modest home, as did Mrs Gandhi in New Delhi). The official residence was at one time an impressive structure left over from British colonial days. Most post-colonial countries take great pride in these buildings and, with their abundant labour supply, maintain them exceedingly well. In Ceylon, however, the old colonial buildings were quite run down and had become musty and seedy. The household staff were as relaxed as other Ceylonese. Nothing ever got done on time, if ever, but it never bothered them and they continued to be pleasant and laid-back. My bed was never made during my entire stay. I can't recall if the prime minister got his bed made but I don't think so. It's not the sort of thing that would have bothered him anyway since he had the ability to adapt easily to any culture in which he found himself and, besides, he never attached much importance to creature comforts.

The official business consisted largely of signing aid and trade agreements, but it was so relaxed and informal that it didn't seem like business. The Ceylonese joked at their own easy-going ways. A young man from the Bandaranaike family who had studied at the University of Western Ontario Business School told me that the main thing he had learned there was how to work; he hadn't known before what it was like to get up at a set time in the morning, to organize his schedule, set his goals, and measure his accomplishments. My personal counterpart and host was the minister of agriculture, Hector Kobbekaduwa, a thoroughly delightful older man. In commenting on the Ceylonese lifestyle, he told me that his agricultural scientists had developed a strain of rice that grew high enough that the workers could pick it without bending. Makes sense too.

Our visit to Ceylon included a train trip up-country to the old capital of Kandy, which was at a higher altitude than Colombo and had a much more moderate climate. At the former British governor's residence, Trudeau was presented with a specially bred Trudeau Orchid and was asked to plant a tree. Our hosts pointed out another tree planted by another Canadian prime minister, named Diefenbaker. There were some interesting suggestions on how to moisten it, but that would not have been appropriate. The rest of our time in the country was spent on a fascinating tour of temples, the highlight being the Temple of the Tooth, where it is believed one of the teeth of the Buddha is placed and locked up in the altar with large impressive padlocks. The priest pointed out how many of the accoutrements of the temple were gifts of other countries. The pitch was obvious but Trudeau wasn't biting. Mark Gayn of the Toronto *Star* and his wife, Suzanne, were with us, and Mark innocently asked if Canada had given anything. Before the priest could answer in the negative, Trudeau turned and said something akin to "fuddle duddle." The priest might not have known the word but he certainly got the message.

The Ceylon temples and shrines were unique, with Buddhas in every conceivable position. It was a gruelling day since we did a great deal of climbing, particularly up the famous Siqiriya, a mountain-sized boulder that none of us would have attempted had not Trudeau taken it as a challenge. If I recall, the temperature was in the 90s Fahrenheit. It did get cooler, which was a good thing, because Trudeau wanted to see every Buddha in Ceylon. We had a difficult time getting him to stop for lunch, and we were still looking at Buddhas at night by the lights of our car when we finally pried him away to the former governor's residence at 10:30 PM for dinner. All of us, except Trudeau, were exhausted. But there was little time for rest, for we had to be up early the next day to see the famous Kandy elephants before making the drive back to Colombo, holding a press conference, and boarding our plane for a long flight to Tehran.

We were awake at 6 AM for our meeting with the elephants. Both the prime minister and I were assigned elephants, which we mounted. As was usual, the television cameras and press photographers focused on Trudeau; then, however, they changed direction and zeroed in on me and my magnificent bull elephant. I hadn't had the experience of "one-upping" the prime minister before and was rather pleased that the camera operators and photographers recognized my importance. What I had not realized is that my elephant, in all the excitement, had become sexually aroused. The pictures did not make the press but the remarks about that big ... on the elephant were less than flattering. On our way to Colombo we stopped at Mrs Bandaranaike's farm, where she received us and brought out her pet baby elephant to show us. Every one was cautioned about letting me near this little jumbo because I had a strange affect on elephants. The Ceylonese, who have a rather naughty sense of humour, were highly amused. Later, as we boarded our plane, Mrs Bandaranaike and her cabinet were lined up near the aircraft ramp for the final farewell. As I came to my friend Hector, the minister of agriculture, he took my hand and whispered in my ear, "Remember that an elephant never forgets." For quite some years after this, I couldn't go to any Ceylonese event where someone didn't bring up the subject of my elephant.

It is incredible that these otherwise kind and gentle people are now engaged in slaughtering one another in a fratricidal conflict. I can't help but notice that political tension and all too frequent violence appears to afflict some of the world's most beautiful island states, such as Sri Lanka, Cyprus, and Ireland. I can only hope that peace and sanity will soon return to all these countries, particularly Sri Lanka, whose otherwise beautiful people will always have a special place in my heart.

Iran and the Shah

The visit to Tehran had not been on our original schedule but since we had to make a refuelling stop between Ceylon and our NATO base in Lahr, Germany, it was a good choice. It was not a state or official visit but the Iranian prime minister, Abbas Hovaida, was a warm and gregarious host. We were thoroughly exhausted after our full schedule and early rising in Ceylon and were anxious to take advantage of an overnight stay in the Tehran Hilton Hotel just to catch our breath. As we entered the hotel, everyone else was pushed aside by large and fierce-looking security guards. There were others at the elevator reserved for our party and they didn't look like people to be trifled with. Other than in Indonesia, I had never experienced such heavy and obvious security. Hovaida hosted an informal party at his official residence, more like a palace, where he feasted us royally, entertained us (there was an orchestra and singers), and introduced us to his other guests, a very jet-set group indeed. The women were stunningly turned out in the latest Paris fashions but I was told that these were copies produced by Iranian seamstresses at a fraction of Paris prices. At the buffet there were platters of the finest Beluga caviar in huge mounds. When I gingerly put a tablespoonful on my plate and was about to move on, the hostess assigned to me asked, "Don't you like caviar?" When I admitted I did — and she likely knew that it wasn't standard fare in the Danson home — she proceeded to pile my plate with it. I couldn't finish the caviar or much else for that matter. I was too tired to enjoy myself, and had a splitting headache to boot. I excused myself and got a lift to the hotel to collapse.

There had been no formal planning but there was some suggestion that we were to visit the shah before our scheduled noon take-off. We were then advised that the visit was on and were taken to his modern and opulent palace. The shah was not a warm person and I didn't detect any positive chemistry between him and Trudeau. He spoke quietly and deliberately as he discussed world events, and was surprisingly well informed. When he was discussing Israel, with whom Iran had friendly relations at that time, he pointed to the jewelled Koran mounted on his desk and said; "You know the Jews mention us in their Holy Book." It was a simple statement but uttered with pride. His knowledge of regional and global military-security matters was expansive, and so was his grasp of Iran's economy and industry. I knew that the Romanians had licensed Iran to manufacture their farm tractors and I mentioned to the shah that they were anxious to license a Canadian manufacturer as well. He then proceeded to talk about the engineering, manufacturing, and marketing of tractors. He listed all other manufacturers and the only mistake I caught was when he referred to "Massey-Harris" rather than Massey-Ferguson. Not a bad slip. The visit lasted about an hour.

On leaving Tehran, Prime Minister Hovaida saw us off at our plane. I was to meet him once more when he visited Canada. When the shah was deposed, and the Ayatollah Khomeini came to power, he was shot. This was a fate that would befall all too many of the leaders I met over the course of my political life, including Mrs Gandhi, Anwar Sadat, and Itzhak Rabin (all shot by assassins) and Ali Bhutto (executed by the regime that replaced his in Pakistan). I prefer the Canadian democratic process even when it doesn't go my way.

On the Road Again: The "Evil Empire"

We arrived home, via Lahr, to a blustery, freezing Ottawa. We had not spent much time on the flight reflecting on our trip. We were just too tired. Nor, once we arrived in Ottawa, did we have time for sentimental farewells to one another. We would be seeing enough of one another in the future. Besides, we had spent some twenty-eight days in very close and continual contact and were more interested in getting back to our families. Except for one of us. The prime minister got into his car for an empty and lonely 24 Sussex Drive. I got myself from the military terminal to the civil terminal at Ottawa's Uplands Airport and on to the first flight to Toronto, where we still kept our home. Without going into detail, it was a very happy homecoming.

A few weeks later, in early March 1971, I was at home asleep when there was a phone call at about one o'clock in the morning. Isobel answered and I heard her say "Who? When did it happen? Where was it?" I was certain that the prime minister had been assassinated. But I was wrong. Colin Kenny, then special assistant to the prime minister, was calling to tell us that the prime minister had been married to Margaret Sinclair in Vancouver. The prime minister, he said, didn't want us surprised when we heard the morning newscasts. I was caught completely off guard. I had recently spent almost a month with this man, all day, every day, yet I hadn't the slightest notion that he was planning on getting married. While I had seen Margaret with Trudeau, I also saw a lot of other beautiful women with him. I had no idea that Margaret had a hold on him. In any case, I was happy to hear the news since Margaret was a mightily attractive girl from a great Liberal family. A small postscript. While in Ceylon, Trudeau had shown a special interest in moonstones. Later, I saw Margaret with what looked like a pewter choker set with moonstones and remarked on them to her. "But Barney," she said, "moonstones are my favourite."

USSR

Margaret was part of the next prime ministerial trip abroad.[1] Our official visit to the Soviet Union, postponed in October 1970 because of the FLQ crisis, was rescheduled to May 1971. It was to be a two-week tour and was to take us not just to Moscow but to central Asia and Arctic Siberia. If I recall correctly, we flew non-stop on the 707 to Moscow. Margaret sat reading in the back part of our capsule while we worked at the tables in front. She seemed like a terribly lonely girl who was to play an official role but was not part of the working sessions and her husband was totally preoccupied. We did not know at the time that she was pregnant with their first son, Justin. We had always travelled "stag" while Trudeau was a bachelor, but, looking back now, I believe that it was a mistake not to have invited Isobel to join me on this trip. Margaret would have benefited from the company of another, and more mature and politically experienced, woman. Fortunately, once we arrived in Moscow, Theresa Ford, wife of ambassador Robert Ford, took Margaret under her wing and was the first

---

1   These accounts of our trips to the Commonweath Conference and the Soviet Union consist of recollections and impressions which do not attempt to deal substantively with the background and official discussions. These are superbly covered in Ivan L. Head and Pierre Elliott Trudeau, *The Canadian Way: Shaping Canada's Foreign Policy 1968–1984* (Toronto: McClelland and Stewart, 1995).

one to guess Margaret's pregnancy. We males were kept in the dark and lacked the intuition that might have given us a clue.

We taxied to the VIP receiving base, coming perilously close to one of two, I believe, Soviet supersonic jets, similar to the British-French Concorde. It was obviously parked there to impress us. As we came down the aircraft ramp, Premier Alexei Kosygin, our host, moved forward to greet Mr Trudeau and asked if we had happened to see their supersonic jet, which we couldn't have missed had we tried. Kosygin, a widower, was accompanied by his daughter, Ludmilla Gvishiani, who acted as official hostess and spoke reasonably good English — certainly better than our Russian. The official interpreter for Kosygin was Victor Sukhodryev, who spoke an excellent English scattered with colloquialisms, some of which were a decade or more out of date. He had learned his English as the son of a Soviet diplomat in London and was the best and most trusted of the Russian interpreters for the highest-level contacts at that time.

After the band played "O Canada" with verve and the very beautiful Soviet anthem, Trudeau inspected the guard of honour. Then our entourage, with Kosygin accompanying Trudeau, travelled by motorcade to the Lenin Hills of Moscow where the Soviets kept a number of guest-houses in a tightly secure compound. These houses had, I understand, been built originally as homes for the highest Soviet officials but whether or not they were occupied by them I do not know. The grounds were well landscaped and the fruit trees were in full spring blossom. There was a separate building with a large modern swimming pool, much to Trudeau's delight and, at Soviet insistence, for his exclusive use. The prime minister's staff included executive assistant Tim Porteous, principal secretary Marc Lalonde, special advisor Ivan Head, press secretary Peter Roberts, and deputy secretary to the cabinet Marshall Crowe. I shared a guest house with Ed Ritchie, under-secretary of state for external affairs, and Jake Warren, the deputy minister of trade and commerce — two of the most senior and respected Ottawa mandarins, extremely bright, pragmatic, and great fun. The main party of advisers, senior officials, security personnel, press, and support staff were ensconced in the Hotel Moscow, a huge modern structure said to be the largest in the world, with some eight thousand rooms, and not far from Red Square.

It was a bit dreamlike being in the heart of the "enemy." Our central point of activity was the Kremlin itself, where all meetings were held. It was a historic walled compound with a variety of buildings for government functions as well as museums. The Supreme Soviet was a large modern building that reminded me of Toronto's O'Keefe (now Hummingbird) Centre. Premier Kosygin took us on a personal tour and was explaining where the different people sat. I was at the back of the group and I said to the members of our party close to me, "I wonder where the opposition sits?" This was overheard by some of our hosts, a few of whom broke into wide smiles, but it did not seem so funny to our uptight Canadian officials. When we got down to business, several meetings took place in the Kremlin, chaired by Premier Kosygin and attended at different times by Foreign Minister Andrei Gromyko or his deputy and Yuri Andropov, KGB chief and future Soviet leader. Also attending were Dimitri Polyanski, first deputy chairman to Kosygin, Mikhail Suslov of the Council of Ministers, and Boris Miroshnichenko, the Soviet ambassador to Canada. Leonid Brezhnev, general secretary of the Central Committee of the Communist Party and the most senior leader in the Soviet system, did not attend. It was Premier Kosygin's show.

While not reflected in any protocol, there were two matters of special interest. The prime minister had raised the matter of Canada's concern about the reunification of families and about Soviet Jews who were restricted from emigrating to Israel. Kosygin answered in no uncertain terms that this was an internal Soviet matter and, by implication, no business of ours. Nevertheless, he did agree to accept a list of relatives of Canadian families whom we asked to be given permission to emigrate to Canada. He also went further and said that he would allow all to leave except those who had broken the law — a big exception since one could have broken the law simply by expressing a desire to leave the country. This response was only what we expected, for it was the official Soviet line and Kosygin was not about to soften it in an official meeting with his most senior people present. But Trudeau had his own way of getting around these entrenched positions. As happened often with other leaders, he and Kosygin, along with translator Sukhodryev, went to a corner of the room where they could talk frankly and without attribution. They spoke as politician-to-politician and man-to-man. No position papers, no witnesses, no officials. Trudeau pointed out that Canadians were greatly concerned about the issues he had just raised, and that he could not go back with the packaged answers he had received from Kosygin. He would be prepared to discuss the subjects that the Soviets were interested in, such as greater cooperation in the Arctic, or scientific and cultural exchanges, or just better and friendlier relations. But these goals would be hard to achieve if there was no progress in the area of emigration. Kosygin listened, apparently understanding but remaining noncommittal. In the following months the small and uneven flow of Jewish immigrants increased astronomically for a while, as did the number of Soviet citizens — a large number from Ukraine — reunited with families in Canada. This may not have been totally attributable to Trudeau, since U.S. President Richard Nixon had raised the same issue during a recent visit and had received the same sort of reaction. Yet there is no question that Trudeau's representation and the very high regard in which he and Canada were held by Kosygin was a significant influence.

The other matter — and one that caused some confusion — concerned the Canadian gift of a pair of musk ox, the tough buffalo-like beast that still survives in our Arctic but was extinct in the Soviet Arctic. Jean Chrétien, as minister of Indian affairs and northern development, had thought of this idea and asked us to relay it to our Soviet hosts; he would follow it up on a subsequent visit of his own later in the year to the Soviet Union. The translators couldn't handle musk ox. It wasn't in the curriculum of the Soviet translation schools. Even our Canadian translators, or, more accurately, interpreters, who made certain that the Soviet translators were accurately reflecting our words, were stymied. Still, although our hosts were confused about the generous offer Canada was making, they were not about to look a gift musk ox in the mouth. Ambassador Miroshnichenko came to the rescue and leaped at this opportunity to impress his Moscow superiors. He had made the initial indication to Canada that a gift of two, healthy, sexy musk ox would be highly acceptable, providing that one was male and one female. Apparently, the Soviet hierarchy was not familiar with the love life of musk ox, but Boris, with great enthusiasm, delivered an impressive explanation to his duly elected (Soviet style) political masters. There were smiles all around and the ties between the USSR and Canada were bound even closer. As planned, Jean Chrétien renewed the offer when he visited the Soviet Union — this time it was for a herd of ten musk ox — and, after various bureaucratic delays at the Soviet end, these animals arrived in their new home in 1974. Since then, I'm told, they have multiplied to 2,500, and the Russians have ambitious plans to increase the population to 250,000 and harvest the animals for their meat and wool.

The substantive portion of the talks dealt with trade, scientific cooperation, particularly in the Arctic, cultural exchanges, and other such matters, all of which were inscribed in protocols signed by both prime ministers in an elaborate Kremlin ceremony in elegant white, gold, and crystal surroundings. The protocols were not binding agreements but expressed the intention of both countries to pursue these matters and provided guidance for our bureaucrats. The Soviets put great emphasis on the protocols and the prodigious quantity of champagne that followed the signing demonstrated their sincerity. Indeed, if champagne, vodka, and caviar are any indication, they were very sincere at every opportunity.

Trudeau had two special meetings on his schedule, one with President Nikolai Podgorny, properly titled chairman of the Presidium of the USSR Supreme Soviet, and the other with Leonid Brezhnev, the real power in the country. He was to be accompanied at each meeting by only one person and it was agreed that Ivan Head and I would fill this role. I believe that we decided who would go where by the toss of a coin. I won Podgorny and Ivan won Brezhnev, to my envy (in the end, Ed Ritchie, as under-secretary of state for external affairs, was also invited to attend the Brezhnev meeting). Nothing of great note came out of either meeting but the one with Brezhnev went well past its allotted time, taking an hour and forty-five minutes. This was the result, we learned, of the ebullience and garrulousness of Brezhnev, a dynamic restless bear of a man, fully aware of his power, who paced the floor constantly and talked so intensely about a range of subjects that Trudeau found it difficult to get a word in. I imagine, however, that he enjoyed the performance.

The Podgorny visit was scheduled for a half-hour. As we entered his office, we saw this little man behind a very large desk. At first glance, I was sure that I was looking at Nikita Khrushchev, which would have been impossible, or, even more unlikely, Lord Beaverbrook. But it was indeed Podgorny, who talked in generalities and was impressively unimpressive. There must have been more to him than what I saw, given that he was one of the troika — the others being Kosygin and Brezhnev — who held the reins of power in the country. Once the courtesies had been observed and there seemed to be nothing further to talk about, Trudeau excused us and we proceeded to our waiting cars and motorcycle escort. Since we were much earlier than expected, the rest of our party and the press were not there as planned and likely wandering in the Kremlin compound with Soviet guides and security. While waiting for them, Trudeau took an interest in the motorcycles of the escort. He displayed a knowledge of motorcycles that surprised the Soviets, and us, and mentioned that he had not driven a bike with a drive shaft. Examining the machine closely, he sat on it and, to everyone's surprise or delight or fear, put it in gear and took off for a solo performance, circling around the relatively small courtyard. Later, the press was crestfallen to have missed this great photo opportunity, much better than Indian camels and Ceylonese elephants. It went unreported in the Canadian papers.

After our Kremlin sessions, we returned to our guesthouse to discuss the day's events and plan for the next day's meetings. Fortunately, it was balmy weather and we could walk the grounds talking in subdued voices without fear of intruding microphones, although I swear that some of the blossoms looked suspiciously mechanical. After our garden walk, when our assessment of the day's events was complete and our strategy for tomorrow set, we returned to our quarters to talk to the chandeliers. Ed Ritchie, Jake Warren, and I were certain that our guesthouse was efficiently bugged — not an unusual practice even in some friendly countries — and the ornate crystal chandeliers were the most logical place to pick up conversations. We sat back, drinks in hand, and discussed information that we felt would help direct the next day's discussions to our benefit. For instance, if a subject had been dealt with previously but we wanted to open it up again, Ed might say, "Surprisingly, they closed off discussion on C when they should have realized we were prepared to go further than we did." We, of course, had no intention of going further and didn't, but we wanted them to do so in an effort to draw us out. Sure enough, they would open the next meeting noting that they wanted to discuss Item 6 of yesterday's meeting further and had added it to that day's agenda. We restrained ourselves from smiling smugly.

Overall, we had full and fruitful discussions, as the communiqués say, and were treated to sumptuous banquets with ample servings of caviar and continuously topped-up small glasses of vodka. In a spare moment, Trudeau and I went to see the eerie and highly air-conditioned tomb of Lenin in Red Square, a Soviet shrine that every Russian wants to visit once in his or her lifetime, just as a Muslim wants to visit Mecca. There was a considerable line-up but our Soviet guides/security detail took us ahead of everyone else. Ambassador and Mrs Robert Ford gave a reciprocal dinner at our embassy residence. Robert Ford was a distinguished diplomat who spoke and wrote Russian fluently and was the highly respected dean of the diplomatic corps in Moscow. While the embassy accommodated both the ambassador's mouse-infested residence and the overcrowded chancery, Theresa Ford managed to introduce a certain restrained elegance in the pre-revolutionary mansion. Trudeau, as official host, made the traditional personal gift to his political counterpart — a spanking new Bombardier Ski-Doo. Premier Kosygin was not a demonstrative man and it was difficult to perceive any excitement as he pondered what he would do with it. Apparently, there were few snowmobile trails in the Soviet Union at that time but they probably cut some around his dacha.

When I say that Kosygin was not a demonstrative man, I certainly don't mean to imply that he was cold. Rather, though a bit reserved, he had a soft smile and was a most considerate host. Among the many world leaders my job brought me in contact with, I rate Kosygin at the very top as a person I could both like and trust. Trudeau seemed to share my feelings and we sometimes discussed the anomaly of a man who had worked or fought his way up in one of the most brutal systems known, who could be firm, even tough, in negotiating sessions, and yet who always remained a gentleman. One didn't want to be naive in international relationships, particularly with the Soviets, but I said to Trudeau that anyone who could raise a daughter like our official hostess,

Ludmilla, couldn't be all bad. She could have been the nice "girl next door" in a Canadian setting. Unfortunately, she died prematurely of cancer in her mid-fifties. I shall always remember her with fondness. I was to meet Kosygin again in October 1971 when I acted as a host on his official visit to Canada. I accompanied him on his trips outside Ottawa (where, of course, the prime minister was his host). My impression of him remained the same. A measure of his quality as a man is that, after the end of the Cold War and the break-up of the Soviet Union, none of the streets, parks, and buildings named after him (he died in 1980) had their names changed, an honour, so I'm told, bestowed on no other Soviet leader of the past.

The respect that Trudeau had for Kosygin was mutual. When we were leaving Moscow, Kosygin turned up personally to escort Trudeau to the airport and bid him farewell. Again, I had the duty to wait with Kosygin until Trudeau turned up in one of his less than light moods. (For a man in superb physical condition, especially for one of his years, he required a good night's sleep.) Apparently, it is good form and good manners in Russia to offer a guest a glass of cognac or, more likely, Georgian brandy when departing. Kosygin offered such a drink to Trudeau, who declined it. Kosygin insisted. Trudeau, who rarely drank alcohol at all, asked for fruit juice but Kosygin replied that this toast had to be drunk with alcohol. Remembering Kosygin's official responses on the emigration of Jews, Trudeau wryly said, "You don't tell me how to run my country and I don't tell you how to run yours. So don't tell me how to drink." What might have been taken as offensive by others was taken in good stride by Kosygin who got the point.

That was typical Trudeau — frank, direct, and irreverent. Later, when he was being criticized in the press for getting too close to the Soviets or for referring to the United States as an imperial power, he said something in French that defined him as a person. It translates roughly as, "Do what your instincts tell you is right, and let the asses bray." Not a bad credo, especially for a politician. It may have gotten him into trouble once in a while, but it likely accounts for much of the respect he attracted. There was more to him than uncompromising frankness, of course. Another characteristic of his that left a lasting impression on me was his unique combination of brilliance and charm. On our trip to the

Soviet Union, for example, there was an occasion when Trudeau was introduced to members of the Moscow diplomatic corps. As he met the ambassadors, he said a short greeting in the language of each. This was a masterful performance that impressed everyone and surprised those of us who, while close to him, had no idea of his facility with languages, although I suspect that a short greeting was all he knew of some. The Chinese ambassador had tears in his eyes.

From Moscow we embarked on an extensive tour of the Soviet Union, beginning with Kiev, the capital of Ukraine, and then proceeding almost two thousand miles to Tashkent and Samarkand in Uzbekistan, to Norilsk in Siberia (two hundred miles north of the Arctic Circle), across the Barents Sea to Murmansk, and finally to Leningrad. Most of the journey until Leningrad was done on an Aeroflot turbo-prop, since many runways in our itinerary would not accommodate our Boeing 707. These arrangements probably suited the Soviets' security concerns, because a NATO aircraft would not be a welcome observer over the great expanse of their country. In Kiev, we met with the premier of the Ukrainian Soviet Socialist Republic, Bolodymyr Shcherbitsky, a tough KGB type, totally humourless, the kind of guy you could imagine breaking your fingers one by one.

Tashkent, the capital of Uzbekistan, was our next stop. There, we met with the prime minister of the Uzbek Soviet Socialist Republic, Narmakhonmadi Dzuraraevich Khudaiberdiev, whom we called "Premier" for short. He was as mild a man as his Ukrainian counterpart was rough. At our formal talks we had the usual soft drinks and mineral water but they also offered us bowls of the largest, most succulent strawberries that I had ever seen and that Trudeau devoured with glee. Actually, the strawberries were the most memorable part of our official meeting, since the premier focused on relaying all the statistical information on the Uzbek Republic at his command. From Tashkent we flew some 200 miles to Samarkand, also in Uzbekistan, the ancient city astride the trade routes in central Asia to China and the east. We saw fascinating architecture reflecting the city's founding by Alexander the Great in 329 B.C., its destruction by Genghis Khan in 1221 A.D., and its subsequent rebuilding as Tamerlane's capital in the fourteenth century. Samarkand was not yet easily accessible to Soviet and foreign tourists and a visit such as ours aroused great curiosity among the populace. Our own curiosity about the ancient, meticulously preserved mosques in this very old centre of commerce and power was just as great.

We then went back to Tashkent where we switched to a larger Aeroflot turboprop for the long flight to Norilsk in Siberia. We were surprised to find that our hosts had divided our party in two, with half of us up front and the remainder in the rear. The accompanying Soviet party was seated mid-ship. We couldn't understand these arrangements until we landed at the airport serving Norilsk. As we disembarked, we realized that the vibration from the turboprop's engines was intense in the middle of the aircraft. The victims were our hosts, who staggered down the gangway, glassy eyed and disoriented — not an experience to inflict upon their guests. They attempted smiles and cordiality but were obviously hurting.

On arrival in Norilsk the temperature was 0° Celsius, quite a contrast from the heat of Samarkand. No motorcade greeted us but we did have a comfortable slow train ride into the city. At the train station there was a motorcade waiting and it whisked us to the city centre where great cheering crowds had assembled to welcome these distinguished foreigners. Whether they had been ordered to or whether they were merely treating the occasion as a break in their dreary, day-to-day, routine we will never know, but we accepted the accolades with waves and smiles. We drove up to our quite large hotel while the car carrying the Trudeaus slipped imperceptibly off to a special guesthouse. The crowd didn't notice this and thus cheered me and the rest of our party as we climbed the steps to the hotel entrance and I waved my hat as a prime minister would, to resounding acclaim. After checking into the large multi-bedded room which I shared with Jake Warren and Ed Ritchie, we realized that there was not much point in trying to sleep in the perpetual daylight — there was no such thing as window blinds or curtains. Having slept on the plane anyway, we decided to walk the streets at what could have been midday rather than midnight. We met others of our party doing the same thing and I recall Tim Porteous pointing out two very large women with mops and pails. "Arctic Chars," I explained.

Though Norilsk was bleak, it was a large mining centre. Indeed, it is the largest nickel mine in the world. Housing was in massive, bulky apartments built at ground level, whereas in our Arctic they would be built on piles and stilts so the heat from the buildings would not melt the permafrost and cause the buildings to buckle or sink. When I questioned our hosts on this point, they told me that the buildings were supported by piles that employed heavy steel beams sunk into holes drilled into the permafrost for stability. These holes were filled with water, which quickly and permanently froze, providing greater stability and at less cost than steel beams alone could. The building seemed solid, if quite unattractive, while in the Canadian Arctic we continue to build on stilts for smaller, lighter, and more attractive structures.

There had to be some alleviating distractions for the people in such a place, if they weren't to go stir-crazy, and there were. Workers were given generous leave at resorts in the south (three months each year, I was told). There were also organized sports, and it was enlightening for us to visit indoor hockey rinks where we saw Russian kids playing with the same enthusiasm as youngsters in our little leagues back home. Perhaps some future NHL stars were getting their start in Norilsk. Marshall Crowe, a cultivated man, and I visited a music academy with a large performance theatre and listened attentively to a young pianist who was apparently rehearsing under the watchful supervision of her teacher. It was quite an improvement on what we might find in our Arctic at that time and Marshall and I displayed our cultural superiority by guessing the obviously Russian composer of the work being practised. We called out the names of every Russian composer we could conjure up, impressing ourselves if not our hosts; when we were told it was Kabalevsky, whom we had missed completely, we slunk out quietly. The people of Norilsk were warm and obviously curious and pleased to have any visitors from the outside. There were no attractions for tourists.

From Norilsk we flew to Murmansk, the major Arctic port and naval base. It was the centre of shipping activity in the Soviet Arctic and was well remembered by Canadian sailors who in the Second World War accompanied convoys carrying military equipment to our Soviet Allies in the most difficult winter conditions, through waters infested with German U-boats. We found it to be an impressive sheltered seaport bustling with activity and were given a tour of the world's first nuclear-powered ice breaker, the *Lenin*, which even at that time was being superseded by more advanced nuclear technology. Then, it was time to fly to our last official stop, Leningrad (now, once more, St. Petersburg).

Ludmilla Gvishiani, representing her father, Premier Kosygin, met us there. Soon afterwards, I had a unique experience involving that favourite Russian pastime, drinking. It began when I was taken down to the port one morning to meet a ship, the *Stanislawski*, which had just arrived from Canada with a cargo of Calgary-built all-terrain vehicles for use over the Arctic tundra. On board, the captain kicked off what seemed an endless series of toasts with vodka and brandy — to the ship and its cargo, our two countries, our wives, our allies, our adversaries, and just about anything else that came to his mind. The cumulative effect of these toasts left me quite sloshed. What is more, Jake Warren, who was supposed to have accompanied me on this visit, caught up with me just as I was staggering down the gangplank. The Russians would not forgive us if we didn't do the whole round of toasts all over again for Jake's benefit, and so we did. To top everything off, I had an official luncheon to attend at the city hall with Trudeau. Once I had staggered back there with my KGB escort, I told him that I was just not up to the luncheon; if I went, I feared that I would embarrass my country and insult his. He then drove me back to the Hotel Leningrad, where I was comatose for the rest of the day. Not my finest hour. That night, an antidote of white wine and straight vodka provided by the mayor, who had heard of my plight, allowed me to make a mild recovery. I don't know what the Russians called their hangover cure, but it must have been something like our "hair of the dog that bit you." In any case, I felt well enough to be able to attend the Kirov performance of *Swan Lake* at the Mariinsky Theatre. The ballet was superb, and I found it particularly enjoyable because we were sitting in what had been in pre-Soviet days the Royal Box of the Tsars.

Before departing there was still lots to do. We paid a remarkable visit to the Hermitage Museum, where some of the great art of the world is hung. Regrettably, the light and humidity levels would not have been tolerated elsewhere, but, as I understand, the conditions are much improved today, partly as a consequence of associations with the Art Gallery of Ontario and others. I find it remarkable that, after the 900-day siege of Leningrad in the Second World War, which brought almost total devastation to the city, the Soviets gave the highest priority to restoring such national treasures as the Hermitage. And restore it they did, the whole structure being lavishly and superbly decorated with the plentiful use of costly gold leaf. The same was true of the royal summer palace of Peterhof in nearby Pushkin, which had been almost totally destroyed in the war by the German army.

The memory of the "Great Patriotic War," as it is known, exercises a great hold on the Soviet psyche, hanging over the people like a pall — some 28 million died, 18.5 million of them civilians — but it is also a source of fierce pride. On our visit, veterans — who are called "Heroes" — still wore the ribbons from their wartime medals on their civilian suits. Wherever we went, the first place our hosts were likely to take us was to the local war memorial, which paid tribute to the millions of war dead. The Young Pioneers, the Communist equivalent to our Boy Scouts and Girl Guides, took great pride in being chosen to stand ceremonial guard at the memorials. Newly married couples first went to the war memorial to leave flowers before the post-nuptial festivities and honeymoon. All in all, it was enough national pride and sense of history to turn any Canadian historian or veteran green with envy. Russians have experienced war in a manner almost beyond the imagination of Canadians and they are not about to let their own people or any other people forget it. I have little doubt that we may well have lost the Second World War if Hitler had not made the fatal mistake of attacking the Soviet Union, gravely underestimating its strength and determination while overestimating Germany's.

Back Home: Kosygin, Tito, Heath, and Nixon

Before leaving Leningrad, we received word of a crisis in Parliament. It gives some idea of the magnitude of the crisis that I can't recall what it was about, but at the time it seemed important and the prime minister was to intervene in the debate some few hours after our landing in Ottawa. Notes for his speech were drafted on the long flight home, and this speech apparently saved the day for the government because we weren't forced into a premature election.

Two special jobs that came my way in the fall of 1971 involved acting as host to two foreign visitors after they left Ottawa for other parts of Canada. One, as I've already recounted, was Alexei Kosygin, who visited Canada in October. Accompanied by his daughter Ludmilla and an official party of twenty-three, Kosygin began his tour in Ottawa, with Trudeau as host. During his visit to the capital, while he was strolling between the Centre Block and the East Block of the Parliament Buildings, an expatriate from the Soviet bloc leaped out from the curious crowds lining the route and jumped on him. Paul Martin (senior) and I were watching in disbelief from my office in the Centre Block as it happened. Martin, particularly, was aghast, saying that the rest of the world would not be impressed with such bush-league security.

In Ottawa, as at the other stops on the tour, Kosygin was met with angry anti-Soviet, anti-Communist protestors, some of Baltic and Ukrainian origin but largely Jewish Canadians, many of whom had escaped Soviet oppression and were now demanding the release of political prisoners and the right of all Soviet citizens and particularly Jews to emigrate to Israel and elsewhere (especially but not only when it was a matter of family reunification). While I was accompanying Kosygin on a drive from Parliament Hill to lunch at 24 Sussex, there was a large demonstration outside the then Rideau Club. Kosygin asked why the Canadian Jews wanted the Soviet Jews to go to Israel rather than Canada. He certainly must have been aware from his briefings that I was Jewish and I'm equally certain he knew the answer to his own question, but I gave a deflective reply since I was sure he realized that it was not my job to involve the Soviet premier in a serious political discussion on a highly sensitive issue.

The protests were just as large in Montreal, Toronto, and Vancouver but less so in Edmonton where we were hosted by the new young premier, Peter Lougheed. Toronto was a special experience. The official dinner, hosted by the province, was held in the impressive Ontario Science Centre in Don Mills. When we were about to leave we were told by the RCMP security people to stay put. Unknown to us, there was a large, vociferous demonstration outside, complete with anti-riot police forces and horse-mounted constables pushing the protestors aside. After well over an hour, the protest had subsided sufficiently to allow us to beat a hasty retreat to the nearby Four Seasons Inn on the Park, where

Kosygin and the official parties were billeted in luxurious, un-Soviet-like accommodation. As on other such visits, the delegations became remarkably friendly with each other; in my case, I was quite chummy with Kosygin's friend and Georgian prime minister, G.D. Dzhavakhishvili (pronounced, at least by me, "Java-hash-veeli"). Since my Toronto home was just a few minutes away, I asked Dzhavakhishvili and some of the others if they would like to visit a Canadian worker's house, to which they enthusiastically assented, particularly because I said "for drinks." Thus, a group with RCMP escort departed for 88 Old Colony Road. To my embarrassment, I had nothing alcoholic in my house but Walker's Imperial Rye Whiskey and Beefeater's Gin, which didn't phase them one little bit — as long as there was lots of both. (Such were the hazards of having two homes and forgetting how much liquor you had in each; the same applied to shirts, socks, and underwear, which were not as critical to the Russians.) Dzhavakhishvili presented me with a beautiful silver-encrusted drinking horn. In fact, it was just a cow horn but, because of its shape, could not be put down when filled with booze without spilling the contents. My Georgian friend explained that I had to fill it and drink it all, without putting it down. Quite a challenge but I later learned that the proper protocol was to fill it with Georgian wine — or whiskey or gin in this case — take a sip, and pass it around for everyone to participate until the horn was ready for refill. This was not in our briefing notes. During these Canada/USSR festivities, my youngest son, Tim, who was still living at home and not away at university as were his brothers, arrived. Bearded, and with his immaculate hair hanging down to at least his shoulders, he was in his early Marxist phase and a great fan of Che Guevara — which was all received with enthusiastic good humour by my guests if not by the RCMP contingent surrounding my house. Somehow, sometime, we all got back to the Inn on the Park and were ready for business the next morning. Soviet-Canadian relations remained intact except for the small matters of NATO and the Cold War and Soviet emigration.

The other visit was a quieter affair. President Josip Broz Tito of Yugoslavia, along with his wife, Madame Broz, and an official party of twenty-five or so, was in Canada in November, starting in Ottawa and then proceeding to Quebec City and Halifax. In Ottawa, the formalities were observed but there was just no magic or warmth between Tito and Trudeau. Quebec City was highlighted by a spectacular dinner hosted by the premier, Robert Bourassa, in the excellent dining room of the National Assembly. Strangely, Bourassa offered his official greetings and toast while remaining seated and speaking into a small microphone. Tito was his unsmiling self, but a lighter spirit was injected into the event by Mirko Tepavac, the Yugoslav foreign minister, his vivacious and distinguished actress wife, Renata, and Madame Broz, also a former actress.

Halifax was the real focus of the trip since, some months previously, Fitzroy MacLean, a British MP and Churchill's liaison with Tito during the war, had visited Ottawa. McLean was a good friend of the late David Groos, the MP for Victoria, and one day the three of us met in David's office. MacLean was anxious that Tito, with whom he was on close terms, visit Canada, but no invitation was forthcoming and such a visit was not high on Trudeau's priority list. As we were talking, Senator Henry Hicks walked by the office, and David's face lit up. Inviting Hicks in, Groos said that if Dalhousie University in Halifax, of which Hicks was chancellor, offered Tito an honorary doctorate, this would virtually force an invitation from the government. And that's what happened. The visit to Halifax was a great success.

The convocation at Dalhousie was impressive, with the Atlantic Symphony Orchestra playing enthusiastically under an expatriate Yugoslav conductor. Victor Oland, the lieutenant governor, was on the stage and fell asleep periodically through the ceremony. As for Tito, even in his declining years, he was in total command. He was one tough guy and not a little intimidating. Even his associates kept their distance and treated him reverently. Though his health was fragile, his doctors reluctantly allowed him one cigar a day and he made certain it was a big one; his staff handed it to him as if it were a holy offering and he smoked it with great relish. Madame Broz fussed over her husband constantly but even she never seemed completely relaxed with him.

Tito and company were travelling from Halifax directly to Cuba in a Yugoslav air force aircraft and we were all on hand for the official departure. Isobel had been with me for the entire trip and was present on this occasion too. At this point, the reader should know that my wife calls me either "Danson" or "darling" or sometimes a combination of both. This amused the Yugoslavs as much as it has always delighted me. Mirko Tepavac, the foreign minister, who, along with his wife, Renata, had become quite friendly with Isobel and me, said as he shook my hand, "Goodbye, Danson Darling." A postscript. Some twenty years later we found ourselves in Belgrade and phoned the Tepavacs, who thought that we were confused and were looking for their son who was a student at the University of Alberta. I insisted that we had met when they were in Canada. Renata, who spoke excellent English, said that they hadn't been in Canada for over twenty years, to which I replied, "Do you mean that in all those years you have forgotten Danson darling?" "Danson darling!" she shrieked and called Mirko to the phone. It was the beginning of a very happy reunion.

In April of the next year, President Richard Nixon visited Ottawa, accompanied by a large entourage including his secretary of state, William Rogers, and his national security adviser, Henry Kissinger. Nixon was not an easy man to be with and there seemed to be no natural affinity between him and Trudeau. Though their discussions were cordial enough, Nixon never seemed to relax and appeared distracted, perhaps not surprisingly since things were going badly in Vietnam at the time. There was one moment, however, when he did let down his guard a bit. As he and I sat alone in the cabinet room just before his speech to a joint session of the House of Commons and Senate, his manner changed when I asked him about his children; he then spoke with some warmth, just like any caring father. But the moment soon passed, and the barriers went up again. Perhaps he was thrown off by the fact that his speech was to be televised and his face was heavily pancaked with make-up to hide his quite dark beard, which gave him a sinister image on TV.

Rogers, for his part, was an easy-going man who could charm the birds out of the trees. But it was Kissinger, whom I would meet again when I was defence minister and he was secretary of state, who was the really intriguing character. Confident to the point of arrogance, he always seemed to be performing. Isobel and I sat with him at a dinner following a gala performance at the National Arts Centre, along with Ivan Head and his wife and Kissinger's escort, Charlotte Gobiel, resplendent in a deeply cut gown that exposed her considerable endowments.

While Charlotte was enchanting, Kissinger continued to pontificate throughout the evening. He had few doubts about anything, certainly none about himself, and showed little interest in his hosts. Indeed, almost all the official Nixon party gave the impression that the whole visit was a crashing bore and that this foray into the "sticks" was something that had to be endured. This attitude filtered right down to Ron Zeigler, the press secretary, and Rosemary Woods of later Watergate tape-erasing fame, both of whom attended the governor general's dinner at Rideau Hall. All in all, it was an awkward visit, yet an enlightening one, shedding light on the kind of people who were then leading the most powerful nation in the Western world.

These types of encounters helped make my two years as parliamentary secretary among the most fascinating periods of my political career. The job came to an end with the election of 1972, when I returned to the backbench as was then the practice. Trudeau never again appointed a parliamentary secretary of his own. Read into that what you will, but it had been a great experience for me.

Chapter Five
Backbench and Cabinet, Minister of State for Urban Affairs, 1972–76

As the government moved into the fourth year of its mandate, I was finding my work as stimulating as ever, but, like other Liberals, I was also anxious about the political climate. Through 1971 and 1972, the government's popularity fell sharply. There was no single reason. Trudeau's style was beginning to wear thin with some — we were now hearing even from Liberals that he was too arrogant, too cocky — and the economy was troubled by continuing high unemployment and high inflation, a combination, dubbed "stagflation," that economists had previously not thought possible but that would nonetheless bedevil the country for the next several years. The government alone was not to blame for this, but the perception had begun to take hold among the public that Trudeau wasn't paying as much attention to the economy as he should, that he was too preoccupied with such things as bilingualism and national unity. On top of that, bilingualism itself was an irritant to many, who saw no reason why French had to "be shoved down their throats," as it was put at the time. Their attitude was wrongheaded, but it was deeply felt all the same.

A Rude Awakening: The Election of 1972

In the fall of 1972 Parliament was dissolved and an election was called. The Conservatives, under Robert Stanfield, seemed to be in a strong position to defeat the government; indeed, I am convinced that if

Stanfield hadn't bungled a football pass at an event on the eve of the election — an embarrassing moment caught by press photographers and published on the front pages of newspapers on election day — he would have won enough additional votes to make his party rather than ours the minority government. And, if Stanfield had become prime minister, I believe that he would have been a solid one and difficult to dislodge the next time round, for by now he was clearly showing himself to be a person of significant talents and great integrity, and with a personal style sharply different from that of Trudeau. (Apart from Stanfield and Tommy Douglas, I cannot recall any other provincial premier who made a successful transition to federal politics.) But history is full of "'ifs." What did happen was that the Conservatives ran a good campaign and we did not; in fact, ours was a weak, flimsy affair, with Trudeau musing aloud about lofty subjects in his best philosophical fashion rather than taking the battle to the enemy. Our approach was summed up in the campaign's tepid slogan, "The Land Is Strong." No one knew what it meant, particularly since, in the minds of many voters, the economy was weak and jobs were disappearing.

In my own riding of York North, my Conservative opponent, Stephen Roman, the wealthy owner of Denison Mines, mounted a strong challenge. Roman was not a particularly effective candidate — he was right wing, short-tempered at all-candidates' meetings, and not very articulate — but such was the hostility to the Liberal government that I had a hard fight on my hands. It was also expensive. I spent $50,000 on my campaign, which was less than half of what Roman spent but still double what I intended, and it was tough for my fundraisers to come up with such a large amount in the difficult political environment of the time. Complicating the picture for me was the government's proposal, announced in March 1972, for a second Toronto airport at Pickering. Though the airport proper was to be located not in York North but in Norman Cafik's adjoining riding of Ontario, its flight paths did cross my riding and so local opposition was intense.

On election night, October 30th, I was delighted to emerge victorious, but my margin of victory had shrunk from about 8,000 to 2,000 votes. For other Liberals, it was more grim. No fewer than twenty-seven

Liberals went down to defeat in Ontario alone, and in the country as a whole we were reduced from 155 to 109 seats, just two more than the Conservatives. The NDP, with thirty-one seats, held the balance of power. And those were the final totals — the initial numbers were even closer. Norman Cafik was first reported to have lost his riding by a handful of votes — four, I believe — to Frank McGee, a former Diefenbaker minister. He demanded a recount and in the end came out on top by twelve or so votes. Had he not prevailed, our position would then have been even more precarious than it turned out to be, a 108-seat tie between the Tories and us Grits.

From Minority to Majority: The Election of 1974

For the next two years, the government was dependent on the support of David Lewis's NDP to ward off defeat in the House at the hands of the Conservatives. For all that, however, the minority Parliament was a highly productive one, and, as someone on what I call the sensible left wing of the Liberal Party, I was not uncomfortable with a situation in which the NDP kept our feet to the fire on social issues. At the time, I supported wholeheartedly the act creating the Foreign Investment Review Agency (FIRA) as well as the government's oil strategy, which controlled domestic prices, stressed national self-sufficiency, and created the national oil company Petro-Canada.

I backed, sometimes strongly, occasionally reluctantly, a variety of other measures which the NDP could not help but support, including increases in old age pensions and family allowances, the removal of the sales tax on children's clothing, and cuts in personal income taxes. In addition, as someone who had just gone through an exorbitantly expensive election campaign, I welcomed a new law that placed controls on election spending. However, in the event of an election being called, the act was not to come into effect until six months after the writs were issued, which meant that it did not have any impact on campaign expenditures in the election of 1974.

In April 1974 I introduced a private member's bill providing for the collection of alimony and child-support payments from errant husbands and what we now call "deadbeat dads." The reaction to the bill was excellent in the House — Conservative MP George Hees in particular gave the bill his strong support — but it never advanced beyond first reading, thus sharing the fate of my earlier private member's bill on Remembrance Day. While this is the fate of virtually all private members' bills, such legislative proposals serve the purpose of drawing attention to issues and sometimes, as in the case of my 1974 bill, lead to action by governments.

As far as I was concerned, the minority Parliament was humming along nicely and there was no reason to cut short its life. My leader or the people around him, however, may not have shared this opinion. It has since been said that, in the spring of 1974, Trudeau, Keith Davey, and Allan MacEachen, believing that the time was ripe for another election, decided to insert provisions in a new budget that neither the Conservatives nor the NDP could support. At the time, however, I knew nothing about this, nor, I am sure, did most Liberal MPs. For my part, I thought that the budget that Finance Minister John Turner introduced in early May, whatever its shortcomings, did not warrant the government's defeat in the House. When that did happen and an election was called — an election is mandatory whenever a government is defeated on a finance bill — I said to David Lewis, "David, you will regret this, your seats will be cut in half." I can't remember his words in reply, but they were something to the effect that he had no choice; the budget was unacceptable and the people would have to pass judgment. And so the government was defeated on 8 May and an election was called was called for 8 July 1974.

The ensuing campaign was a much happier experience than that of 1972, both for me and for the Liberal Party. Nationally, it was a brilliantly run campaign, with the Liberals able to take credit for all the achievements of the minority Parliament and Trudeau bashing Stanfield's call for wage-and-price controls to subdue inflation (his memorable "Zap! You're frozen!" moved a lot of workers to the Liberal camp). Margaret was pressed into service, too, and the effect of her activities was to soften the image of her often-aloof husband ("He's a beautiful guy," she said at one rally, "he taught me a lot about loving"). In York North, I was up against Stephen Roman again, but the campaign was different this time. Roman used many of the same, tired arguments he had used before, and resorted to the same kind of right-wing rhetoric — tax cuts for business, less government, anti-bilingualism — but none of this seemed to resonate with the electorate. Though there was still considerable distrust of Trudeau, the visceral hatred of him that had marked the 1972 campaign had abated significantly, especially among people who had shifted their votes to the NDP and the Conservatives in the 1972 election. As for the proposed Pickering airport, the opposition was as intense as ever, but, here again, the old fires were not burning quite as fiercely. As the campaign wore on, I grew increasingly confident about my chances as well as about the prospects of my party. And, as it turned out, my political antennae were working correctly. On election night, the Liberals were returned with a majority government, winning 141 seats to the Conservatives' 95 and the NDP's 16 — almost dead-on what I had predicted to David Lewis — and I was re-elected in York North by a margin four times larger than the one I received in 1972, with about 33,000 votes to Roman's 26,000. (The victory was all the more to be savoured since Roman had broken his previous all-time record for spending, and I had not even tried to compete in that field, proving the point that bigger campaign spending alone cannot win elections.) My political career was going to continue — for now.

Minister of State for Urban Affairs

Making it into cabinet is the ambition of most MPs, certainly those who belong to the party in government or to one that has a reasonable chance of getting there. Some people manipulate their way to a cabinet post; some reach their goal because of considerations of regional or ethnic representation; still others do so because of their outstanding qualifications or their political clout. And there are those who, for no earthly reason, believe that they're entitled to cabinet rank. Bizarrely enough, some of the latter actually succeed, in most cases for a short period of ineffectuality before being summoned to the Senate where they won't be noticed and can't do too much harm. Most MPs, though, have a different experience, putting in their time on the backbench, working on committees and as parliamentary secretaries, and all the while hoping that one day their abilities and hard work will be recognized. When there is a cabinet shuffle rumoured, a person's name may be mentioned as a possibility and some may actually see their dream come true while others suffer disappointment.

I have already told of the circumstances in which I learned of my appointment to cabinet: Prime Minister Trudeau's phone call to me while I was barbecuing a flank steak in July 1974, just after the election, his offer of the portfolio of the Ministry of State for Urban Affairs, and, in response to Isobel's inquiry about how I was doing — with the steak, that is — my "Not Bad for a Sergeant" reply. The smugness of that answer notwithstanding, I had not been consumed with cabinet ambitions from the time of my election in 1968, but I confess that my ambitions had grown over the years, especially as I saw certain people being appointed in whom I did not detect any outstanding qualities. It wasn't a matter of arrogance. I just believed that I could do as good a job as most ministers, and a better job than some of them. In any event, by mid-1974 there were the usual rumours of a post-election cabinet shuffle, and there was also scuttlebutt that I might be included. I wasn't hoping for any particular portfolio; I would have been satisfied with just about anything, except national revenue, the lowest rung on the ladder apart from minister without portfolio. When the call eventually came, I was not completely surprised that the prime minister had designated me for urban affairs.

I had developed a keen interest in policies relating to urban issues, particularly as Toronto's urban sprawl began threatening the rural and small-town environment of my constituency. Yet there was no voice for the cities in Ottawa; municipalities were the creatures of the provinces. While I, like others in Ottawa, recognized this jurisdictional reality, I also believed that the federal government could constructively influence the development of all cities. In addition, I had become the founding chairman of the Toronto Liberal caucus, formally known as the Metropolitan Toronto Area Planning Committee, thankfully given the acronym "METPAC" by Alastair Gillespie. This body focused the interests of the hefty caucus of Toronto-area MPs, and it was the first such grouping in Parliament relating to a city. METPAC became a force to be taken seriously. I also had been vocal on such issues as the need for high-speed rail transit, the threat of uncontrolled urban sprawl, and the value of urban "green belts." Among my other interests in those years — it was long before the Pickering proposal surfaced — was the building of an international airport at Kingston to serve both Montreal and Toronto; this airport would be linked to cities in New York State by Hovercraft and to Ottawa and other centres in Ontario by high-speed railway transit. The objective was to siphon off some of the growing charter and overseas traffic from the overburdened Toronto and Montreal airports. The special bonus was high-speed rail transit between Toronto and Montreal, which would relieve both road and short-haul air traffic and would be the main trunk line in the Quebec-Windsor corridor, enhancing the attractiveness of the areas in-between for residents and industry. It was a vast project involving new train technology and new railway rights-of-way and roadbeds. None of it happened, of course, but the prime minister was intrigued with the proposal and evidently thought of me as someone with an interest in the whole area of urban policy.

Whatever the reasons, I was chosen. The shuffle that brought me into the cabinet was announced on August 8th. As shuffles go, it had been a major one, involving the temporary departure of such important ministers as Herb Gray (in later years the dean of the House of Commons and deputy prime minister) and Robert Stanbury (who went on to a senior role in the private sector); the moving of a numbers of others, including Jean Chrétien, André Ouellet, Bud Drury, Jeanne Sauvé, Bryce Mackasey, Mitchell Sharp, Allan MacEachen, and Ron Basford; the replacement of Paul Martin as government leader in the Senate by Ray Perrault (Martin then became our high commissioner to the United Kingdom); and the arrival of three newcomers — Judd Buchanan, Romeo Leblanc, and me.

The next morning I flew to Ottawa to find out what a new minister was to do. Very much a sink-or-swim operation. Nobody was around to hold my hand and steer me through the shoals. And this wasn't unusual. As is always the case in cabinet appointments, a minister's predecessor — if still in office — is either busy learning a new portfolio or licking his or her wounds after having been dropped from the cabinet. After the swearing in of the new cabinet at Government House in a brief ceremony conducted by Chief Justice Bora Laskin, acting in the absence of an ailing Governor General Jules Léger, I was whisked back to my office to get to work. Phone calls and hand-delivered messages were coming in faster than my lone secretary and I could handle. Many were from people "on the Hill" who wanted to join my staff. Others were for essential meetings with my deputies. There was a deluge of requests for press interviews — hard to turn down for anyone with the necessary ego to become a politician in the first place. Notices of cabinet meetings to attend. Dozens of messages from total strangers who had to see me immediately to plead for some pet project which probably had already been rejected by one of my predecessors but which, in their view, was certain to enhance my stature.

Being a minister, as I quickly learned, requires instantaneous focus. You have so many, often disconnected, things on your agenda as you hurry from meeting to meeting that you must focus on the most immediate, as opposed to the most important, giving it all of your attention and then moving on to another meeting on a totally different subject. You soon learn to take this in your stride, but you absolutely must have a competent and dedicated staff to support you. They keep the briefing notes flowing and move you from one meeting to the next, providing you with last-minute updates or with gossip on the political priorities of the others you are meeting with. At the same time, they are constantly taking notes, or gathering the notes I have taken, for later consideration or immediate action. Many ministers blame faulty performance on weak staff. In my experience, good ministers have good staff. To be sure, staff can let a minister down occasionally: they are no less human than ministers. Yet in the long run, or short run for that matter, the minister is the person accountable and blaming his or her staff is a cop-out. If there are any weak links, the minister must recognize them and replace them.

In terms of my political staff, I chose an experienced "political junkie" and all-round great guy, Peter Connolly, as my executive assistant, or EA. Peter, who had cut his political teeth with the master tactician Keith Davey at the National Liberal Federation, had held similar posts with such senior ministers as Allan MacEachen, Herb Gray, Edgar Benson, John Turner, Bryce Mackasey, and Judy LaMarsh. He knew the system thoroughly, having been weaned on it as the son of Senator John Connolly, a leading figure in Liberal politics for as long as I could remember and a good personal and political friend. Big, bluff, affable, and always great fun, an effective operator who organized my office and me efficiently, Peter steered me around the political and bureaucratic obstacles. He remained my EA for about a year before moving on to another challenge. He remains a good friend of mine to this day. His successor was Eric Acker, who had begun as one of my parliamentary interns and then become a special assistant at Urban Affairs (another was Jeffrey Simpson, today the distinguished political columnist of the *Globe and Mail*). From Shelburne, Nova Scotia, Eric was a quiet, immensely competent young man who always told me what I needed to know, not what he thought I wanted to hear. I had complete confidence in him, so much so that, when I later moved to the Department of National Defence, I took him with me. Also invaluable to me was my secretary, Eunice Bartolucci, a true "girl Friday" — to use a term that is now politically incorrect but was acceptable then — who was a ruthless gatekeeper intent on making the most effective use of my time.

The Ministry of State for Urban Affairs, or MSUA, had three separate areas of responsibility: the ministry itself; the Central (now Canada) Mortgage and Housing Corporation (CMHC), which worked with the provinces and municipalities in financing and developing moderately priced or "affordable" housing across the country; and the National Capital Commission (NCC), which was responsible for the physical presence of the federal government in the National Capital Region on both sides of the river, mainly Ottawa and Hull and contiguous municipalities, including parts of the Gatineau, with its beautiful park lands and ski trails. CMHC and NCC had their own boards of directors but fell under my jurisdiction. The overall budget of the ministry, including its CMHC and NCC branches, was not piddling, amounting to $1.5 billion annually, and there were 4,000 employees in all. The ministry proper, as separate from CMHC and NCC, was not a "line department" like Health, Defence, Transport, or Justice, which had massive programs and statutory responsibilities in addition to very important policy roles. In that sense, MSUA was like its sister, the Ministry of State for Science and Technology; it was primarily a policy ministry, with the mandate of coordinating the urban presence and interaction of all federal departments and lands and liasing with the provinces on urban issues, particularly when there were areas of federal jurisdiction involved, such as railways, ports, and defence installations. The ministry also developed new thinking on urban issues, especially those where the federal presence could act as leverage for optimum urban development. It was quite a young ministry, having been established only in 1971, with Bob Andras as the first minister, followed by Ron Basford before me. Dwarfed in size by CMHC and NCC, it had just a few hundred employees.

Because of the ministry's tripartite structure, I had in effect three deputy ministers, each with a different title and area of responsibility: Jim McNeil, Bill Teron, and Ed Gallant. Jim McNeil (who later became the director of the environment program at the Organization for Economic Co-operation and Development, or OECD, and later still the secretary of the Bruntland Commission on Sustainable Development) was the senior civil servant at MSUA, his official title being that of "secretary," considered equivalent to the rank of deputy minister. McNeil was a talented civil servant who had come to Ottawa from Saskatchewan, where he, like many other federal civil servants of distinction, had served in the bureaucracy of Tommy Douglas's CCF government. Ross Thatcher, the new Saskatchewan Liberal premier elected in 1964, had wanted to clear the socialists out and replace them with his own gang of rogues. And so the federal government benefited from a migration to Ottawa of members of the "Saskatchewan Mafia," such as McNeil, Tommy Shoyama, and Al Johnson, who were highly respected and experienced, knew the workings of government well, and had a somewhat left-of-centre orientation which could adapt to the Liberalism of the Pearson and Trudeau eras. Under McNeil at MSUA were two talented assistant secretaries, Paul Tellier (later clerk of the Privy Council and currently president and chief executive officer of Canadian National), responsible for policy, and André Saumier (later deputy secretary of the Quebec cabinet and president of the Montreal Stock Exchange), responsible for coordination. They are two men for whom I still have the greatest respect and affection.

Bill Teron was the chairman, president, and chief executive officer of the Central Mortgage and Housing Corporation. He was a dynamic, youngish man who had been tremendously successful in the private sector as a builder and developer in the Ottawa region. He was not a person to adapt easily to the role of "deputy" to anyone. Teron became acting secretary of MSUA on McNeil's departure in 1975 and in June 1976 was formally appointed to the post, which he held while retaining his job as head of CMHC. The next year, under my successor as minister, André Ouellet, the ministry was disbanded. By then the government had concluded, as had I, that while the ministry was doing good work, urban affairs was a jurisdiction best left to the provinces and the coordination of the federal urban presence with the provincial and municipal governments didn't require a separate ministry.

Edgar Gallant was the chairman of NCC, the third element of my portfolio and in some ways the most interesting. Ed was an experienced mandarin and a somewhat low-key but polished operator who knew his way around Ottawa very well and was highly regarded. He was an invaluable person to have around at the meetings with my two other "deputies," since he had a knowledge of the federal system that Jim and Bill, newer to the league, respected mightily.

Before entering cabinet, I thought that I was a pretty busy MP, immersed in constituency work and parliamentary business. Being a cabinet minister, though, put my earlier workload into perspective. Ever since, I have felt that the prime qualities a minister must possess are reasonable intelligence, sound judgment, and the constitution of a horse. Every afternoon and Friday mornings when Parliament was sitting and I was in Ottawa, I, like all ministers, was in the House for Question Period. Lunch was generally in my office and consisted of sandwiches brought up from the West Block cafeteria. I usually tried to be at home by 6:00 for dinner with Isobel and the CBC Radio news (all politicians are news junkies). More often than not, further meetings, House duty (it was essential that a number of ministers be in the House at all times to cope with unexpected motions or procedural surprises), and official functions of one sort or another followed in the evening. Weekends, I was usually back in the riding for constituency business, the first priority of an MP. It was a demanding schedule, to put it mildly, and frequently the day ended with me falling asleep in bed surrounded with cabinet documents.

Though I was a junior minister, I felt comfortable in cabinet from the beginning. It was a collegial group, and the heavy-hitters (Chrétien, Jamieson, Turner, Sharp, Drury, and MacEachen) had been around a long time. The prime minister himself performed as brilliantly in cabinet as he did in caucus. To watch him deal with subjects you hadn't been able to keep up with in your own job, zeroing in on just about every paper that came before the cabinet, always asking probing questions, and almost always in a very gentle, almost conversational way, was really quite an experience. And, yes, I said gentle. This may surprise people accustomed to Trudeau's public image as an intellectually arrogant man with a confrontational streak, but the fact is that in cabinet he was the soul of patience, listening quietly, letting us talk almost as long as we wished, and almost always seeking consensus. The atmosphere was anything but adversarial. Certainly there were flashes of impatience or temper but more often it was his cabinet colleagues who were impatient for a decision. I can recall several occasions when, after lengthy discussion and failure to reach a consensus, Trudeau would throw his hands up in exasperation and say, "Well, I guess someone has to be the boss around here," and then indicate what his decision was. He exhibited incredible forbearance with our irrepressible minister of agriculture, Gene Whelan, who would find the most tenuous relationship between almost any topic and farmers and would go on and on and on, trying to make his case. Sometimes, when Gene or another minister was clearly enjoying the sound of his own voice (and some were not as loveable as Gene), I thought that we would have benefited from having a chairman more like Captain Bligh, but the mood soon passed.

Still, Trudeau, with his formidable intellect and memory, could be intimidating. A typical situation would find me bringing a document before cabinet. I had worked on its subject matter over a period of months and had studied its details over a period of weeks with my officials and often with caucus members. It contains a covering document very like an executive summary. I really don't expect that my colleagues have studied the full document and its supporting material unless they have a personal or departmental interest in it, and even then they are likely to be familiar only with those parts brought to their attention by their officials, who had, or should have, read every word. By now, I have dealt with the document in at least one cabinet committee and before

Treasury Board, and so I feel that I am thoroughly familiar with it. In fact, it has been on the cabinet agenda at least once before and deferred through lack of time or because some urgent priority had developed. Today, it is coming before cabinet the morning I've arrived back at 3 AM from a foreign capital, after having passed through several time zones. But Trudeau has done his homework. He has been well briefed and he has not only read the document but also retained its contents in that vacuum-like sponge he has in his head.

I am trying to give as positive a presentation as possible. Just when I make what I think is a strong point, the prime minister intervenes. "That's not what you said when we were driving from Jogjakarta to Solo, Barney." He's referring to a conversation we had some four years previously in Indonesia when I was his parliamentary secretary. I don't know what I said four years ago, but he does and repeats it. I explain my inconsistency or change of thinking as best as I can and go on. Then Trudeau intervenes again and says, "But Barney," or if he really wants to be kittenish, "But, Bernie Dawson," "that's not what the document says on page forty-five, para 2(a)." Now I flip through the document until I find page forty-five and, completely off stride, explain it as effectively as I can before continuing my presentation. Trudeau hasn't interrupted me to throw me off; he just wants to be certain that he understands what I am proposing and, perhaps just as important, that I understand it and can hold my own. If I try to bluff, it will soon be apparent to my colleagues and Trudeau. Admittedly, I have seen some great bluff artists in cabinet who survived, Bryce Mackasey being the master. In any event, I move through the rest of my presentation and, after a long discussion, my colleagues decide to support my planned course of action. Everyone around the table now knows, if they didn't already, that they had better be on top of their subject when Trudeau is in the chair.

Katimavik

The single achievement of my political career that gave me the greatest satisfaction was unquestionably Katimavik, a national youth service that was the most successful of all the varied youth services attempted in

Canada over the years but that was tragically terminated by the Mulroney government. I had been promoting such a service since arriving in Ottawa, and, though it didn't come to realization until my appointment to the Defence portfolio in 1976, it began to take concrete shape during my days at Urban Affairs. Most initiatives in government are part of a continuum, germinating over a period of time through caucus discussion and bureaucratic deliberations and often spanning a series of ministers. In this case, I know that Katimavik is a program that would not have happened had I not initiated it; nor would it have been the success it was without the passion, excitement, and drive of its first chairman, Jacques Hébert, now a retired senator and one of the three people I thought of as a close personal friend of Trudeau's, along with Gérard Pelletier and Jean Marchand. Years later, Hébert was to give a moving eulogy at Trudeau's funeral.

The genesis of my concept was my own experience as a young soldier. In those days, I came to have a deep appreciation of the value of a sense of purpose, teamwork, structure, discipline, and physical challenge, and I developed close bonds with other young men that turned into deep friendships. It was then, too, that a sense of commitment and service to our country, as well as a passionate loyalty to our comrades, took root in all of us. The war was our crucible. It also gave us the opportunity, as I said earlier, to get to know many parts of Canada — in my case, virtually every part of Canada. And, because of the structure of the Canadian army at that time, with its component divisions representing each region of Canada, we came to meet people from all areas of the country and from all socio-economic and various ethnic backgrounds. Perhaps most precious of all was the opportunity the war gave anglophones to meet francophones, and vice versa — for many of us, this was our first experience of our country's other "solitude."

I never had any fundamental objection to a mandatory national military service — nor do I have any today — but I also realized that such a system was not part of the Canadian tradition and would never fly politically. How, then, could we duplicate and expand the positive experiences of the military for young people in a peacetime environment? Actually, there was a precedent of sorts in post-First World War Germany. In 1921 Kurt Hahn, a distinguished German educator, established Salem School, which, while avoiding the militarism so ingrained in German society, had many of the same objectives I have just outlined. There were differences too, however, the most important being the elite nature of Salem's student body: Hahn's school drew its students largely from the ranks of the privileged in Germany and other European countries. Though Salem was highly successful, Hahn was a Jew and in 1933, after Adolf Hitler's rise to power, he left Germany for Great Britain, where he became headmaster of the renowned Gordonston School in Scotland, whose graduates over the years included Prince Philip, then of Greece, soon to be Duke of Edinburgh, and his son, Charles, the Prince of Wales.

Inspired by Hahn's example, and also by the Outward Bound Movement and the Atlantic Colleges (now United World Colleges) that embodied his ideas, I wanted a youth service that offered the opportunities I had enjoyed as a young soldier — the physical challenges, the opportunity for service to community and country, the chance to get to know Canada and to interact with a wide range of other Canadians — but without the casualties. I kept raising this issue with the prime minister whenever I could, in writing, in conversation, in caucus, and, after 1974, in cabinet. He always listened attentively but never picked up the ball. One day, however, he spoke to me of his friend, Jacques Hébert, who led a successful overseas youth program, Canada World Youth, better known by its francophone name, La Jeunesse Canada Monde, which gave Canadian youth the opportunity to work in developing countries. Jacques had spoken to Trudeau about his hope that some elements of his program could be built into a national youth service in Canada. Trudeau told Jacques of my hopes for such a program and asked me if I could see him, which I did with alacrity. The rest is, as they say, history.

In exploring this history, it is important to know that both Jacques and I had yet to develop confidence in one another and we were feeling each other out — sort of like shadow boxing — since we had strong, and somewhat differing, ideas about what a national youth service should be. Even though I was minister of urban affairs at the time, the youth program I had in mind had absolutely nothing to do with my regular daytime (and night-time) job. Jacques, for his part, already had experience in running his own, highly successful, program, and in this capacity he had demonstrated his commitment and skill. My concept, unlike that underpinning La Jeunesse Canada Monde, drew on my own background to give the program a military component — something that Jacques was not at all enthused about. I feared a lack of toughness, discipline, and structure, and I was convinced of the need for young Canadians to understand the valuable role the military had played in our history and was still playing in our society today. The experience of several other youth programs had ended in "hippie" disasters! I wanted no part of that. La Jeunesse Canada Monde, however, was in a different category altogether, being universally well regarded. I realized that Jacques would be essential to the success of the program I envisioned, for I had no faith in the bureaucracies that had produced the earlier free-wheeling flops and the political fallout they generated.

Ultimately, it was agreed that the program would be national in scope and allow all social, economic, regional, and linguistic elements of Canada to be proportionately represented. It would represent the age group of seventeen to twenty-one, serving as a transition from secondary school to university, community colleges, or careers, an opportunity for the participants to experience other aspects of life and other parts of their country and, in the process, to help them sort out what they wanted to do with their lives. In order to have both a civil and a military component, we decided that the program would consist of three, three-month periods, for a total of nine months' enrolment, one of which for anglophones had to be in a francophone environment and vice versa. The participant could choose to serve one of these periods in a military environment. This idea was to cause some apprehension in the military, which did not particularly like these "debutante" recruits, particularly since many of them would be women and at the time there was little acceptance of the view that the armed forces should be open to women, except in the traditional administrative, technical, and nursing roles. In the end, however, the military component of the program was hugely successful. (It also resulted in the program acquiring the nickname "Barney's Army," which was catchy but off the mark.) Participants were to be paid the princely sum of one dollar a day for pocket money and, if they completed the full nine-month program, they would receive an honorarium of $1,000 towards their future education or other endeavours. It was not a job-creation program.

The prime minister was supportive of our plans and encouraged me to submit a formal proposal to cabinet, which I ultimately did in November 1976. By this time, I was minister of national defence and I had serious reservations about keeping responsibility for a program that might be perceived as a form of national military service. But Trudeau was adamant; he said that it was my baby, for which I had lobbied for years, that I had developed a good working relationship with Hébert, and that I was the only minister he wanted to head the program. There was great curiosity in cabinet, but no real opposition, and I received approval for a program initially involving 1,000 participants, to commence the following July. A not-for-profit corporation, OPCAN (acronym for Operation Canada), was established to administer the program and report to me. A board of directors was established with Dr Howard Nixon, a distinguished educator from Saskatoon, and Jacques Hébert as co-chairs. Donald Deacon, then of Toronto and now P.E.I., subsequently succeeded Nixon, and both men served ably with Hébert and with strong commitment to the program.

None of us involved was enthusiastic about OPCAN as a name, and Jacques soon came up with an alternative, Katimavik (pronounced cat-im-a-vik), an Inuit word, we were told, for "place of meeting." It wasn't the easiest name to pronounce or even remember at first, but it was impossible to forget once you got accustomed to it — and it was the same in English and French. As the program's chairman, Hébert established offices in Montreal and ultimately in each region of the country. The authorized budget was $10 million.

The public reaction was positive from the beginning, much like that of cabinet. People were intrigued with the concept. Though some were sceptical, there was no significant opposition except from those who feared a repetition of past disasters. But Hébert's day-to-day direction, the support of his stalwarts Nixon and Deacon, and our regular, even constant, discussions reduced the chance of failure substantially. Hébert attacked his new role with almost ferocious passion, engendering an enthusiasm in the program's staff and leaders that was contagious. Some four thousand young Canadians applied, and while it was initially planned to hold interviews in each region, this proved impractical in terms of travel costs and staff time. Selection was thus made by the impersonal computer to reflect the demographic criteria essential to the program. This antiseptic approach did not appeal to me but the costs of the original plan were really quite staggering. Besides, the computer selection had, in addition to the economics, the advantage of fairness; there was no possibility of bias on the part of interviewers dispersed across the country. It also permitted a faster start. In any event, it worked. One thousand candidates were chosen from the total pool of applicants.

Communities, cities, towns, villages, and remote wilderness areas expressed interest in hosting Katimavik projects, which included environmental clean-up, building or upgrading playgrounds, flood and erosion control, forest-fire prevention, and working with senior citizens and the handicapped, all under the supervision of instructors. The community-service orientation of the program appealed to the values of the young men and women involved, not to mention their parents, the host communities, and us. New skills were acquired. There were, to be sure, a lot of bruises, fingers hit by hammers, and likely new expletives in both official languages — a bonding element in any group activity. All the time, the participants were fully aware of the two basic rules in this co-educational adventure: drugs and cohabitation were definitely prohibited, on pain of expulsion. Obviously, this did not produce a group of angels, but infractions were relatively few and handled expeditiously.

The program was renewed annually while I was in office but in 1979 the Clark government decided to close it down. By the good fortune of the Liberals' return to power in 1980, it was reinstated before the scheduled termination and remained in operation until the Mulroney government delivered the *coup de grâce* in 1986. An enraged Hébert, now a senator, engaged in a prolonged hunger strike in his Senate office, attracting enormous media attention and embarrassing the government. Ultimately, the promise of an alternative program caused Hébert to end his strike. As it turned out, however, this program never achieved anything remotely resembling the quality of Katimavik and put paid to the dream of enlarging Katimavik and making it accessible to all Canadian youth. At the time of writing, the Chrétien government is in the process of restoring Katimavik but it is still a very long way from achieving its earlier stature and meeting its full potential. At times like this, I wish that I were back at the cabinet table, and that Jacques Hébert, whose name will always be associated with Katimavik, was in charge of the revived program. Even in his late seventies, I'm sure that he would jump at the chance.

Today, if you should speak to any Katimavik alumni, you will almost always learn that it was a defining experience in their lives, one that resulted in lifetime friendships, bonds of attachment to the families with whom they were billeted, new skills, acquisition of a second language, values that have enriched their lives, and, above all, knowledge and love of their country.

Waterfronts

To get back to Urban Affairs, immediately after my appointment to the portfolio, I had blurted out to the press that "I felt like an alcoholic let loose in a liquor store." I suppose that I could have chosen my words more carefully. What I was trying to say was that Canada's cities did face challenges and I was eager to start working on them. One of those challenges was a housing crisis that had become evident that summer, a crisis triggered by high interest rates (12–13 percent) and manifested in a sharp decline in housing starts and a tight rental market. A variety of steps were taken to stimulate the construction of affordable apartments and encourage home ownership. Particularly successful were the Assisted Home Ownership Plan (AHOP) and the Registered Home Ownership Savings Plan (RHOSP). AHOP provided grants to first-time home buyers; RHOSP, a CMHC program administered by the Department of Finance, was set up to allow people to set aside $1,000 annually, tax-free, towards the purchase of a home, to a maximum of $10,000. A less politically sexy measure was the Sewage Treatment Assistance Program, which subsidized the building of sewers on unserviced land or in housing developments — a very successful initiative that allowed the construction of low-cost housing on land that was not otherwise capable of development.

I held several federal-provincial meetings of municipal affairs ministers, who usually had responsibility for housing. Most of these were low-key and, after the showpiece of the opening session, their real business took place out of sight in a suite in the Chateau Laurier, usually with only one official per minister present. This allowed us to get right down to work, avoiding the grandstanding for other officials and the press that is part of the game in the Ottawa Conference Centre. In private, we could be frank and cut away all, or most, pretence.

One of my particular interests was the future of the country's waterfronts. I had always felt that cities with waterfronts, like Toronto, Montreal, Quebec, Halifax, and Vancouver, should maximize them for their recreational potential. During Ron Basford's, André Ouellet's, and my time as minister, we had the satisfaction of seeing exactly that happen. Waterfront-improvement programs were begun across the country, at Halifax, Saint John, Quebec City, Montreal, Toronto, and Vancouver's Granville Island. In my home city, Toronto, the evolution of the present-day Harbourfront area took place over many years. Shortly after we were elected in 1968, Prime Minister Trudeau and his Toronto MPs went for a tour of the waterfront in a large Toronto Harbour Commission launch and I pointed out the potential of this area and the fact that nothing was being done about it. The waterfront was filled with derelict old warehouses from bygone days when there was heavy water traffic — before trucks and rail containers took over the common transportation of goods. The Redpath Sugar plant was the only structure of architectural note on the central waterfront. This was before Ed Zeidler's spectacular "Ontario Place" was completed. A few years later, just days prior to the close election of 1972, Mitchell Sharp, the senior minister from Toronto, announced the government's purchase of a large parcel of land in Toronto harbour for transformation into a dynamic cultural and recreational centre. Both the provincial government and the city were furious over the lack of consultation, but MSUA began cleaning up the land and planning cultural activities for the area. When I became minister, a management structure was established, including appointees from Metropolitan Toronto and the city of Toronto but not from the province, which, under municipal affairs minister Darcy McKeough, still refused to have anything to do with what it viewed both as a federal boondoggle and as an outrageous intrusion by the federal "Grits" into an area of provincial Tory jurisdiction.

With André Saumier, the second senior official at MSUA, playing a particularly active and vital role, much progress was made in the redevelopment of Toronto's waterfront. At this point, we had no intention of building housing in the area — the horrendous condo towers that blight the area came much later. We aimed only to create a recreational area of which the city could be proud. The success we had was largely the result of the partnership that developed among myself, Paul Godfrey, the chairman of Metropolitan Toronto, and Toronto's "tiny perfect" mayor, David Crombie. Unlike the provincial government, Godfrey and Crombie, both Tories themselves, saw our plan as a great boon for Toronto and had no compunction about working with the federal Liberals to realize it. When the three of us agreed to pull together, it was a partnership based on mutual respect, trust, and self interest — an unbeatable combination — and my admiration for these men has never faltered.

Railway Lands

Most cities had extensive railway yards in their central core. They were the hub of the country's transportation network, and many Canadian cities, particularly on the prairies, had grown up around them, with quite majestic railway stations at the focal point of central business districts. But transportation had changed immensely over the years. Not only had marshalling and railway yards moved to the outskirts of cities, but trains were being used more and more for freight as the airplane, car, and bus became the preferred modes of passenger travel. Under my predecessor, Ron Basford, MSUA developed a program to help finance the redevelopment of these largely derelict railway centres across the country. The Railway Relocation and Crossing Act, as it was bureaucratically called, had a $100-million budget. This was intended as seed money only, however; the hope was that it would be supplemented by additional funds from other levels of government and the private sector. Unfortunately, a single railway-lands project could use up $100 million easily, and partners with additional money were found only in two cities, Regina and Quebec City. But a lack of sufficient funding wasn't the only problem. Though the concept was beautiful, putting it into practical operation was a hugely complicated task beyond MSUA's capacity and jurisdiction, involving as it did planning matters that were properly the jurisdiction of the cities. Railway track could not be moved, and railway lands redeveloped, without long and hard negotiations with the host of players involved: provincial and municipal governments, private and corporate landowners, developers, and the railway companies themselves. Such negotiations as there were did not get far in most cities; the huge issues at stake defeated a subtly conceived and well-motivated program. Contributing to this outcome, too, was a gradual revitalization of railway travel in major urban centres. In mid-1976 it was generally thought that train travel was doomed; yet within a few years, as concern over urban sprawl, pollution, and traffic congestion mounted, trains came to be seen as an environmentally friendly alternative to other modes of transportation. And so in the end, for all our ambitious plans and despite the yeoman efforts of Jim McNeil and, once again, André Saumier, we seldom were able to get projects beyond the initial-planning stage.

At one cabinet meeting in 1978, when we were trying to find new ways to reduce expenditures, I said that I had a $100-million program that was not accomplishing what it had been created to accomplish and I would throw its budget back in the pot. I hoped that this would encourage others to examine and discard some of their ineffective programs, but it served only to rile them. They had never heard of such a thing: nobody ever gave back money without blood. Maybe I was naive, but I just didn't think that the railway-relocation program was going anywhere. The program was eventually killed, and I'm sure that Jim McNeil, who had taken a special interest in it, never forgave me. In any case, the dreamers at MSUA kept dreaming. They just started dreaming about more realistic things, like waterfronts, where there was clear federal jurisdiction and we had greater municipal support.

Habitat

"Habitat" was the United Nations conference on human settlements that Canada hosted in 1976 in Vancouver. It was one in a series of global UN conferences — earlier conferences had dealt with such issues as the environment, food, trade and economic development, and population growth — but had the highest profile of them all, with the exception of the 1972 Stockholm conference on the environment. Its purpose was to catalogue and study the array of settlement problems (congestion, pollution, poor housing, lack of infrastructure, and others) facing countries around the world, to explore possible solutions to these problems through "demonstration" projects undertaken at the national level, and, via partnerships among UN member states, to encourage developmental projects for the long term. As host minister, I was assumed to be the chairman of the conference, although my chairmanship wouldn't be confirmed until the first plenary session of the conference, when the chairman would be elected. In preparation for the event, I was expected to meet with other people who had been responsible for earlier UN conferences, particularly the Stockholm conference on the environment. The secretary general of that conference had been Canada's Maurice Strong, who had gone on to head the United Nations Environment Program in Nairobi, Kenya, and subsequently many other key UN roles. There were several regional preparatory conferences, which led up to the main "prep cons" in New York and, just prior to Habitat's opening, at Harrison Hot Springs, British Columbia. I didn't attend the regional conferences, but I did go to the New York conferences. These were my first exposure to the United Nations secretariat and the whole maze of the UN's member countries. The secretary general of the Habitat conference was a former Colombian cabinet minister, Enrique Penelosa. The Canadian secretary general of Habitat was Jim McNeil (who had left the ministry for the OECD by the time the conference convened), and he and Penelosa worked extremely closely together for many months. Theirs was a mammoth job, coordinating and leading the work of delegations and accredited observers from some 140 nations. Each participating nation was expected to initiate demonstration projects that addressed domestic human-settlement problems and that could be transferable to other countries. Of particular interest to me was the need for clean water in the developing world.

According to a report of the World Health Organization in 1970, one billion people in the world lacked safe water. In many villages in the developing world, there was just one well. In others, people had to depend on a nearby stream. If it was a stream, it was the women who went with jugs on their heads to return with their heavy, daily family supply, sometimes walking several miles each day. If it was a well, it was used for all purposes — drinking, cooking, laundry — and so was a breeding ground for disease in the community. Against this background, I believed that, because Canada is a country with great water resources — there is more fresh water per capita here than in any place on earth — our foreign-aid programs should focus on the provision of fresh water and the cabinet agreed. We also thought that this should be one of our priorities at Habitat, proposing a ten-year target for clean-water supplies around the world. At a "prep con" in New York, I proposed that fresh water be the main focus of the conference. This proposal was accepted unanimously, but the secretariat then came up with the goal of giving every dwelling its own water supply. The term was "a stand pipe in each home." A laudable objective but a completely unrealistic one. When this became apparent, the bureaucrats changed the policy to "a stand pipe for each four family units." All of this was a bit bewildering to the Third World delegates, and it was so far from reality in the foreseeable future that I suggested that we start off with a minimum objective of each village having a single standpipe to provide potable water. It was an achievable goal rather than a utopian, unachievable dream. The reaction was as if someone had said something quite revolutionary or possibly outrageous. But many sombre black faces lit up with wide smiles. One after another observed that this was something that they could identify with.

As part of the preparation for Habitat, I (accompanied by Isobel) travelled to a number of countries around the world to brief and encourage them in their plans for the conference. There were several messages I wanted to deliver about Habitat as I visited these countries and a great deal I wished to learn and discuss. While officials from each country were deeply involved, I wanted to make certain that the political leadership and particularly my counterpart ministers, who were most likely to lead their delegations at the conference, were also fully engaged. They were the people who would be responsible for the extent and quality of their contributions to the conference and the implementation of the lessons learned from others. I also wanted to acquire a better understanding of the different needs of countries at quite different stages of development. In the developing world, urban problems centred on the squatter settlements surrounding cities, with their makeshift housing constructed from scavenged materials, open sewers, and lack of clean water and of infrastructure of any kind. Socially, they were urban jungles. By contrast, the developed countries presented problems that the Third World countries could not believe were problems at all, and more than one of the latter said that they would happily trade theirs for ours. Ours largely revolved around dealing with the consequences of over-development, such as urban sprawl and air pollution and improving an already high quality of life. The strategies being employed to achieve these ends included the creation of "green belts" and the building of efficient transportation systems to tie communities together and to reduce the impact of the automobile, which was and is polluting our air and strangling our city cores.

Perhaps my deepest concern was to keep the conference focused on its purpose — human settlements — rather than the seemingly intractable political issues which found their forum in the United Nations General Assembly and Security Council but which were extraneous to the business of Habitat. The overriding and most divisive of these was the cleavage between Israel and its supporters and its Arab neighbours and their supporters, a split that itself overlapped with the larger chasm between the communist bloc and the capitalist West. Most of the Third World nations had banded together into what was known as the Group of 77, which had grown by 1976 to 134 states. Within the UN, there was a clear majority of states that were routinely against anything that didn't include the condemnation of Israel. Furthermore, in late 1975, the Group of 77 had succeeded in getting the UN General Assembly to pass a resolution equating Zionism with racism. In the midst of all this, my position was especially delicate because I was a Jew and, while making every effort to be balanced on Middle East issues, I was a strong supporter of the state of Israel. Still, I realized that, if Habitat were to be a success, we would have to avoid being derailed by such issues. I did my best during my Habitat-related trips in 1976 to keep the focus of everyone squarely on human settlement, and, when I said something along these lines in Arab countries, our hosts would smile politely but say nothing.

My first visits were to Britain, France, the Netherlands, and Sweden, where I met with ministerial counterparts and other government officials and saw many of their demonstration projects as well as a number of experimental satellite communities with easy access to major cities. As developed nations, their problems were similar to ours. Later, a tour of several African and Middle Eastern countries awakened me to the massive human-settlement challenges facing those societies struggling with spontaneous development amidst crushing poverty. We began in Senegal, where the government had grand plans for developing a huge housing project near the capital of Dakar. For some strange reason, Queen Farah, the then wife of the shah of Iran, who was also the developer, was financing this. The architect and planner was a Canadian, Moshe Safdie, whom I knew and who was in Senegal at the time of our visit; he briefed me at the site of the proposed project. We were next to go to Lagos, Nigeria, to meet with our counterparts of this, the largest of the African nations, but our ambassador in Senegal, André Couvrette, alerted us that a military coup was taking place in Nigeria. It was not exactly a propitious time for an official visit. This was unfortunate, not least because the Nigerian delegation was to play an important role in the difficulties that were to beset the conference in Vancouver.

We then flew right across the continent at its widest point to Nairobi, capital of Kenya. Our Canadian Air Force Falcon Jet had bathroom facilities but, because it didn't have enough baggage space for our group, the toilet area was filled with luggage. This made for a long and uncomfortable trip and we were always anxious to get to the next fuelling stop. The first leg was fairly easy, to Abidjan, Ivory Coast, but the next leg was very long, to Bangui in the Central African Republic. We landed there in the middle of the night and thought that it would be a simple refuelling stop, with no protocol or contact with the government. We did get word as we approached, however, that there were to be protocol officers to greet us and facilitate our refuelling and the most important task of going to the bathroom. As we taxied to stop in front of the terminal, the gangway was lowered and we noticed four or six men in pinkish jump suits — almost like overalls; people dress for comfort and tradition in these countries. I walked along the line and shook their hands, assuming that they were the protocol people. But in fact there were no protocol people around, just the ground crew to get us refuelled and turned around and who were somewhat bewildered by the V.I.P. reception. What nobody had expected was that we desperately wanted to get into the terminal to go to the bathroom and nobody could or would let us in without approval from immigration officials, who were wisely at home fast asleep. This became a greater crisis as the minutes went by, but we eventually got into a bathroom and accomplished what we had to do. It had been touch and go.

My host and counterpart in Kenya was the minister of housing and social services, Taita A. Towett, and an active participant in our meetings was the mayor of Nairobi, Margaret Kenyatta, daughter of the legendary president, Jomo Kenyatta, now old and ailing. A mind-boggling experience was a visit to the politely called "spontaneous development" in the Mathare valley, on the outskirts of Nairobi. An impressive Kenyan woman from the World Council of Churches (WCC) guided us through this teeming, ramshackle squatter settlement, sadly typical of the squatter settlements surrounding many cities in developing countries. Drinking a locally made brew that was equivalent to what we think of as "fire water" was commonplace. It was cheap, accessible, and offered an escape from lives of misery and boredom. Our WCC guide directed my attention to an obviously quite drunk woman, saying, "This is my problem — how do I take a woman like this and try to talk about birth control? How do I take the men and try to get them to show responsibility?" I realized the immensity and frustrations of her job, as well the difficulty of trying to come up with measures at Habitat that would alleviate — let alone solve — such daunting problems.

In preparation for Habitat, I had been advised to visit an Arab country, and I chose Saudi Arabia. Jews were not welcome in that country — there had been one exception, Henry Kissinger, who had visited Saudi Arabia on behalf of President Richard Nixon — and I wanted to test the system (and especially the Saudis' reaction to a Canadian minister who happened to be Jewish). This was the first time I was introduced to the need of having two passports. I was travelling on a diplomatic passport but my officials gave me a second one for the Arab countries because I had been in Israel before and my passport had been stamped — someone whose passport had an

Israeli stamp could not travel to most Arab countries. I didn't like the apparent subterfuge, but if you are to play in this league you have to make compromises. Anyway, the Saudis would certainly know that I was Jewish and that I was to go to Israel afterwards. I was anxious to see if I could make a dent on their intolerance.

Jeddah, the capital of Saudi Arabia, was our first stop. We were greeted by our ambassador, Michael Shenstone, whom I had known previously from the Helsinki Conference on Security and Co-operation in Europe in 1973, and by Prince Majid, my counterpart minister in Saudi Arabia. After staying just long enough to refuel and go through the protocol of arriving in the capital city, we went on to Riyadh, where the real action was (and is). Riyadh was then in a state of explosive growth; there were new roads, new schools, and new hospitals, and new housing was being built on a massive scale. The first really modern hotel, the Riyadh Hilton, had just opened and we were escorted into a large and well-equipped, if not lavish, suite that even had an unstocked bar — rather unusual in this strict Muslim country. It was, however, soon adequately stocked when the ambassador arrived laden with two Addida sports bags carrying liquor from the embassy's special reserve. Though such liquor was intended for use within the embassy only, we did not object. To us, our hotel suite was an extension of the embassy.

I had cordial but rather stilted meetings with several ministers, all of whom were princes of the Saudi royal family. I was meeting with one of these, the governor of Riyadh, who had to excuse himself since he was summoned to a council of state. In our terms, that's a cabinet meeting, though in this case all the ministers were brothers or cousins. King Fahd had recently succeeded the assassinated Faisal. When he had something to discuss, he called the council of state and everyone dropped what he was doing and went to the palace — not terribly unlike our system although we generally get advance notice.

Since all the Saudi ministers were at the palace, we had a little time to kill before lunch, which was to be at the Jockey Club. There, the ambassador advised me, we would see a lot of men standing around drinking fruit juices. It always ended up with a quick buffet and everyone leaving shortly afterwards. Ambassador Shenstone explained that this was a common practice and counselled me not to be offended, saying that Allan MacEachen, Donald Macdonald, John Turner, Alastair Gillespie, and other Canadian ministers had been to Saudi Arabia and they had not been treated any differently.

When we arrived at the Jockey Club, Michael Shenstone observed that something was different. Our car was greeted with impressively costumed guards with crossed scimitars, and the smell of incense surrounded us as we made our way through an elaborate entrance leading to the reception room. Michael looked around and commented that almost anybody who was anybody, except the king, was here today. This was unusual. But even more unusual was the presence of Isobel, who had been taken on a private tour of Riyadh. Having a woman at such an event in this almost exclusively male society was, to our knowledge, unheard of. After the introductions and three sips of fruit juice, servants opened double doors to the dining room. In front of us was a huge, heavily laden table groaning with food. It was about forty feet long, set with elaborate silver. I sat opposite the prince who was the host at that time. Isobel was sitting at his right. The food was more than we could possibly manage at lunch and they kept bringing more. Indeed, they rolled in large trolleys with huge silver covers under each of which was a whole lamb. I don't know where it all went. We surely couldn't eat it all, but they seemed offended if we stopped. They did ultimately relent after what they considered an appreciative effort on our part. As lunch concluded the prince announced that the king wanted to see me, and he asked Isobel if she wished to visit his wife at their palace — an invitation she couldn't refuse.

We were escorted to the king's palace, which was a modern, low-slung building, and led into a large room with chesterfields lining the walls. We were then seated, but all rose when the king came in. He took a seat and beckoned us to do the same. We were about five feet apart — he was directly opposite me — and a translator was at one side between us. I made the mistake of calling him "Your Highness," when the correct title, as Michael Shenstone reminded me *sotto voce*, was "Your Majesty." It didn't seem to bother the Saudis or perhaps was lost or edited in translation. Things were going quite cordially as we discussed Habitat issues. In a previous conversation with Michael, I had mentioned my interest in horses and how, in my post-political days, I hoped to own and raise them. This was a throwback to my youth and more of a dream than anything else, but Michael latched on to it. Our hosts were Bedouins, who had been brought up with horses and loved them. Michael said to the king, "The minister wants to devote his life to horses." At this point, the king and all others reacted with glee. This instigated a visit to several horse farms and the stables of the National Guard, a security force distinct from the army that, some said, had the task of keeping the army in check if that proved necessary.

From time to time, ministers or other members of the royal family arrived, bowed appropriately to the king, and were introduced to me. It was all quite colourful, for they were in full gowns and djellabas. One of them was the foreign minister, Prince Saud, son of the late King Faisal, who had obviously been briefed on my background. In a short period of time, and in a soft and gentle way, this Princeton-educated man let me know that he was the loyal son of his father, whom he revered, but didn't agree with all his beliefs. It was not a topic for discussion but a pointed message to me, since it was known that I was soon to be in Israel. In fact, the prince's desire to communicate this message may account for the quite elaborate hospitality I was receiving.

Isobel later reported of her own visit that the prince's palace was really a large modern home of great luxury, with twin everythings — his and hers barbecues, his and hers swimming pools — which is in keeping with the social and religious protocol in Saudi Arabia. The women were all beautifully dressed in Western style. In the midst of the visit, the prince himself arrived, following the meeting with the king. He was very hospitable and asked Isobel if she would like a drink. She tentatively suggested tea or coffee. He said that he meant a real drink. She settled for the traditional coffee, but he had the biggest Scotch whiskey Isobel had ever seen. When he had finished and it was time for him to depart, he took an atomizer out of his pocket and sprayed his mouth to cover his breath before going on to his next engagement.

In the evening we had a gathering with Canadian businessmen in Riyadh. This was held in our hotel suite and the ambassador's stock of embassy spirits was put to good use, enhancing Canada-Saudi trade —

a relaxing interval in a very hectic schedule, without the need of translators. It was an interesting event, as we learned of opportunities and the
do's and don'ts of doing business in this rapidly growing oil-rich economy with its very different customs. Many of the businessmen said that,
like me, they were intrigued by the unusual, truly royal attention being
lavished on us.

So ended my visit to Saudi Arabia. But a short postscript is now in
order. In late 1974 I had drafted a letter to King Faisal of Saudi Arabia,
without a doubt the most anti-Israeli, anti-Semitic leader in the Arab
world at the time. Reflecting my belief that a Palestinian state was an essential part of any viable plan for Middle East peace, as well as my conviction
— obvious enough — that one makes peace only with enemies, not
friends, and one must always let them save face — the letter read as follows:

Your Majesty,

As a child of God, I am distraught over the misunderstanding and even hatred which exists between elements of humanity. Misunderstanding and hatred
which should more properly be directed to mutual
respect and love.

As a citizen of the world, and in a small way, as a
political leader in my own country, I fear the consequences of current economic disruption and the possi-
bilities of military conflict in the Middle East which
could engulf that region and reverberate throughout
the world.

As a Jew, I have an understanding of the anxiety
of Israelis and Jews elsewhere about the future, even
survival, of that state. The anchor it provides for a
people whose past gives justification to their aspirations for a homeland.

As a Jew, proud of my tradition, fiercely loyal to my
own country, but above all, sensitive to and dedicated to
justice and respect for all people, I am profoundly dis-
turbed by the animosity between Arab and Jew. Between

people whose faiths, traditions and history should motivate them to live in harmony and mutual respect.

It is from this perspective that I have found little to offer solace or hope in existing circumstances. Not believing in miracles, I have felt that only a miracle could bring a satisfactory conclusion.

Complex problems defy simple solutions, yet, it occurs to me, sir, that you have the power, resources and universal respect to create such a miracle. The miracle of peace and harmony in the Middle East, renewed hope and opportunity for both Arabs, especially Palestinians, and Jews.

You must wonder why Providence has endowed you with such awesome power, problems and resources. At times, you must wish for simpler times and simpler problems. To be able to serve your peoples' needs and live in reasonable tranquility. The tranquility of your faith which obviously motivates you so deeply. I too have so wondered.

It is strange that the possession of such immense economic resources can cause overwhelming unease when it is possible that these have been given to you to create the miracle about which I write. To continue the Arab renaissance and give it special impetus by building a new Palestinian state with its own viable economy, society and institutions. With its energies directed towards its real fulfillment as a nation living in harmony with its neighbours, be they brother Arabs or Israelis.

To make this possible, the Israelis must revert to former boundaries but be given your guarantee of their perpetual security. This, I realize, is not an easy undertaking when insecurity and mistrust abound. The evidence of good faith which I almost impudently suggest is within your hands to provide. Appropriate economic support to help enable Israel to achieve economic stability in a peaceful environment. This might even be conditional on other sources providing equivalent assistance.

The establishment of a co-ordinating government, consisting of both Arabs and Israelis to oversee the total development of a still politically divided Jerusalem. A form of metropolitan government which recognizes the political division but is charged with the responsibility of bringing harmony into the lives of its inhabitants through joint services provided but, more importantly, to enrich the religious and historical presence so sacred to so many faiths.

A further dimension could be the establishment of a Moslem, Jewish, Christian university or institute of world stature, dedicated to knowledge, understanding and full appreciation of each of the component religions and cultures. A centre which could harness the genius of the people of the region towards the development of their potential in a dynamic society based on peace and mutual respect.

It is a simple thought put forth for its own sake and in the absence of other initiatives. I do not propose it as an alternative to other approaches but as one that holds hope and which only you are in a position to lead. Indeed, it would further enshrine your name, and that of your illustrious family, in the history of mankind.

In March 1975 I sent a copy of this letter to the prime minister, with the request that in view of the fact it had nothing to do with my portfolio and the political fallout if it became public could be disastrous, he might wish "to keep … at home rather than at the office." I wouldn't mail the letter, of course, until I had heard his reaction.

As it happened, however, I was still waiting for Trudeau's feedback when King Faisal was assassinated. There matters rested until early 1976, when I decided to visit Saudia Arabia as part of my Habitat tour. I remember vividly the day of my departure. I was in Trudeau's office, briefing him on my departure later that day for Habitat-related visits to Aftrica and the Middle East, including Saudi Arabia. At once, he urged me to follow up on my letter of the year before, by which he had been deeply moved. I replied that obviously I hadn't sent it, I didn't know where it was, and I wouldn't have the time to search my files before leaving. He said that he still had his copy and went over to a cupboard in his office which had a filing cabinet for private material After rummaging around for a few minutes, he suddenly announced, "Here it is!" and walked briskly out of his office to a nearby photocopy machine. He then returned and gave me a copy to take with me.

At the end of my 1976 trip to Saudi Arabia, I showed my letter to Ambassador Shenstone. He said that he liked it and that he thought it should be addressed to the current king, with a few additional changes to reflect the just completed visit. I followed his advice and sent him a new version of the letter after my return to Ottawa. It is unclear to me whether it ever found its way into the Saudi system.

This story is interesting, I think, because of what it reveals about Trudeau's memory: not only had he remembered my letter, but he knew exactly where to find it. Also, in the wake of the March 2002 peace proposal of Saudi Crown Prince Abdullah — calling for Israel's return to its 1967 borders in exchange for complete normalization of relations with the Arab world — I have been thinking again about my 1975 letter. I wouldn't think of claiming that the thoughts I expressed there had any influence on the crown prince's thinking — that would be absurd — but I do find it encouraging that the Saudis appear to have come around to a conclusion somewhat similar to the one I had reached a quarter-century earlier. I fervently hope that something comes of the Saudi initiative as a basis for serious negotiations. Indeed, I hope that they are able to convince their dissidents and other Arab states to join with them and stick with whatever commitments they make. The initiative has been one of the few glimmers of hope in the long-running conflict between Arabs and Jews that has become even more intractable and tragic — if that is possible — since the outbreak of the second Palestinian *intifada* in 2001.

From Saudi Arabia we flew to Cairo, where I met with my ministerial counterpart and a number of other officials before making a side-trip to visit our peacekeeping troops at Ismailia, commanded by my old army friend Brigadier General Don Holmes. It was always fun to be with

Don. We wound up the tour in Israel meeting with Dr Josef Borg, the minister of the interior, my host and counterpart. Isobel, Dr and Mrs Borg, and I were to meet for lunch with Prime Minister Itzhak Rabin and his wife, Leah, at their home. Isobel and I arrived first, as planned. We found Rabin introspective and courteous. That he, like President Anwar Sadat of Egypt, whom I was to meet the following year, was destined to be assassinated speaks volumes about the hazards of moderation in the cauldron of Middle East politics. When Josef Borg and his wife were about to arrive, Leah Rabin said, "Just watch him. As soon as he arrives he will go into the kitchen to make certain it meets his high standards for a kosher kitchen." That is exactly what happened: Borg inspected the kitchen and gave it his blessing. I briefed Rabin on the arrangements and expectations for Habitat and expressed my hope, which I had relayed to Arab leaders and others, that the conference would stick to matters of substance and avoid extraneous political issues, particularly the Arab-Israeli dispute. Rabin was sceptical, and, as events proved, his scepticism was well founded.

At the final "prep con" at Harrison Hot Springs the weekend before Habitat convened, I met with UN officials to review procedures for the conference. This was an important matter, because everyone knew that procedural wrangles of various sorts were certain to occur as the different factions among the UN's member nations came face to face at Habitat. Indeed, the danger signals were everywhere. Not only had the Arab states made trouble at a number of UN conferences held recently, but the Group of 77 was now making noises about tackling the Israeli issue as soon as I called Habitat to order. Given all of this, I was furious when I arrived at Harrison Hot Springs and learned that no UN legal advisers were there. I was told that I shouldn't worry: legal advisers would be at the conference to offer procedural advice when it was needed. It didn't turn out that way. Once the conference convened, the principal UN legal adviser informed me that in a few days he would have to leave for another conference in Rome. He assured me that his deputy could handle any problems that arose, but I did not share his optimism and asked that his superior be sent from New York, a request that was either lost or ignored since this gentleman never arrived. Then, when procedural nightmares did materialize, the UN legal officers at the conference didn't have a clue what to do. This did nothing to give me confidence in the UN bureaucracy.

Habitat, or, to use its official name, the United Nations Conference on Human Settlements, opened on 31 May in Vancouver and ran until June 11th. The largest UN conference to date, it was a major affair. In all, about 5,000 delegates were present, and in addition there were 7,000 more in attendance at a parallel conference, the Habitat Forum, on the campus of the University of British Columbia, for representatives of non-governmental organizations (NGOs), various advocacy groups, and individual citizens. The Canadian delegation alone, headed by Ron Basford, my predecessor at MSUA and a Vancouver MP, had seventy-two members, drawn from all three levels of government, native organizations, and NGOs. The city's hotels were overflowing, not only with conference delegates, but also with heads of state, press representatives from around the world, and assorted luminaries, such as Barbara Ward, Margaret Mead, and Buckminster Fuller. Country delegations presented audio-visual displays of demonstration projects (there were more than 200 of these). There were sessions on low-cost housing, transportation, resource conservation, water and irrigation, employment, city government, town design, waste management, and much more. Yet, in the end, the conference's good work was overshadowed by political manoeuvring that would have left even Machiavelli breathless.

The conference opened amicably enough with an inspiring address by Prime Minister Trudeau and another by the secretary general of the United Nations, Kurt Waldheim. As expected, I was elected conference chairman. But the happy mood did not last. Mid-way through the first week, delegates from the Group of 77 and others left the hall when the Israeli delegate, Josef Borg, started addressing the assembly; this was standard practice, but I found it offensive. Afterwards, when a delegate from the PLO (Palestinian Liberation Organization), which had observer status, spoke, the Israelis returned the compliment.

There was also trouble behind the scenes. The Group of 77 had prepared a statement of principles emphasizing the need for a "new international economic order" — one of the buzzwords of the time, hurled by Third World and communist states against industrialized Western democracies — and also including an Iraqi attack on all "forms of racism and discrimination condemned by the resolutions of the General Assembly of the United Nations," a not-so-subtle reference to the UN resolution, passed the previous year, equating Zionism with racism. One of the principal committees of the conference, concluding that it was unable to recommend either this document or three others that were before it, turned the matter over to the plenary assembly. A new committee was struck to deal with the impasse, but it got nowhere. And so another plenary meeting was convened. At that time, the Group of 77 statement was presented to the conference, along with a Cuban amendment that attacked settlement planning that was intended "for the purpose of prolonging occupation and subjugation." A Pakistani delegate then proposed that all amendments to the statement of principles before the meeting — he clearly had the Cuban amendment in mind — be decided on the basis of a simple majority; this was a clear violation of rules previously agreed on, namely, that procedural changes required a two-thirds majority to pass. Sensing that the conference was to collapse in disarray, I turned to my UN legal staff for advice, and when they couldn't offer any, I urged the delegates to reconsider. "This is a moral matter," I told them. "For the sake of God and the sake of our children, I beg you — and I do not beg easily — to stay with what this was all about." It was all for naught. The Pakistani resolution scrapping the two-thirds rule carried by 69 to 28, with 20 abstentions, and then the Cuban amendment passed by a like margin. Thinking of resigning as chairman, I retired to my hotel room to have a stiff drink, leaving one of my vice-chairmen in the chair. A number of delegates came to offer their support, and so I returned to the hall. But things didn't improve. The conference, to my astonishment, accepted a United States proposal to vote on the statement of principles as a whole rather than on its individual paragraphs in succession. By now, everyone just wanted to pass something and go home. The result was that the Vancouver Declaration on Human Settlements, based on the Group of 77 text, passed 89–15, with 10 abstentions; the nations voting against it were Canada, Israel, the United States, the United Kingdom, France, West Germany, the Netherlands, Luxembourg, Belgium, Norway, Denmark, Italy, Ireland, Australia, and New Zealand.

And so it was over. For all the hard work that had gone into the conference — more than two years of it — we couldn't even agree on a statement of principles. Specific recommendations on settlement issues were passed, but these were phrased in such general terms that no one could have any illusions that progress would be easy or quick — or that it would take place at all; for example, on the issue of water, my special interest, the conference passed a resolution urging governments to aim for clean water by 1990, but there were no specific mechanisms suggested to achieve this goal and no targets were set. The failure to devise hard targets was a particular disappointment to me.

In spite of all this, there were achievements. Nations that never before addressed their problems of settlements were now to do so as a result of the Habitat process. A secretariat was established in Nairobi alongside the United Nations Environmental Program to monitor progress and facilitate the exchange of information among developing countries, and provision was made for further conferences on the issue of human settlement every twenty years. Habitat II was held in 1996 in Istanbul and Habitat III is scheduled for 2016. In addition, "mini-Habs," actually "prep cons" in a sense, have been held every five years since Habitat I to monitor progress and ensure that ongoing problems are addressed on a regular basis.

It is commonly said that if the UN did not exist it would have to be invented. It is the only truly international forum that addresses the major problems of the world. That doesn't mean by any possible stretch of the imagination that I am one of its greatest admirers. In its efforts to represent all of its members fairly, it all too often settles for the lowest-common denominator. And, in order to reflect its diverse membership, its secretariat is often comprised of people of dubious competence, too frequently selected on the basis of their political or family connections to sometimes-despotic rulers. Having said that, any organization of such size and diversity would be difficult to manage under the best of conditions, and the UN, despite all its faults, has attracted people of great ability and integrity. One of these is the current secretary general, Kofi Annan. Under his leadership, one senses a tightening of the UN's organizational structure, as well as an honest assessment of its weaknesses and failures and a new resolve to correct them. It is a tough assignment, and I can only hope that the political determination of the secretary general — aided by Canadians such as Stephen Lewis, Maurice Strong, and Louise Fréchette, the deputy secretary general — results in real progress.

When the Habitat conference closed, I was eager to get back to Ottawa, where politics could be brutal but never as vicious and unprincipled as what I had just witnessed. Little did I know that, a few months after returning to my office in Ottawa, my political career would take a new turn.

Chapter Six
Minister of National Defence, 1976–79

By mid-1976 I was becoming frustrated in the Urban Affairs portfolio. At first the job had been appealing to me because of my interest in urban planning and development, but over time I came to the realization that the federal role was severely constrained. The municipalities were constitutionally "creatures of the provinces" and we had little clout. Certainly, we had jurisdiction over federal lands, railway lines, airports, and waterfronts, but we couldn't exploit these assets without the full cooperation of the provinces and without adhering to their planning guidelines, and they were not likely to relinquish their role, nor should they have been. They were intimately and consistently engaged with "their" cities and towns and physically and politically closer to them than the federal government was. As a result, when we devised a superb initiative like the Railway Relocation and Crossing Act, the municipalities, who had the most to gain, were reluctant partners who participated to the extent of the federal money available. Occasionally, provincial and municipal planning did involve areas of federal jurisdiction, but when, for example, the federal government chose to turn over valuable federal lands such as the Canadian Forces Base, Downsview, and the costly and defunct Pickering airport lands adjacent to Toronto for use as parkland, the transfer was grudgingly accepted with hardly a word of thanks. All in all, there seemed to be a huge gap between the world of municipal politics and that of Ottawa — a fact reflected perhaps in the difficulty most municipal politicians (like provincial premiers) have had in making the transition to federal politics, cases in point being Phil Givens and David Crombie, both former mayors of Toronto who never seemed fully at home on the federal scene.

The Department of National Defence

In the summer of 1976 there were rumours around Ottawa of a cabinet shuffle and I mentioned to the prime minister that if, as I heard might happen, Jim Richardson left Defence for another portfolio, I would be interested in taking it on. Trudeau listened closely but was non-committal, since he was probably still juggling his options. In any case, Defence was operating well under Jim, and, for that matter, so was Urban Affairs under me, notwithstanding my concerns there. And so I was not surprised when a cabinet shuffle on 14 September brought about a variety of changes — including the appointment of a number of talented newcomers, John Roberts, Francis Fox, Monique Bégin, and Iona Campagnolo — but left me in my place and Jim in his. I was disappointed, but not terribly. Jim Richardson had not intimated to anyone that he wanted a change and Trudeau seemed content with the way things were.

Then something surprising happened. Out of the blue, Jim Richardson told the prime minister of his intention to resign. The issue was bilingualism, or rather the plans currently being discussed both in Ottawa and in the provinces, as part of ongoing negotiations regarding constitutional patriation, to give Quebec a constitutional veto over language rights. Trudeau urged him to reconsider his decision, but Jim's mind was made up. On 13 October, the day after the speech from the throne, he again informed Trudeau of his decision to resign effective immediately. His letter of resignation, though not expressing opposition to bilingualism in principle, asserted that "Canadians will be put into a linguistic and cultural 'straight-jacket' if they agree to additional language rights in the patriated Constitution and, *at the same time*, provide a perpetual veto to Quebec, the one province that has a special interest in French language rights." The conclusion of the letter also referred to Jim's annoyance over the government's "apparent indifference" towards the "reasonable aspirations of Western Canada" and its neglect of "the energies and creativity of Canadian entrepreneurs." But these issues were secondary; bilingualism was the heart of the matter.

We were all puzzled. I did not share Jim Richardson's views on bilingualism and I wondered, as did all of his colleagues, why he had not raised the matter before, either in cabinet or in caucus. But the die was cast, for me no less than Jim. At the same cabinet meeting at which Jim's resignation was announced, the prime minister asked me if I was still interested in becoming the new defence minister and my reply was immediate. I definitely was! The Defence portfolio was one I had long wanted. It and Industry, Trade and Commerce, as it was then known, were the two portfolios for which I had always thought I would be well suited. I also noted, however, that I had a few things to clear up at Urban Affairs before I would be in a position to move on. Within three hours of Jim's resignation I was made acting minister of defence, and I combined this job with my Urban Affairs portfolio until 3 November, when I was sworn in as the defence minister and André Ouellet succeeded me at Urban Affairs.

One of the pieces of unfinished business at Urban Affairs concerned a housing project in Cape Breton that didn't quite meet CMHC specifications but that the people at St Francis Xavier University in Antigonish — for whom I had high regard — told me had great value; the housing we were planning, they said, would be better than anything the miners currently had. I flew to Cape Breton to make an announcement that the housing was to be built, and CMHC then had no option but to proceed with the project. The other loose end I wanted to tie up before moving on to Defence involved the city of Ottawa. At this time Ottawa's downtown business core was becoming run down as large shopping malls began sprouting up on the city's outskirts. At my direction, a concept was being developed at NCC for strengthening the downtown and we were in the midst of talks with city politicians on this matter when I became acting minister of defence. These talks continued for another month before collapsing because of the opposition of Mayor Lorie Greenberg, who only reluctantly acknowledged the importance of the federal government and NCC to Ottawa and viewed our plans as a further federal intrusion into the city's affairs.

From the moment I stepped into the job at Defence, I felt at home: here was a job I really could get my teeth into, not least because defence, unlike urban affairs, fell squarely within federal jurisdiction. It was certainly a much bigger home than the one I was used to at MSUA, with about 78,000 armed-forces personnel and 40,000 civilian employees, to say nothing of a $12-billion annual budget. Fortunately, I had first-class help. The chief of defence staff (CDS) in 1976 was General Jacques Dextraze, an outstanding officer and remarkable human being, a veteran of both the Second World War and Korea. I was to develop a very close relationship with "Jadex," as he was known. Though we had our differences, he was the kind of crusty, no-nonsense soldier you would want at your side in battle. Sometimes, when we reached an impasse in discussion, he would stand to attention. I was his superior, and if I wanted something done he would treat it as an order and get on with the job. After his retirement in September 1977, Jadex became chairman of Canadian National Railways and was replaced as CDS by his vice-chief, Admiral Bob Falls, the first sailor to hold the position.

When I arrived at Defence I asked Eric Acker to come with me from MSUA as a special assistant. I didn't make him my executive assistant because someone else was already filling that role, Major-General Gus Cloutier, who had been with the department for a long time, knew everyone, and was a vast fount of knowledge. Eric, however, soon became familiar with defence matters and the key players in the department, and he grew restless. In early November he wrote me a touching letter expressing his respect and affection for me and explaining why he thought he should get on with his career elsewhere. To my surprise, Gus Cloutier soon told me that he himself thought it was time to move on to something different. I asked Eric to hang in, which he did, and in the spring of 1978 a solution suggested itself that accommodated both Eric's desires and Gus's. Colonel David Currie, VC, the sergeant-at-arms of the House of Commons, retired, and when I raised with Gus the possibility of his taking on the job, for which I believed he would be eminently well suited, he responded with enthusiasm. The prime minister agreed to the appointment, and today Gus is still weaving his magic in the corridors of Parliament. Eric became my EA on Gus's vacating the post.

Ministerial Trips, Part One: Europe

From my first morning on the job, when Jadex and my deputy minister, the former naval officer Buzz Nixon, landed on me with their enormous briefing books, I was on the move. Much of my time, as before, was spent in meetings; the most important of these were the meetings of the Defence Council every Monday morning at National Defence Headquarters (NDHQ). A meeting with the CDS, the Deputy Minister, the senior representatives (known as "chiefs") of each of the three services, and other senior officials — but much time, too was taken up by travelling.

The road show began almost immediately. Shortly after taking over at Defence, I was off to London for a meeting of the NATO Nuclear Planning Group (NPG). The NPG, along with the Defence Planning Committee (DPC), constituted the governing military structure of NATO. The larger of the two groups was the DPC, which consisted of representatives of all NATO countries and was located at NATO headquarters in Brussels. The NPG was comprised of the two nuclear powers, the United States and Britain, as permanent members, along with a rotating membership of six other countries. (France, the third Western nuclear power, was a member of the North Atlantic Alliance but had withdrawn all its forces from NATO command in 1966.) The chair of both the DPC and the NPG was NATO's long-time secretary general, Josef Luns, the former foreign minister of the Netherlands.

The November 1976 meeting of the NPG was my introduction to NATO and its senior officials. Before leaving, the chief had given me detailed briefing books that were so gargantuan that there was no way I would be able to read them, let alone digest them, in the limited time available. I wasn't overly concerned, feeling confident that Jadex would be able to fill in the blanks on the flight over. He didn't. In fact, he fell asleep, whereupon I did too.

At the NPG meeting, I remember being apprehensive. I was able to read aloud a position paper, but that was about all. More than anything, I was an observer on this occasion, and there was much to observe. As secretary general, Josef Luns was in firm control of NATO's political and administrative arm. A tall, austere, sometimes gregarious, often domineering chairman who in his not infrequent lighter moments had a dry and always well-timed sense of humour. Josef had been associated with NATO longer than anyone else around the table and enjoyed the respect or occasionally fear of everyone else. He was NATO's senior bureaucrat and as such was responsible to his political masters, the presidents and prime ministers and foreign and defence ministers of each member country, and he balanced his authority and responsibilities well. I would come to have a particularly warm relationship with him, as would Isobel who, at 5'1," always looked up to his 6'4" except when, in a massive sweep, he would bend to put her hand to his lips. The meeting was also my first meeting with General Alexander Haig of the United States, who held the post of SACEUR (Supreme Allied Commander Europe), NATO's military commander. Immaculately trim in uniform, he was a man of immense charm. His rise in the military from the rank of lieutenant-colonel in Vietnam had been spectacular, almost as spectacular as his later political rise to chief-of-staff in Richard Nixon's White House and secretary of state in Ronald Reagan's cabinet.

I would attend many meetings of the NPG and DPC over the next few years. The contents of the discussions at both bodies were and still are highly classified, so I cannot discuss them in any detail here — a slippery excuse often used by politicians but in this case true. In general terms, however, both the NPG and the DPC essentially validated decisions already taken by the governments of NATO's member countries. The NPG dealt with matters of command and control, logistics, and procedures relating to NATO nuclear capabilities, while the DPC focused on the larger strategic issues, the global arms race, budgets, national troop contributions, and the all-important nuts and bolts of keeping a vast array of military capability functioning efficiently.

The DPC was the principal forum for defence ministers, with the day-to-day work carried on by each country's ambassador to NATO, known as the permanent representative or "PERMREP," who was supported by both diplomatic and military staff. All DPC meetings began with comments by the secretary general (Josef Luns, during my tenure as minister) on the general political situation, followed by an analysis of the strategic military scene by the chairman of the Military Committee, a position filled at one time by Canada's Admiral Bob Falls. A subject of constant discussion was NATO standardization, which referred to the adoption of common standards throughout the alliance on such matters as ammunition sizes, couplings (to allow the refuelling of ships and aircraft), and fuel types. As logical as all this may seem, each country had it own styles, traditions, and substantial military and industrial investments in its own hardware. NATO infrastructure expenditures — bases, communications, surveillance systems such as AWACS (Airborne Warnings and Control System), and, of course, headquarters — were another frequent topic of discussion at DPC meetings. Each nation was expected to pay a proportionate share but the ability of some to pay was limited and wealthier nations frequently paid a disproportionate amount. It was also a bit of a game getting facilities or equipment manufactured in one's own country designated as infrastructure. And then there was the just as never-ending pressure on each member nation to provide more people and formations.

One of the most valuable features of DPC meetings was the informal dining arrangement in the NATO cafeteria, where, surrounded by PERMREPS, defence chiefs, and other NATO personnel, your tablemates might be Josef Luns or Alex Haig and almost always a defence minister from another country. This provided the opportunity for informal conversation on personal and political subjects. Private meetings provided more structured contact with other defence ministers in your or their office, always with your own PERMREP present. These were designed to coordinate or determine positions on subjects to be discussed at the DPC itself. They were also an occasion to extend or respond to invitations to visit one another's country, always an interesting, informative, and enjoyable part of the job and essential to creating the political understanding that was so vital when our armed forces had to work closely together in potentially hazardous circumstances.

To return to November 1976, after the NPG meeting in London was over, I was scheduled to visit our main NATO base in Lahr and its satellite base at Baden-Solingen in Germany's Black Forest, and I arranged for our aircraft to stop en route in Normandy for my first pilgrimage to the Canadian War Cemetery at Beny-sur-Mer, close to the beaches at Bernières-sur-Mer, where my regiment had landed on D-Day. This cemetery is particularly sacred to the Queen's Own Rifles and all Third Canadian Infantry Division troops as the burial ground for our comrades who died on the D-Day landings and the Normandy battles in Caen and its environs. It, like all of our war cemeteries, is beautifully landscaped and meticulously maintained by the Commonwealth War Graves Commission. The magnificent appearance of these cemeteries gives solace to veterans and the families of the fallen, who see that their friends, sons, husbands, and brothers are so well cared for, and gives all Canadians who visit them a sense of pride. Each time I visit one it is like entering a shrine, truly holy ground where so many young friends will be forever.

At Beny-sur-Mer, I stopped at many of the headstones, remembering the friend buried there, and told those with me the story of his life and the circumstances of his death, as I best recalled: the Reed brothers, both killed on D-Day but unaccountably buried in different rows; "Colonel" Worthington, in fact a private, a beloved, fun-loving guy with a gift for relieving the tedium of a route march by his tomfoolery (he would flap his arms like a crow, caw like a crow, bark like a dog, baaa like a sheep, keeping us in stitches), who had a wife and family back home when he died on D-Day at age thirty-six, one of the "old guys"; and another fellow, whom I will not name, who gave the impression of wanting to die after learning from his minister that his wife had had a child some two years after he left Canada. Looking at the white tombstones with engraved crosses stretching into the distance, with a sprinkling of Stars of David, I was reminded of how young we all were and of the variety of our ethnic, religious, and linguistic backgrounds — differences that were of no concern to us at the time. It struck me that the multiculturalism of Canadian society was as much a fact of life then as it is now.

I would visit other war cemeteries in later years — Calais, Brettville-sur-Laize, and Adegem in Belgium — and each time my feelings were much the same. As we veterans get older, we remember that, like the men buried in these cemeteries, we were once young, fun-loving, and scared. Deep emotions overwhelm us when we visit these cemeteries and even when we write or talk about such occasions. With our fallen comrades and those days in mind, we find an inner strength in the knowledge that, when our country needed us, we came through. No one can ever take that away from us, but we know that the cost was great in young friends who never lived to be veterans or wear the medals that they, too, had earned.

The pilgrimage to Beny-sur-Mer over, we proceeded to Lahr and Baden-Solingen. Visits to our troops, both at home and abroad, were my most enjoyable experiences as defence minister, and this visit was no exception. Major-General Ramsey Withers, commander of CFE (Canadian Forces Europe), ultimately to be chief of defence staff in Ottawa, was my official host and I'm sure I also met and spoke to almost every other soldier or airman on these bases. I remembered from my army days how important such visits were for the troops, and I soon learned how valuable they were for the minister.

Once back in Ottawa, I barely had time to unpack before I was on the road again. After a meeting with Jadex and Ramsey Withers at Lahr, we were off to Cyprus to visit Canadian peacekeeping troops serving with the United Nations forces there. Landing at Akrotiri, the British base in southern Cyprus, we were met by the young and impressive Colonel John de Chastelain, a later chief of defence staff and ambassador to the United States who was also to play a distinguished role in the decommissioning of arms in the Irish "troubles." He escorted us by helicopter to Nicosia, the divided capital of Cyprus, where the large modern airport was a virtual no man's land and inoperable, with Turkish troops on one side and UN troops on the other. At the time, Canada had 500 troops, mostly of the Royal Canadian Regiment (RCR), serving with the United Nations forces in Cyprus (UNICYP). The peacekeeping operation was the classic UN kind, where both sides agreed on a cease-fire and the UN brokered the actual Green Line, as dividing lines were known in UN parlance. The UN force then had the responsibility of monitoring the cease-fire — a relatively straightforward task compared to the situation so often facing peacekeepers of today, when there is often no peace to keep and *peacemaking* plays an increasing role.

There was an eerie atmosphere in the Nicosia section of the Green Line, which ran through the centre of the city: everything remained exactly as it was the moment the cease-fire was brokered in 1964, with restaurant tables still set and cars in garages still on their jacks. Outside the city, the atmosphere was different but still odd: the opposing lines and outposts were in sight and earshot of each other, and curses and shouts (as well as, sometimes, slingshot projectiles!) flew back and forth. I felt a bit nostalgic, too, since the military conditions in Cyprus resembled those I was familiar with from the Second World War, with junior officers enjoying great operational independence in their command of platoons located far from the overseeing eyes of their military superiors. Speaking to one young officer of the RCR, Lorne O'Brien, I could see myself in the same role, thirty-odd years earlier. Cyprus was no holiday for our men there — quite the contrary. The situation was a dangerous one — hostilities had broken out as recently as 1974, when Turkey invaded and occupied 40 percent of the island — and offered as close to actual fighting conditions as our troops had experienced since Korea. Despite the dangers, however, I recognized not only the critical nature of our peacekeeping role but also the island's great importance as a training area for our troops. It offered the kind of experience that could be had nowhere else — an experience invaluable at the battalion level and down. Here our troops, far from home, had real-life operational responsibilities.

From Cyprus we made our way to Brussels, where I joined Don Jamieson, secretary of state for external affairs, at a meeting of NATO's DPC. I felt more at home at this meeting than I had at the earlier NPG one, being now part of the club, along with Harold Brown of the United States, Fred Mulley of Britain, Georg Leber of Germany, and Rolf Hansen of Norway (with whom I had the closest working and personal relationship), and other NATO defence ministers. It was an occasion to meet again with Henry Kissinger, now the American secretary of state, whom, as I have already said, I had first met in Ottawa in April 1972 when he was national security adviser to Richard Nixon. At the Brussels meeting, Kissinger seemed to wallow in the level of security that enveloped him. A ten-man guard surrounded him at all times, and, I am told, two Secret Service officers even accompanied him to the washroom. The security was undoubtedly needed, but I also have the sneaking suspicion that Kissinger enjoyed it. Many more encounters with him would follow, and he would always have a large entourage, the entire party resembling an imperial procession. I certainly respected Kissinger's brilliance (as did he), but there can be no doubt that he was a difficult customer. Always speaking with the greatest confidence and authority, he was abrasive and overbearing, with an ego of mammoth proportions. There is an amusing story about him that bears repeating. Kissinger's brother, like him an immigrant to the United States from Germany, spoke with no accent at all. When asked why Henry had such a heavy German accent, he replied, "That's because Henry never listens."

Military Renewal

With no travel scheduled for a while, I had a better chance to become familiar with the nuts and bolts of my job. While the Department of National Defence had considerable resources, few Canadians, including parliamentarians, had a clear idea of what our defence priorities were and how well DND's money and people were being used and for what purpose. The last White Paper on defence had been published under my friend, and then defence minister, Donald Macdonald, in 1971. The priorities articulated at that time were: the defence of Canada; the defence of North America with our U.S. allies through NORAD; membership in NATO; peacekeeping through the United Nations; and aid to the civil powers in Canada (for example, during internal crises, such as the FLQ kidnappings of 1970, and at times of natural disasters such as floods and hurricanes).

Reflecting on these broad objectives, I could not fault any of them. I briefly toyed with the idea of a new White Paper, but there seemed little need for one since the strategic situation and the Cold War environment hadn't changed materially since 1971. We were highly successful peacekeepers and domestic crises had given us a dependable capability at home. Furthermore, quite substantial resources had been committed in support of these priorities and even the intimation of a further White Paper would put these in question. Major re-equipment programs would likely be put on hold, our armed forces would be put in limbo, and our NATO allies would question Canada's military and political dependability. The system wasn't broken — in fact, it was on the upswing — so I saw no need to fix it. I was satisfied that we were on the right track and wanted to avoid any delay or derailment.

Change was needed in one area, however: public relations. From the time of my own military service, I had identified with the men of the Canadian armed forces, and my experience as minister only confirmed me in this feeling. The personnel I met were performing superbly in often difficult conditions, and the officers were most often people of considerable ability. (I made an effort to get to know as many officers of the rank of colonel and higher as I could, since it was at that level that I became involved in the promotion stream, responsible for authorizing all promotions to brigadier-general and above.) In addition, our troops, all volunteers, were highly respected abroad; in fact, they were generally regarded as among the best-trained troops in the NATO alliance. But there was a problem: our military was not communicating its accomplishments to the public at large. Accordingly, I brought in a public-relations firm to assess the department's work in this area and suggest changes. The changes recommended, though not dramatic, were eventually implemented and may have had something to do with results of a January 1979 magazine poll, which showed that almost 90 percent of Canadians believed the size of the Canadian Forces should be maintained at its present level or increased. We must have been doing something right.

Yet there was more than public relations on my mind in these days, for, after years of neglect, the Canadian military was experiencing something of a renaissance. The roots of this development could be traced back a few years. Unification of the armed forces, proposed by then Defence Minister Paul Hellyer in a White Paper of 1964 and implemented in 1967, had been designed to avoid duplication of units in the three services, save manpower, and increase efficiency across the board, thus freeing up revenue for the acquisition of new military hardware. This was not how things turned out, however, though not all attributable to unification. In 1968–69 the newly elected Trudeau government launched a review of defence policy that led to a freeze on all defence expenditures from 1970 to 1975 as well as a reduction in personnel. No new weapons were purchased, manpower declined from 120,000 in 1963 to 78,000 in 1977 (our NATO forces in Europe were cut from 12,000 to 5,000), and overall defence expenditure dropped to 2.3 percent of GNP, placing Canada in the second-to-last position among NATO countries, ahead only of Luxembourg. In these years, Trudeau not only had a high degree of openness to the Soviet Union, he simply did not recognize the importance of the military; not militaristic by nature, he didn't even think Canada needed tanks — he thought they were too aggressive! By the mid-1970s, however, it was becoming apparent that Canada could not continue on this course without inflicting irreparable damage on our relationship with our European and American allies. In this regard, Trudeau was particularly influenced by Chancellor Helmut Schmidt of Germany, a towering figure for whom he, like all Western leaders, had the greatest respect. According to rumours at the time, Schmidt cautioned that hopes for improved economic links between Canada and Europe were doomed unless we more vigorously pursued our NATO responsibilities.

And so the government decided in 1975 that the time had come for substantial investment in our armed forces. Though the ceiling on manpower remained in place, the Department of National Defence was assured a 12 percent annual increase, in real terms, in its capital budget for equipment acquisitions in each of the next five years, the result being that, from 1977 to 1982, an estimated $4 billion was to be made available for this purpose. Under my predecessor, Jim Richardson, several studies of possible new weapons systems were launched, and in 1976 decisions were made to purchase 18 U.S Lockheed Aurora long-range patrol aircraft for the monitoring of our east and west coasts and the Arctic (cost — $1.1 billion), 128 West German Leopard tanks ($200 million), 700 Canadian-built light armoured vehicles ($400 million), and more than 3,000 trucks ($50 million).

As a backbench MP, I was not as focused on defence matters as I was on economic ones, but I nevertheless was deeply disappointed at the reduction in our European forces. Later, while minister of urban affairs, I was a strong supporter of the increased defence expenditures under Jim Richardson, as were other ministers with only a few exceptions (and even the latter were not especially strong in their opposition). There was a consensus around the cabinet table that our defence forces were in an inadequate state and that upgrading them was essential both for our own security and for our reputation on the world stage; what disagreement there was involved details of costs, choice of manufacturer, timing, and other such matters. I was part of that consensus, and, on taking over the defence portfolio in 1976, I had Trudeau's blessing to continue along the same path as I thought fit, provided that I stayed within the expanded budget limits and respected the manpower ceiling.

The cover illustration of the *Globe and Mail*'s *Weekend Magazine* on 16 April 1977 featured a larger-than-life me standing in the midst of a jumble of ships, tanks, trucks, missiles, and assorted other hardware while two fighter planes circle my head and outstretched hand. This image inflated my own importance but it did convey the significance of the equipment acquisitions I was overseeing in those days. All of the equipment ordered under Jim Richardson — the Aurora patrol aircraft, the Leopard tanks, the light-armoured vehicles and trucks — were delivered on my watch, and so I had the satisfaction of seeing them put into use for the first time. (One of the peculiarities of cabinet portfolios is that ministers inherit both the successes and the failures of their predecessors, and while they always take credit for the former, they are also saddled with responsibility for the latter.) But I was not a mere spectator to the military build-up: I was an active participant. One of my most important responsibilities was the acquisition of new fighter aircraft. This process had begun years before I arrived on the scene, but it accelerated and intensified under me.

Enter the CF-18

In 1976 we had three main fighter aircraft, the CF-101 (Voodoo), the F-104 (Starfighter), and the CF-5. All were at least twenty years old, the upper limit of a fighter aircraft's life expectancy (the Germans called their F-104s "Widow Makers"). There was a clear need for a new tactical aircraft in Europe, but planes with long-range capability were required as well: while short-range aircraft were fine for Europe, we also had to have aircraft suited to our strategic role in North America as part of the NORAD alliance. Rather than acquire two different types of aircraft, one for Europe and one for North America, I came to believe strongly that we should obtain a single aircraft that could serve both purposes, with a common training and maintenance system and consequent reduction in spare-parts inventory. To select the new aircraft, a NFA (New Fighter Aircraft) Program Office was established in March

1977. Under DND leadership and involving as well the departments of supply and services and industry, trade, and commerce, the office began with about seventy-five members but ultimately grew to hundreds. It was headed by Brigadier-General Paul Manson, who went on to become commander of the Canadian Air Group in Europe, chief of the air force, and CDS. (A measure of Manson's integrity was that he never allowed his team to accept offers of hospitality from foreign governments or aircraft manufacturers.) Our goal was 130–150 planes; the budget for this acquisition was $2.34 billion, plus the special inflation rate designated for defence expenditures, to be distributed over the period 1977–88.

At the outset, there were about fourteen candidates under consideration, but these were eventually pared down to five: the F-15 (McDonnell Douglas); the F-18L (Northrop/McDonnell Douglas consortium); the British-German-Italian Tornado; the F-14 (Grumman), and the F-16 (General Dynamic). A sixth aircraft, the F-18A (Hornet), a McDonnell Douglas/Northrop product, was not part of the initial list but added later, as Manson's team learned more about it. The F-14, F-15, and F-18L were eventually ruled out for a variety of reasons: the first partly because it was too expensive and had little room for "growth" as new electronics and other equipment became available, but mainly because it lacked air-to-ground attack capability, essential for our European role in NATO; the second, the F-15, which was the air force's first choice, also for reasons of cost (we could afford only ninety-six and I believed that if we didn't have at least one hundred aircraft we didn't have an air force); and the third because it was still in the planning stage and none had been built or orders received. We were then left with three aircraft, the European Tornado, General Dynamic's F-16, and McDonnell Douglas/Northrop's F-18A. The first was included partly not to offend Britain, Germany, and Italy, all NATO allies; however, we never could get a fixed price from the Tornado's manufacturer, the Panavia consortium. Eventually, it was bumped from the list, and so we were down to two candidates, the F-16 and F-18A. Negotiations — involving the drawing up of actual contracts — were conducted with both companies through 1979, but Manson and everyone else on the team were clearly leaning more and more to the F-18A. The F-16 was the cheaper of the two but lacked all-weather capability as well as long-range radar and the ability to accommodate new equipment. Of great importance was the fact that the F-16 was a single-engine plane, a feature I didn't like: if that one engine failed, particularly in our NORAD role where long range and reliability were essential, the aircraft was doomed — and likely the pilot too, especially if the crash occurred in the Arctic. The F-18A, for its part, was a twin-engine aircraft, and, because it was designed for the pitching decks of aircraft carriers, was sturdy and stable (a definite plus, as evidenced in the long life of our Tracker aircraft, which were designed for carriers but did yeoman service in coastal patrol long after our last aircraft carrier was decommissioned). It met all our other specifications and was in production for the U.S. Navy and Marines.

Despite our interest in the F-18A, by late 1978 McDonnell Douglas had become convinced that we preferred the F-16 and were merely using them as a stalking horse in negotiations. Rumours about the state of the negotiations were soon being reported in the press, and, since we were very interested in the F-18A, we had to assure McDonnell Douglas that they were still in the running. To that end, in February 1979 I phoned a former cabinet colleague, Donald Macdonald, who was then on the board of McDonnell Douglas Canada. Negotiations of this kind are a delicate business, but, without telling McDonnell Douglas that we were leaning towards their bid — there was still a competition to go through — I needed to keep them on board. I took this approach in my conversation with Don Macdonald and added that I wanted to meet with "Mr Mac," James McDonnell, the legendary founder of the company. Don phoned me back and said there wasn't a chance of such a meeting taking place; M. Mac was in his late seventies (which seemed very old to me at the time) and did not involve himself in negotiations any more. I should speak instead with Sandy McDonnell, James's nephew and the person now actually running the company. But I replied that I had already spoken to Sandy. I wanted to see Mr. Mac

An hour later the phone in my office rang. Picking it up, my assistant, Eric Acker, heard a voice growl, "This is McDonnell in St Louis." It was Mr Mac himself. "I understand the minister wants to see me?" "How's he fixed for 10 o'clock tomorrow morning?" He said that he could fly to Ottawa the next day and arrive in the late morning. It seemed a bit much to ask such an elderly man to undertake this kind of trip — especially when he said he intended to get up at 5 A.M. and drive to the airport himself! McDonnell brushed aside this concern. "I'll be there tomorrow," he said.

And indeed he was. We met, both privately and with company executives and staff, for about four hours in my parliamentary office, working through a lunch consisting of salmon sandwiches (my favourite) brought up from the West Block cafeteria. "Old Mac," as he called himself, was a real delight — direct, plain-spoken, sharp as a whip, brimming with knowledge about an industry that he knew like the back of his hand. He was the sort of man I had liked to do business with during my days in the private sector. You knew that if you shook his hand and looked him the eye, he would play straight and in the end you would have a good agreement. Yet, once again, I had to communicate our strong interest in the F-18A without in any way tipping our hand. I told him that we were "dead serious" in our interest in the F-18A and that the competition was a fair one. I even went so far as to say that McDonnell's chances were at least fifty/fifty.

My assurances were evidently convincing, for McDonnell Douglas did not withdraw from the competition, a very expensive process for vendors. Owing to the extensive negotiations with two possible contractors and the need to cover the myriad of details in what was the largest defence procurement in Canada's history, negotiations continued throughout my time as defence minister, but towards the end it became plain to all that the F-18A was to be the government's choice. The actual contract was not signed until the early 1980s and the first aircraft were delivered in 1985. There was nothing unusual about this lengthy time-frame in terms of major peacetime procurements; all such procurements proceed slowly from the investigative phase to the moment of contract signing and ultimate delivery. The initial order was for 123 aircraft, at a total cost of about $3 billion. Though we could have bought 142 F-16s for the same price, I have no doubt whatsoever that we made the right choice. From the first, the F-18A performed brilliantly, and in the 1990s, at the time of the Persian Gulf War and later NATO's intervention in Kosovo, it again met and even exceeded expectations.

Personally, I was fascinated by the whole process of selecting a new fighter aircraft. I had always loved airplanes. When I was a boy, an aunt once gave me a birthday present of five dollars, and as soon as I had the money in my hand — it was an almost unimaginable sum in the 1930s — I hitchhiked up Dufferin St to a local flying club, Leavens Brothers, and bought a ride on a single-engine plane. It was thrilling and terrifying all at once. Much later, during the war, my platoon won the divisional championship in aircraft recognition, an important skill in those days. But I digress. The point I wish to make is that, with this fighter-aircraft file, I had a chance to pursue a long-standing interest while accomplishing something of considerable military importance. It was big, big business, and the lobbying, while completely above board, was incessant and intense (this was in the days before professional lobbyists became a fixture on the Ottawa scene). It was the most important procurement issue I ever handled in government and had the great advantage of a superb project manager in General Paul Manson. I was completely immersed in it, and, looking back now, I get great satisfaction from knowing that I was part of a process that reached such a satisfactory conclusion.

Other Acquisitions

The need for new equipment did not end there. Still with the air force, if getting new fighter aircraft into the air was one of my priorities, protecting our bases was no less important. Once, on a visit to Baden-Solingen, I witnessed a display of a mock attack on the base. Turning to the officer in charge, I asked when it was to begin. "It's over, Sir," I was told. I had heard a noise but hadn't seen a thing, and, much more worrisome, most of the gunner crews hadn't either: only one of them had had a plane in its sights at any time. If there ever was conclusive proof that we needed better radar and anti-aircraft weaponry — the current stuff was Second World War vintage, designed before the era of high-speed jets — this was it. On returning to Canada, I made my pitch to the prime minister, and he not only supported my decision to acquire new hardware but also approved the additional fifty or so men needed to operate it, notwithstanding the ceiling on manpower that remained in place. This made the air force happy, and the army was pleased, too, since its artillery would be responsible for operating the new weaponry. In retrospect, I'm not sure that the whole thing wasn't a set-up on the part of the military to get my support in this matter. In any event, it worked.

Meanwhile, the other branch of the armed forces, the navy, had a shopping list of its own. Topping it was a request for new patrol frigates, the purpose of which was to protect what was known as SLOC — sea lines of communication — from the threat of submarines. When I saw the hefty price tag this involved, I suggested, half-facetiously, that it might be cheaper to purchase a fleet of Boeing 747s and transport our troops and supplies by air. The admirals were horrified and came back with briefings to prove that planes, no matter how large they were or how often they flew, could not carry the volume of supplies that ships could and these ships needed to be protected. I eventually authorized the navy to continue its studies into the question, and in late 1977 I obtained cabinet approval in principle of a plan to replace twelve of Canada's twenty-four frigates. The new ships, costing something in the order of $9 billion, were acquired some ministers later. Again, the long time-frame was not unusual, especially when it is kept in mind that the new ships were required to be built in Canadian shipyards rather than acquired "off the shelf" from a foreign supplier. From the beginning, the new "City-Class" frigates were considered superb, setting new standards for design and performance in NATO and elsewhere while bringing Canadian component and systems suppliers into global prominence.

Industrial Benefits

In the negotiation of contracts for new military hardware, I encouraged a significant change in the way procurements were handled. In the past, Defence had insisted that "industrial offsets" should be part of any military contract, meaning, for example, that if a company agreed to manufacture aircraft, the wings of those aircraft would be built in Canada. There was nothing wrong with this, but it did not contribute anything enduring: once the wings were built and the aircraft delivered, the company that had constructed the wings closed down that operation and that was the end of it. A better approach was one that I termed "industrial benefits to Canada." This meant that, if a company wanted to sell equipment to the Department of National Defence, that company would have to agree to initiate industrial activity in Canada (whether by establishing a new facility, making a further investment in an existing one, or transferring new technology to a Canadian company) that might or might not be directly related to the purchased equipment. I was determined that the industrial-benefits approach be pursued consistently in all DND procurements and with access to markets globally.

Industrial benefits were part of every proposal and of every large contract during my time as minister and remain so. Usually, we tried to obtain strategic investments focusing on things that were either not being done in Canada or not being done well, while also keeping regional-development concerns in mind as much as possible. The policy led to the creation of numerous companies in Canada, some of which remain operating today, as well as to the expansion of others. It also led to the forging of long-lasting relationships between foreign and Canadian firms. We never selected a company on the basis of its industrial-benefits program alone, but those benefits were one of the key factors that we considered when negotiating contracts. As for the suppliers themselves, not only did they not balk at our demands, they were imaginative in endeavouring to meet them. In the case of the new fighter aircraft, the contract eventually signed with McDonnell Douglas/Northrop for the F-18A provided Canada with a wide range of industrial benefits: IMP, Halifax, and Enamel and Heating, Amherst, Nova Scotia, obtained contacts for the manufacture of structural parts for McDonnell Douglas's civilian DC-9s: Canadair was contracted to build airframe components for the F-18A; Menasco (then in Quebec, now in Oakville, Ontario) obtained a contract for building landing-gear hydraulic systems both for the F-18A and for the DC-10; General Electric, Bromont, Quebec, contracted to build "blades and vanes," the heart of all jet engines, and set up a new plant for that purpose which involved the most leading-edge technology of the day, technology that was used in a wide range of GE jet engines beyond that the of the F-18A; Fleet Manufacturing, Fort Erie, Ontario, was contracted to build structural parts for the F-18A as well as for other McDonnell Douglas aircraft; Orenda Engines, Malton, Ontario, obtained a contract for F-18A engine parts; Toronto's Litton Industries, the Canadian arm of a U.S.-based company, was contracted to build the highly sophisticated inertial navigational system for the new fighter and much of this work was subcontracted to other Canadian suppliers (it was later to develop the same system for the Cruise Missile); Garrett Manufacturing, Rexdale, Ontario (now part of Allied Signal), and Computing Devices, Ottawa, were contracted to supply electronics and avionics for the F-18A; and CAE Electronics built the flight simulator for the CF-18A, which clearly established the Canadian company as the world leader for flight simulators.

I made a point of explaining the industrial-benefits policy to my cabinet colleagues, including the prime minister, all of whom backed it although, at first, some had only the foggiest idea of what it involved. In fact, while the social-affairs ministers were somewhat less enthusiastic about defence spending than the others, I generally had little difficulty mustering support for my department's initiatives. Credit for much of this must go to the defence bureaucracy, which briefed their counterparts in other departments who in turn briefed their ministers. Fortunately, too, there was none of the inter-departmental infighting that had marred an earlier defence procurement. In the case of the Aurora long-range patrol aircraft, Jim Richardson had been embroiled in a nasty dispute with Jean-Pierre Goyer, the then minister of supply and services, with Goyer accusing Defence of financial waste. Such battles are not unusual in government — it was the business of Supply and Services to act as the purchasing agent for all departments — but in this instance the feuding struck me as avoidable. In late May 1977, therefore, DND and Supply and Services, still under Goyer's leadership, signed a memorandum of agreement covering both the Aurora purchase and the proposed purchase of fighter aircraft. Everything went smoothly after that, with nary a word of recrimination between the two departments of which I was aware.

August 1978: Fiscal Crisis

Trudeau stirred up a hornets' nest on one memorable occasion. In July 1978 the prime minister attended an economic summit in Europe in which Western governments pledged to cut back on unnecessary expenditures in order to devote more money to alleviating the economic problems then afflicting the industrialized nations. After the summit, he went sailing in the Baltic with German Chancellor Helmut Schmidt, who, no doubt, helped to add to his resolve. Shortly afterwards, on August 1st, he went on national television to announce that current and planned government spending was to be cut by $2 billion, a gargantuan amount in those days, thereby enabling increased expenditures on such projects as job creation, industrial investment, and social assistance to those hurt most by inflation.

It was a Sunday, and a long weekend, and most cabinet ministers were away from the capital. I was at my Georgian Bay cottage when I turned on the television and heard the prime minister make his announcement. I was astounded. Cabinet had been discussing a range of restraint measures for some time, but nothing had yet been decided and we were thinking more in terms of $1.4 billion in cuts, not $2 billion, with Defence's share pegged at $100 million. Evidently, Trudeau had grown impatient with the interminable discussions and decided to force the issue.

I reached Jean Chrétien, the minister of finance, at his summer cottage at Lac-des-Piles, near Shawinigan. He had just turned off his TV, and, astonishingly, he had heard the news for the first time too. I then called Bob Andras, the president of the Treasury Board, at his Ottawa home; he expressed equal surprise, which left me sceptical since he was the minister responsible for coordinating the new expenditure reductions and was sworn to secrecy. In any event, a crucial cabinet meeting was called for 9 August. On that day, it was a grim lot of ministers who sat around the huge round cabinet table in the Langevin Block, the home of the prime minister's and the Privy Council offices. Trudeau proceeded to read off the cuts he and his advisers had decided were appropriate. As he came to each department, the minister responsible either went glassy-eyed or slumped in his or her chair — or both. None, to their credit, actually collapsed. We all made the best pitch we could for our individual causes, but Trudeau was unbending on the principle of the cuts. DND's share of the pain was to be $100 million. The prime minister told us to consult with our officials on what programs or operations we would cut and give the details to Bob Andras, who was to prepare the critical press release that was to be the basis of the policy implementing the restraint measures. This, presumably, would be followed up with proper cabinet documentation, but a simple press release was the operative document that we were to address.

I instructed my officials to continue looking for areas where cutbacks could be made. A couple of weeks later, during a cabinet meeting held on 16 August, Bob Andras itemized the cuts expected of all departments — and Defence's share was now set at $150 million. Each minister was asked to report back to cabinet on 30 August with details of how the cuts were to be made. I was speechless. Even the earlier proposed cut of $100 million would essentially have abrogated Canada's existing commitment to its NATO allies to increase Defence's capital expenditures by 12 percent in real terms, a commitment that the prime minister had made at a NATO summit in Washington in May, with Don Jamieson and me in attendance. This still higher reduction was making a bad situation worse.

Taking the prime minister aside during a break in the cabinet discussions, I stressed that his plans threatened not only the future of our military but also our relationship with our allies, to say nothing of his relationship with his NATO peers. We just couldn't do this. I asked if we could meet privately that night to discuss the matter, perhaps over a Chinese dinner (both of us loved Chinese food). He agreed to meet with me, but instead of a dinner in town, he invited me to his summer place at Harrington Lake, where he was going to be with his three boys. The two of us could have dinner there. By now, Trudeau was a single father, having separated from Margaret the previous year, and his devotion to his sons was total.

Before that meeting took place, Andras issued an internal government document listing the departmental cuts, and there was Defence's figure in black and white: $150 million. The very matter that I hoped to discuss with the prime minister was now being presented as a *fait accompli*. I felt like resigning, a common reaction when a cabinet minister becomes very frustrated but one rarely acted upon in the cold light of day. In my case, before I could do anything rash, the prime minister phoned to say there was no food at Harrington Lake, except for one lonely pork chop — so I should eat in Ottawa and come up to Harrington Lake afterwards.

When my corporal driver Robert Joly, and I arrived at Harrington, Trudeau came to greet us with Michel, his youngest boy — who later died so tragically in an avalanche in British Columbia — cradled in his arms. He showed Michel Joly's gold corporal's stripes and brass buttons and let him touch them, something he was fond of doing when introducing his sons to military personnel. Then, in a typically considerate gesture, he invited Joly in to have coffee while we had our discussion, rather than let him sit waiting in the car. It was dusk and the prime minister and I went walking on the Harrington grounds to discuss my budget cuts. It was an ominously overcast night and we stayed close to the house, which allowed the Trudeau boys to monitor our movements. One or another of them would occasionally call out to their father from their bedroom window to ask him to come and say their prayers with them, a regular and expected practice. Trudeau explained to me the difficulty he had in making an exception for Defence, which, compared to some other departments, had a massive budget, but he also noted that he was deeply conscious of our international obligations. The discussion was serious, but so was Trudeau's commitment to prayers with his sons. Following a further plea from the bedroom window, he took me back to the house and handed me a large, gold-coloured box of chocolates, for which he had a weakness. (These were likely a gift; he would never have been so extravagant as to purchase his own fancy chocolates.) Taking two chocolates for himself, with obvious, even mischievous delight, he went upstairs to the boys.

Prayers over, the prime minister returned to the discussion and the chocolates. We were nearing an understanding when a violent storm struck. The sky crashed, lightning flashed, and rain fell in torrents, to the accompaniment of screams from upstairs. The prime minister said that Michel was particularly frightened of thunder and excused himself. Returning shortly afterwards with Michel in his dressing gown, he placed him between us on the chesterfield, covered him with a woolly lambskin throw, and explained to him that we were having an important discussion about the army.

With Michel curled up on the chesterfield until he quietly dozed off, the prime minister and I continued our conversation and eventually came to an agreement. Defence was to be required to make a cut of only

$100 million, and this cut would come out of the budget for training, operations, construction, and equipment acquisition but *would not* affect our NATO and NORAD obligations, search and rescue, peace-keeping, and the purchase of new fighter aircraft. I was to give Bob Andras a one-paragraph note to this effect and ask him to insert it into the press release on departmental cuts that was to be read to the cabinet. Furthermore, Trudeau assured me that Defence's cut was to be for fiscal year 1979–80 only, though other departments' cuts were to be annual ones. He told me, however, that I should not share this information with my colleagues. He then excused himself and carried the sleeping Michel upstairs to bed.

Once I got back to Ottawa, I reached Bob Andras at home where he was struggling to draft a document that met the prime minister's objectives, kept ministers reasonably in line, and was sensitive to all political nuances. Bob was shocked when he heard of my agreement with Trudeau. Fortunately, however, he was one of the few ministers who had an understanding of Defence, having been an army major in the Second World War. He was also a dear friend but friendships were off for this exercise. He didn't know how he would get away with it but we agreed on the wording and he said that he would discuss it with the prime minister.

The planned cabinet meeting of 30 August passed smoothly enough. The real action took place at a meeting on 6 September. There, red-eyed ministers, who had sat up half the night with their officials and spent the morning honing their arguments and making deals for mutual support with their colleagues, hunched around the cabinet table, ready to spill blood in defence of their budgets. I prepared for the assault that would follow the announcement of my relatively meagre cut, making notes of the points I would use, as was my practice. I tried to anticipate every argument and thought I had a good case, but not one I could be certain of in view of my colleagues' belief that, in comparison to their departments, Defence was richly funded.

Bob read the press release itemizing the planned cuts, and as he neared the part on Defence, I anxiously peered at my notes. Then, when he read the paragraph on Defence I had given him, the room exploded in rage. If I wanted a friend under these circumstances, I would have had to fetch my dog. Before I could begin my arguments, the prime minister spoke up and the room was suddenly silent. I wish I had a transcript of his exact words, but in essence he said that I had worked this out with him and that he was in full agreement. He went on to say that the military had, in effect, taken a budget cut every year for ten years by having its budget frozen while inflation took its toll. He reminded everyone that Defence was finally catching up and he was not going to see it fall behind again. I crumpled up my notepaper, tossed it under the table, and somehow restrained myself from crying with joy, kissing the prime minister, or even smiling smugly as my colleagues glowered at me. "OK, Bob. What's next?" asked the prime minister, as I said a silent prayer of gratitude. The press release was approved and issued the following day. (As it later turned out, even the cuts that Defence did take were later tempered by Treasury Board decisions.)

We then turned to other matters, one of which concerned the CBC. John Roberts, the secretary of state, warned that the cuts he was being asked to make would emasculate the corporation. He made a strong and moving case, which couldn't help but sway a Liberal cabinet. My colleagues and I loved to complain about CBC news coverage — many cabinet meetings began with someone saying, "Did you see what those CBC bastards said about us last night?" — but this time even the corporation's harshest critics, such as Eugene Whelan, pulled back. We couldn't destroy the CBC; it was too important to the country and our national identity. Each minister agreed to assume a slightly greater burden so that the CBC would not be mortally damaged. It was John Roberts's turn to smile.

While not related directly to the financial crisis of August 1978, the story about the prime minister at Harrington Lake reminds me of another incident when he demonstrated his remarkable relationship with his sons. In early 1978, after the Syrians and Israelis had moved into Lebanon, the United Nations asked Canada to contribute troops for a peacekeeping operation. Don Jamieson, the secretary of state for external affairs, and I were summoned to an urgent meeting at 24 Sussex to determine what our response should be. Don was accompanied by Allan Gotleib, his under-secretary, and I by Admiral Bob

Falls, the CDS, and Buzz Nixon, my deputy minister. I believe that Michael Pitfield, the secretary to the cabinet and clerk of the Privy Council, was also present. We met in the small library that adjoins the main drawing room and entrance hall of the prime minister's residence, and the discussion was intense. In the midst of our deliberations, a horrendous racket came from the drawing room. The prime minister leapt from his seat, opened the door, and found a rambunctious Michel, diaper at half-mast, beating a tin drum with all his might. Rather than shoo him off, as would most fathers in such circumstances, Trudeau swept him up in his arms, nuzzled his cheeks and neck, and introduced him to each of us. He took special pains to let him know who Admiral Falls was, and, as he had done with my driver at our meeting at Harrington Lake, he allowed him to run his hands over the admiral's impressive four-star rank badge on his shoulder boards (navy epaulets). Then, with very little delay, he passed his precious bundle to the nanny, who swept Michel out the other door. Michel, I'm sure, was left with no feeling of rejection, and we were left with still another glimpse into the character of our quite remarkable and unpredictable prime minister.

We resumed our discussion, the outcome of which was a decision to commit a contingent of the Canadian Signals Regiment to run the critical communications arm of the UN force. I would see these men off from their Barriefield base near Kingston, and, because their regiment had been doing more than their share overseas, I promised that they would be back within six months. The UN was on notice to provide replacements. This was a promise I was able to keep and I was on hand at Barriefield to welcome them back along with a bevy of grateful wives.

Operation Morning Light

The thunderbolt over departmental expenditures was not the only crisis I had to experience in 1978. Earlier that same year, I was deeply involved when a nuclear-powered Soviet satellite, Cosmos 954, crashed into Canadian territory. This satellite — the size of a chesterfield — had begun spinning out of control in December 1977, and with a transfixed world wondering where it would come to rest, Canada learned on the 24th of that month, that we were the unlucky ones (the news came via a telephone call from Zbigniew Brzezinski, national security to the U.S. president, to Ivan Head, the prime minister's principal foreign-affairs adviser). I was advised immediately. Fortunately, the satellite debris — most of the satellite had broken up on entering the earth's atmosphere — did not crash into a densely populated city but in the Northwest Territories, between Yellowknife and Great Slave Lake. The task of locating the debris fell to the Department of National Defence, which headed a vast operation involving a number of departments and agencies of the Canadian government, namely, the Atomic Energy Control Board, External Affairs, the Privy Council Office, Emergency Planning Canada, Energy, Mines, and Resources, Indian and Northern Affairs, the Solicitor General, Fisheries and the Environment, and the RCMP. Assisting us were 115 specialized technical and administrative personnel on loan from the United States (under the command of a Brigadier-General Gates). Control of the operation, dubbed Operation Morning Light, was assigned to the commander of the air force, Lieutenant-General Bill Carr, who in turn designated the base commander at Canadian Forces Base Edmonton, Colonel Jack Garland, as the search commander and CFB Edmonton as the operational headquarters.

As the minister responsible, I was intimately involved, overseeing the search mission and coordinating the work of other departments and agencies. In crass political terms, I suppose that the emergency did wonders for me politically. I was the government's spokesman in Parliament and elsewhere, and, thanks to the intense interest in the satellite's fate not only in Canada but around the world, I was the object of extensive media coverage both nationally and internationally, looking and sounding, I'd like to think, bold, decisive, and completely in charge. I'll never forget the huge contingent of reporters from around the world that accompanied me when I travelled to the Northwest Territories in early February to survey the search area, nor a phone call I received from an old long-lost friend in California, an associate from my business days, who said that he hadn't realized I was in politics, let alone minister of defence, until he heard my voice on his car radio discussing Morning Light.

To return to the larger picture, the Soviets were extremely guarded in response to our inquiries about the composition and structure of what we were looking for, mostly perhaps for security reasons but also to avoid financial responsibility for the clean-up operation. Nevertheless, the search proceeded expeditiously and efficiently. Conducted mainly by Hercules aircraft but also utilizing helicopters and other aircraft as required and gamma-radiation detection equipment, it covered almost 50,000 square miles. Reactor core material, in the form of fine particulate, and other radioactive debris were found dispersed over an area of almost 30,000 square miles from Great Slave Lake to the Alberta border; non-radioactive debris was discovered over an equally wide area, including one large piece in Great Slave Lake. It was an expensive operation, costing the Department of National Defence alone about $100,000 daily. By early April, when the intensive period of the search was over, the total DND bill was $8 million. Fortunately, the mission had been successful. By the spring, we were confident that we had found most if not all of the radioactive debris and that any that remained posed only a marginal threat to people, wildlife, and environment. It was the best practical result we could expect, although one can never be certain that at some time a person or animal will not come into contact with a piece of debris we missed. Another thing I recall about Operation Morning Light is amusing now though it didn't seem so at the time. When I asked some of the people in charge of the operation how they proposed to transport the satellite debris out of the area to a nuclear laboratory at Pinawa, Manitoba, I couldn't believe what I heard: some of it had already been sent by Parcel Post on a regular Air Canada flight. Once I regained my composure, I replied that this wouldn't do. I had no wish to be held responsible for a lost box of radioactive material. In the future, all such shipments were to be done by dedicated Hercules aircraft.

Our Role in Norway

An issue that was not as dramatic as Operation Morning Light but that was critically important in NATO terms was the defence of Norway. One of Canada's NATO's commitments was to help deter any Soviet incursion into northern Norway through the deployment of the fully equipped, battle-ready Canadian Air Sea Transportable Combat Group, or CAST. This was a fully armed and supported infantry brigade that was to be transported by air and sea to Norway, supplementing a mobile force (an infantry battalion plus two squadrons of CF-5 fighter aircraft), known as ACE Mobile Force-N [North], that was to be moved to Norway from Canada (London, Ontario, in the case of the infantry, and Bagotville, Quebec, in the case of the CF-5s). It would have been easier to pre-position the vehicles and equipment in Norway, but Norwegian law did not permit the permanent presence of foreign troops or equipment — a prohibition that had originated in reaction to Germany's occupation of Norway in the Second World War. Germany was now a NATO ally, but the Norwegians felt that they could not make this distinction within NATO. After my time, however, Norway did allow a limited pre-positioning of NATO vehicles.

While CAST theoretically numbered 5,000 troops, in my calculations it existed only on paper — its troops were to be drawn from the 5th brigade headquartered in Valcartier (including the Royal 22nd), the Royal Canadian Regiment in London, and the Princess Patricia's Canadian Light Infantry [PPCLI] from Winnipeg — and so the result was that it would have to be assembled before being deployed. This fact, combined with the size of the force and the heavy equipment it was to carry, meant that speedy deployment was impossible; in training exercises, the best we could manage was twenty-eight days from the time the troops and ships were assembled in Quebec City to the time of their arrival and deployment in Norway. What made matters even more problematic was that the force and its supplies were to be boarded on "roll-on, roll-off" ships to be supplied by Norway; these ships, however, had to get to Canada first, and they could be anywhere in the world when the call came.

I was convinced that the whole idea of CAST made no practical sense, for if our object was to get troops to Norway quickly in order to deter aggression, speed was of the essence. The deterrence factor was critical. It was not our intention, after all, to have troops fight their way into Norway to repel a Soviet invasion that had already begun. Instead of CAST, I concluded that it would be better to utilize the Special Service Force based in

Petawawa, our premiere battle-ready formation and one that currently lacked a specific role. This was a smaller force, numbering about 2,500 (including the Canadian Airborne Regiment), but it existed in fact as opposed to just in theory, was highly trained, and, though lightly equipped, had all the weaponry (including artillery) and ancillary services (such as a field hospital) that a deterrent force required. More than that, because of all these characteristics, the force could be transported quickly by air — there would be no need for "roll-on, roll-off" ships. I raised the matter with then Brigadier-General Andy Christie, the commander of the Special Service Force, on a visit to its base in Petawawa, Ontario. Asking him if he and his troops would like a specific role, I explained that in my view his unit was the best suited to the Norway mission. The reply was immediate: "We'd love a role," he said.

The reaction of some of my officials and NATO colleagues, including Rolf Hansen, Norway's defence minister, to say nothing of Alexander Haig, SACEUR, and Josef Luns, NATO's secretary general, was not as enthusiastic; all of these people preferred things as they were, believing that CAST represented a more formidable force. My arguments to the contrary left them unconvinced, until I asked them if they would rather have a highly trained force of 2,500, which existed as a coherent unit and was ready to move quickly, or a widely dispersed collection of 5,000 which was not at the same stage of readiness and which would almost certainly arrive too late. In 1979 the Special Service Force was assigned the task of participating in the defence of NATO's northern flank, and it formally assumed this role in September 1980, after I had left office.

Search and Rescue

Among the more important of my responsibilities was to oversee, in conjunction with the minister of transport (responsible for the Coast Guard) and the solicitor general (responsible for the RCMP), all search-and-rescue missions. Search and rescue, in my view, is one of the hidden gems of the Canadian military — it is something we do magnificently, often at great risk to the men and women involved. From my point of view during my days as minister, the most difficult aspect of SAR, as we called it, was knowing when to tell a family that there was no longer any hope and to call off a search; less difficult, but no easy matter either, was prolonging a search — even for a day or two to ease the anxiety of a still hopeful family — in the face of the military's recommendation against it. Search-and-rescue centres were initially based at Halifax, Trenton, Edmonton, and Comox on Vancouver Island, and to these I added a helicopter unit for Gander, the first military base in Newfoundland (excluding Goose Bay in Labrador) for a long time, a serious gap in our capability since many of the search-and-rescue missions occurred off Newfoundland's coast and the flying time to Newfoundland significantly reduced the chances of a successful mission. In addition, there were SAR personnel at a number of bases elsewhere, for example, at Greenwood and Shearwater, Nova Scotia, and Summerside, Prince Edward Island. The most common SAR missions involved missing pleasure craft on the Great Lakes and in the Straits of Juan de Fuca and the Georgia Straits in British Columbia, and in these areas responsibility was shared by sector with the U.S. Coast Guard; this frequently provoked outbursts in the House of Commons, the opposition charging us with negligence when the United States carried out a rescue of our citizens in their sector, notwithstanding the fact that we often rescued Americans in our sector. The most difficult and costly missions were those involving private aircraft that crashed in the Rockies en route to Alaska or a fishing camp in British Columbia. These aircraft were often piloted by amateur American pilots I called "flying farmers," who navigated with the aid of little more than Shell road maps and had no experience in this very demanding terrain.

The Airborne

The Canadian Airborne Regiment was considered the most highly trained, battle-ready, and high-profile infantry regiment in the Canadian forces. Yet the Airborne was a concern to me. While its culture — noted for a certain swagger and cockiness — was admirable in wartime, it threatened to reflect itself in peacetime both off-base and off-duty. In addition, for most of my term at Defence, the Airborne was different from other regiments in that it did not have an assigned role. Other sources of concern were the marginal role of paratroopers in our military history, the limited success of paratroop formations in the Second World War, and the unlikelihood that the Airborne would have sufficient priority in our battle order to justify a major chunk of our budget.

When I assumed the Defence portfolio, there was a move afoot to move the Airborne from Edmonton to Petawawa, Ontario, which had the approval of all the military brass but was received with less enthusiasm by some members of the regiment itself. Moves in the peacetime army are always difficult for families, particularly for wives who have jobs and children well settled in schools and in friendships, but periodic relocations are one of the factors of military life that go with the job. Then there are the merchants who usually have little interest in the military until there is an actual or threatened move, when they become deeply patriotic and passionately attached to the regiment and all of its traditions and bring great pressure to bear on the local MPs, who then themselves become equally deeply engaged and make emotional pleas to the minister. In this case, the rationale for the move was convincing to me. There was a strong argument in favour of the excellent training area at Petawawa, except for the puzzling lack of any airstrip large enough for the Airborne's assigned Hercules aircraft. Assured that the local runway at Pembroke would be lengthened to correct this small oversight, I acquiesced. Unreported to me was a plan to move one commando, a unit of the Airborne larger than an infantry company but smaller than a battalion, to Ottawa's Uplands Airport. When I learned of this I was puzzled since Ottawa lacked the excellent training areas that were so key to the move to Petawawa. Jadex justified the move on the basis of national security and the threat to Parliament and government institutions.

I was not persuaded. Regular-force combat troops in peacetime in the nation's capital for the first time in history would appear ominous following the earlier invocation of the War Measures Act during the FLQ crisis and in the wake of the recent Parti Québécois victory in Quebec. It didn't make military, or certainly political, sense to me, especially when it meant fragmenting the regiment and when one of the reasons for the move to Petawawa was the proportionate lack of troops in central Canada, from where they could be moved quickly to large population centres in the event of emergency. Petawawa was less than two hours from Ottawa. Jadex resisted, but I was adamant and the Ottawa move was cancelled.

In a press interview over one of the recurring incidents of conflict between Airborne troops and civilians in their neighbouring communities, a reporter referred to the Airborne as Canada's "elite" troops, to which I responded, as I had on previous occasions, that there was no single elite regiment: the Princess Patricia's, the Van Doos, the RCR, and all our other regiments were elite in my books. Colonel Jacques Painchaud, the dynamic but impetuous commander of the Airborne, responded to the press that "the minister was a stupid son-of-a-bitch and should resign" — something that a senior officer was not supposed to say publicly about his minister, even if it were true. I was prepared to let it pass because I knew and liked Painchaud, who had a reputation for shooting from the lip. Admiral Falls, the CDS, was less forgiving and removed Painchaud from his command and assigned him to NDHQ, effectively ending his career. A number of fellow officers said that Painchaud was always a step away from some such incident and Admiral Falls had made the only right decision. It was a rather sad fate for an otherwise fine officer and one popular with his troops.

It was perhaps typical of the Airborne to be attracting controversy. I liked them. They were superbly trained fighting troops with a sense of "regiment" and morale, which was compelling, even captivating. In spite of my reservations, I never seriously thought of disbanding the Airborne, but I can't say I was ever without apprehension. Years later, in the 1990s, I would be horrified but not totally surprised when some of members of the Airborne tortured and murdered a young boy in Somalia. I was, however, both surprised and disgusted on learning of initiation rites for new members of the unit in Petawawa. In my view, this behaviour would not be countenanced in any other unit of the Canadian forces. Defence Minister David Collenette's action in disbanding the regiment was both harsh and sad but it sent a clear message to all soldiers, sailors, and airmen and to Canadians generally that this standard of behaviour was unacceptable and unforgivable. Even more important was the Canadian military ethic and the image that our forces projected both in Canada and abroad, an image that I, as a one-time Canadian soldier, felt deeply: that is, while we were trained to kill or be killed in wartime, we were not trained to be killers in any other circumstances. This is what differentiates Canadian and many other democratic nations and their militaries from the hooligans of other societies who, calling themselves soldiers, have been responsible for both supporting and forming some of the most repressive regimes on earth, against whom we have stood in the past and must be prepared to stand again in the future. The Airborne, as a regiment, was never in that category, but it was an example of conduct that, if tolerated, could lower our military and personal standards to the level of those our armed forces are organized and trained to resist on behalf of all of us.

Women

In 1970 the Royal Commission on the Status of Women had recommended that there not be any restrictions on the employment of women in the Canadian Forces, with the exceptions of combat roles, sea duty, and isolated posts. At the time, there were 1,500 women in the Canadian Forces, or about 1.6 percent of total personnel. This was one of the highest rates of female participation in the world, but more obviously needed to be done. More was done in subsequent years — by the time I became minister, the number of women in the armed forces had increased to 4,880, or 6 percent of the total — yet few were content to stand still, particularly since most women in the military remained confined to clerical jobs. When in early 1978 the Canadian Human Rights Act came into force, DND promptly undertook a review of its policy on women, and in January 1979 I announced a three- to five-year plan that opened all trades in the military to women and that allowed, on an experimental basis, the participation of women in the army up to the brigade level, so excluding them from direct combat roles only. We also directed the opening of all military colleges to women by 1980–81.

There was no resistance from the chiefs, all of whom were thinking in similar terms: each of us knew that the United States was taking bold action to increase the number of women in its military, and we were resolved to do so too. But there were critics. Opening military colleges to women incurred the wrath of many former RMC cadets, one of whom said that he would make me pay for this crime. (In the next election, he appeared at a number of my campaign appearances, heckling and generally making a nuisance of himself while winning few adherents.) The most difficult problems were posed by the navy. Recently, the navy has announced that women are to be allowed on submarines, but in my days no one suggested such a thing: everyone agreed that submarines — given their tight quarters and lack of privacy — were an unsuitable place for mixed crews. As far as the regular navy was concerned, the greatest resistance to permitting women on board ships came from sailors' wives, who didn't relish the idea of their husbands being at sea with other women for six months at a stretch. Gender equality at sea had to be put off for some time. In terms of the air force, when speaking to a number of women's groups, I mused on the possibility of allowing women into fighter-pilot training on a trial basis, and indeed before I left the portfolio the way was made clear for this to take place.

In all of this, I was taken aback by the attitude of some women's groups. There was a general attitude of scepticism as to whether we really believed our fine words about enhancing the place of women in the military, and in addition there was disinterest and apprehension. Were we opening the door to allowing women to kill in war, just as men did? For my part, I, like other old soldiers, had serious reservations. I certainly couldn't abide the thought of women in combat: this might seem old-fashioned, but I thought that the special stresses of combat and the intimate manner of living and sanitary arrangements were barriers in themselves, and, on top of this, the prospect of women coming back from battle with limbs missing or, even worse, in body bags was inconceivable to me. Yet I was convinced that the integration of women in the armed forces was inevitable. Society was evolving in this direction, and the armed forces had to keep pace. We needed to move cautiously, to be sure, but move we must. For some, we were moving too fast, and, for others, we weren't moving fast enough. It was a complicated matter, with many practical problems, from uniforms to living quarters and the intense, often intentionally brutal, physical contact inherent in military life. In the main, however, the process of integrating women proceeded fairly well during my time at Defence, with obstacles being overcome as they arose. This process is not without problems even today, yet women are now an accepted part of the military and essential to maintaining the level of recruitment necessary for viable armed forces. They are no longer confined to providing support in traditional roles but rather perform virtually all the roles open to men.

Ministerial Trips, Part Two:
The Caribbean, the Arctic, and the Middle East

The travelling, meanwhile, continued. By the end of my first year in the portfolio, I had travelled 80,000 air miles within Canada and another 100,000 overseas. I paid regular visits to our thirty-odd bases across Canada and also made three trips to the far north, while, outside Canada, I was off to NATO meetings two times a year at a minimum and combined these trips with visits to our European bases as well as to Cyprus and the Middle East. My first experience at sea was Operation Springboard, a joint enterprise of the Canadian and American navies in April 1977 in the Caribbean that gave me the opportunity to sail, not only on destroyers and supply ships, but also, for the first time, on a submarine. The extremely cramped quarters in a submarine and the creaking sounds of the submarine's hull were a unique revelation to an old soldier. There was a sense of being in another, eerie world — and a vulnerable one at that. Looking through the periscope and seeing the surface ships converging on us in a mock attack, I was struck by how much depended on the eyeballs and judgment of one man, the submarine's skipper. As for the vessels above water, swinging on a jackstay that took me from one destroyer to another was a somewhat harrowing experience. The crews had a lot of fun watching their minister trying to appear nonchalant in this somewhat undignified operation.

The sheer mass of Canada and our three ocean coastlines compels one to come to grips with the impossibility of our defending ourselves on our own and yet, at the same time, the necessity of demonstrating our presence and exercising our sovereignty throughout our territory and territorial waters, including the Arctic archipelago. We must at least know what is going on in its farthest reaches, a difficult job given our relatively small military, which also has important assignments abroad. One of the trips to northern Canada, in late September 1977, gave me an overview of the dimensions of the task and some familiarity with the far-flung bases and communities of the region. It was a cross-Arctic tour, with Isobel accompanying me, which began in Churchill and ended in Goose Bay, with stopovers at Yellowknife, Inuvik, Alert, Cambridge Bay, Arctic Bay, and Frobisher Bay. On this tour, we had a good look at a Russian weather station, known as the Soviet Ice Island, an operation of the Arctic and Antarctic Institute of the Soviet Union. This facility, a cluster of small buildings and radio installations established in 1973, had drifted into what we consider Canadian waters, encompassing the Arctic archipelago from our eastern and western borders to the North Pole, in March 1976. It was important to assert our sovereignty or we would forfeit it. Five overflights had been conducted in the past, but I took the opportunity to raise the exercise from routine surveillance to a ministerial statement. Our party, which included Lieutenant-General Bill Carr, commander of the air force, flew in a Hercules. In spite of the sophistication of the Herc's electronics and the excellence of the navigators, we had some difficulty finding the "island" at first but eventually located it, about 500 miles south of the North Pole. Then, suspended on the lowered ramp at the rear of the aircraft, a "monkey's tail" clamped on to my safety harness, and air crew hanging on to each of my ankles, I dropped a canister with a Canadian flag attached and inside an assortment of gifts: a beer mug engraved with the message "Welcome to Our Soviet Visitors"; two pictures of myself, one for the residents of the "island" and the other for the Soviet defence minister ("My photos scare our allies all to hell, don't know what they'll do to anyone else," I was reported as saying at the time); and, if memory serves me correctly, a *Playboy* magazine. All of this was no doubt gratefully received by the handful of lonely Russians below.

Another highlight of that Arctic trip was the visit to our intelligence base at Alert on the northern tip of Ellesmere Island. About two hundred men were stationed there on six months' rotation — after their tour, they could be transferred to a similar station we maintained in Bermuda — and as part of our reception they invited us for drinks at the canteen, appropriately named the "No Nooky Inn." On our entry, we were asked to observe a standard ritual: male guests were asked to cut their ties in half and hang the severed parts on wall plaques; the women — Isobel and an air force photographer — were asked to donate autographed panties and hang them there too, in a space known as the "Alert Hall of Fame." This, not surprisingly, gave Isobel pause, but I assured her that we couldn't offend our hosts and, besides, no one would find out: we were in the high Arctic, after all. And so we complied with the ritual, only to discover on our return to "civilization" that the *Globe and Mail* had printed a front-page story on the visit, complete with a picture of Isobel's panties. Word later reached us that Maryon Pearson, wife of the late prime minister, was not amused. Ministers' wives should not behave in such an undignified fashion, charged Mrs Pearson, proving that there are no secrets for politicians in this vast land.

In April 1977 I paid my first visit as defence minister to the Middle East, with the goal of meeting both our military personnel and various officials of the host countries, Egypt, Syria, and Israel. Canada had about 1,000 troops stationed in the region, in the Sinai, on the Golan Heights, and on the Lebanese border, a number that represented the largest contribution by a single country (the overall force of 5,400 was contributed by nine countries in all). After stopping in Cyprus, which had the largest concentration of Canadian troops in the area, I made my first and only visit to Syria, where we had peacekeeping troops on the Golan Heights. In Damascus I had what was probably the most difficult official visit of my life, a meeting with Lieutenant-General Mustafa Tlass, who was then, and is still today, Syria's defence minister. Just before my arrival, Tlass, who undoubtedly knew from his briefings that I was Jewish, was reported to have declared in Syria's parliament that his country intended to kill every single Israeli, adding that he himself was ready to "rip out their throats" with his teeth. A sweet guy. For the rest of the evening, the bare minimum of diplomatic protocol was observed, but the atmosphere was tense and there was little conversation in any language. Towards the end, it was time for the traditional exchange of gifts. I presented Tlass with a plaque depicting the coats-of-arms of Canada and the Canadian provinces, the sort of thing one finds in a souvenir shop; to my mortification, Tlass then presented me with a long, plush red box, inside which was a newly mounted, ornate Arab sword. With our reputation for cheapness thereby established, Tlass excused himself with the same graciousness that had marked his behaviour during the rest of the evening.

The purpose of the trip was to visit the troops on the Golan Heights, which I did. One didn't need to be a military genius or have much imagination to see the strategic and intelligence value of the site to both sides. The Golan Heights overlooked the northern section of Israel, where many new Jewish settlements, made possible only by the Israeli occupation of the Heights, were easy targets. Israel, I was convinced, could never give up the Golan Heights voluntarily.

Because one could not then travel directly from an Arab country to Israel, our next stop, we filed our flight plan for Cyprus, flew over Lebanon and the Mediterranean, and then turned around, headed for Israel. I'm sure that Syrian radar was tracking us all the while, but we weren't interfered with and diplomatic protocol was observed. In Israel, our host was my old friend Defence Minister Shimon Peres, whom I had met on my first trip to Israel many years before, in the company of then transport minister Don Jamieson. At an official dinner in Tel Aviv, I took the opportunity to explain to our Israeli hosts that the principal reason Canada and the United States were at peace was that both countries had Jews as defence ministers, me in Canada and Harold Brown in the United States. Now, if Israel could somehow arrange to have Jewish defence ministers in its neighbouring countries, military conflict in the Middle East would be a thing of the past. Peres said that he would work on it. The joke went over well, but I didn't repeat it when we arrived in Egypt for the last stage of our trip.

In Cairo I first met with the Egyptian minister of defence, the Sandhurst-trained General Gamesy, an outstanding soldier and gentleman admired even by the Israelis. Afterwards, we were told that President Sadat wished to meet with me at a presidential palace outside the city. Accompanied by the Canadian ambassador to Egypt, Jean-Marcel Touchette, we were taken there in a motorcycle-accompanied motorcade through the busiest parts of Cairo, horns blaring and our drivers paying no attention at all to the civilians and their animals who had to scurry out of the way. On our arrival we waited in a magnificent receiving room for the president. When he walked in, I, having been told of the Arab fondness for formality and flattery, greeted him more fulsomely than I would normally. He was gracious, and within a couple of minutes it became clear to me that this was not a man who needed flattery; he was comfortable in his own skin — no flattery or flowery language on my part would be necessary. We talked frankly and with the greatest of ease. As the meeting was drawing to an end, Sadat looked me in the eye and said with the utmost seriousness, "If the Israelis want to talk peace, we are ready." The message was duly relayed to Israeli officials, as Sadat no doubt intended it to be. This was clearly the reason why I had been summoned to the palace in the first place. As far as I could determine, the Israelis had never before heard Egypt's desire for peace expressed so explicitly, and it was certainly the first time they had heard it from Sadat himself. A few months later, Sadat made his famous visit to Jerusalem, and so I like to think that, in my capacity as a courier, I may well have contributed to this historic development. At a personal level, I admired Sadat greatly and felt genuine warmth for him — feelings shared, incidentally, by the then prime minister of Israel, Menachem Begin. His assassination in 1981 shocked me deeply.

Menachem Begin

I first met Menachem Begin the following year when he paid an official visit to Canada. At the time, there was a move afoot in the Jewish community to get the government to move its embassy in Israel from Tel Aviv to Jerusalem. I discussed this with the prime minister on a number of occasions, as I did with Don Jamieson at External Affairs. Don's position was firmly negative, based on the anticipated Arab response. The prime minister was sympathetic to the idea from a symbolic and domestic political viewpoint but was sensitive to Jamieson's concerns. External's reading of the situation and its repercussions would be more than confirmed when, in 1979, the Conservative government of Joe Clark attempted such a move and had to back down, a fatal step for the government and a serious setback for those who were interested in Canada-Israel relations.

Begin's itinerary on his 1978 state visit to Canada included not only Ottawa but also Montreal and Toronto, and I accompanied him on the Toronto engagement. On several occasions during this visit, he lost no opportunity to urge the Jewish community to pressure the government to move the embassy. It is not usual for a visiting head of government to lecture a host government publicly on how it should conduct its foreign policy, at least not in anything but the most diplomatically accepted ways. Begin was as subtle as a sledgehammer. He was not much interested in the political consequences for Canada or for the Jewish community in Canada. When Trudeau told him that Canada was not about to accede to his wishes on the embassy issue, Begin replied to the effect that he was going to tell Jewish voters in Toronto and Montreal about their government's position. In turn, Trudeau said, "They already know. You can tell them what you want, but I don't think it would be very courteous — or very effective." Begin told them anyway, and repeated his call for pressure on the government at his other stops on the visit.

I was intrigued by Begin but also apprehensive. He could be immensely charming and was always supremely confident; he saw things in black and white, and regarded anyone who disagreed with him as the enemy. There was both a dignity to his manner and a disturbing crudeness. He would leave nothing to chance and never left himself exposed. His handwriting exemplified those characteristics. I noticed it first when he autographed two of his books for me: small, almost tiny writing, with each letter carefully and slowly constructed. There were no loose ends; not only were the "t"'s carefully crossed and the "i"'s meticulously dotted, but every stroke and loop was fully completed to match up with and close off each character. Nothing unclear or ill-defined. He was not going to make the slightest mistake.

On a platform in a meeting, or just in one-to-one contact, he was aggressive, cocky, and at times warm and engaging, but never with his guard down, never giving an inch. He had a passion that I can only describe as fire in the belly. Of his two books that he gave me, *White Nights* and *Revolt*, the former offered the best key to this complex man. It dealt with his youth in Poland and his imprisonment in Russia. He was a fighter from the beginning and the threats and experience of discrimination, abuse, and imprisonment shaped his personality. He had to scheme and connive just to exist, and these traits were reflected in his every thought and action. He never forgot or forgave.

At a reception before the official dinner in Toronto, I acted as his host before Trudeau's arrival. There were numerous representatives of the Jewish community present, but members of other communities were there as well. Stanley Haidasz, then a senator, brought a group of Polish Canadians forward to meet Begin. They were warm and respectful and one or two spoke to him in Polish. He refused to acknowledge them, acting as if he didn't understand them. I pointed out to him that these were Canadians who had come to pay him tribute, but, as far as Begin was concerned, they were no different from his former tormentors of a more than a generation ago. No concessions, no forgetting, no forgiving. Later at this same dinner, when menus were passed to him to autograph, he took the same meticulous care with his signature as he had in autographing books for me; there was none of the hurried flourish that is common with busy people.

When I took him to the airport in a limousine for his departure, I invited Larry Grossman, the cabinet minister representing the Ontario government, to join us. Larry mentioned that his late father, Allan, a former Ontario minister, had met Begin many years ago on a previous visit to Canada. Begin surprised us by remembering the occasion and relating many details about Allan Grossman — I imagine that he filed every bit of information, every incident, in his brain as carefully as he wrote. His farewell at the airport was warm and effusive, with the handshakes and bear hugs that were his normal style — unless, of course, you were an enemy, like a Pole.

The next time I encountered Begin was later the same year, at a reception in the president's residence in Jerusalem following Golda Meir's funeral. As head of the Canadian delegation to the funeral, I was one of hundreds of foreign guests. Yet, as I came close to the receiving line, he spotted me, opened his arms, and greeted me with all the considerable warmth and charm of which he was capable.

It is interesting to compare Begin to other leaders in Israel with whom I had friendships or at least some contact. Of course, Golda Meir was in a class all her own. Basically, she was as tough as, if not tougher than, Begin but she had a genuine warmth and light touch that eluded him. Itzhak

Rabin, as I said earlier, was not an easy person to be with, somewhat introverted, but always courteous and in control; you knew that there was an inner toughness and determination in the man. Close enough to me to be called "friends" were Shimon Peres and Dr Josef Borg. Peres is the only Israeli leader with the diplomatic skill and vast experience necessary to have brought the Oslo negotiations to what might have been a successful conclusion, had the process not been trashed by Yasser Arafat and Benjamin Netanyahu — this after painstaking, step-by-step progress over many months and the heroic efforts of Ehud Barak. There was no guarantee that Oslo would work but positions had been clarified and there was some hope of success. Regrettably, the bombast of Netanyahu combined with the ineptness of Yasser Arafat proved more decisive and great damage was done. In my view, Peres is the greatest Israeli statesman since Abba Eban and with greater personal warmth. Another of my Israeli friends, Josef Borg led a small religious party which, in the Israeli electoral system, assured him a cabinet post in every government since the founding of the state of Israel. As minister of the interior, he was highly respected and liked. Deeply observant religiously, he could speak many languages and was a true intellectual. In addition, he had a quick and easy, sometimes outrageous, sense of humour. I recall at least two occasions when I was exhausted and emotionally drained and the very presence of this wise friend was an immense source of strength to me. He served Israel and Judaism with great dignity and distinction and, like Rabin, had that inner toughness and determination that has allowed both Israel and Judaism to survive. I continue to mourn him.

Looking Back

Such were my years in Defence, a period of my life that, as I will recount in more detail in a moment, came to an end with my defeat in the election of 1979. Without doubt, these years were the most satisfying period of my political career — certainly more fulfilling than the time I spent at Urban Affairs. Satisfying and fulfilling are terms that apply only if you are a right fit for the job and I believe that, in the case of Defence, my experience and the job matched well. There were very few times

The Habitat Conference, Vancouver, 1976, with Secretary General
Enrique Penelosa and Senator Sydney Buchwald.

Trudeau at Habitat, May 1976.

Campaigning for clean water with Margaret Trudeau, at the Habitat Conference, Vancouver, 1976.

With Prime Minister Trudeau and Chief of Defence Staff General Jacques Dextraze, 1976.

Meeting with Katimavik leaders, circa 1977.

Swinging on a jackstay between ships taking part in Operation Springboard, at Roosevelt Roads, Puerto Rico, April 1977.

Emerging from a Leopard tank, Lahr, Germany, 1977.

At NATO headquarters, 1977, with British Defence Minister Fred (later Lord) Mulley (right) and British PERMREP (ambassador) to NATO Sir John Killick.

With Egyptian President Anwar Sadat, Cairo, 1977. It was at this meeting that Sadat told me of Egypt's strong desire for peace with Israel, a message I relayed to the Israelis – as Sadat no doubt intended I should.

With peacekeepers on the Golan Heights, 1977.

Inspecting peacekeepers in Cyprus, 1978.

Margaret and Pierre at Harrington Lake on the 10th anniversary of his leadership, 1978.

With Prime Minister Menachem Begin and Israel's ambassador to Canada, Mordecai Shalev, Ottawa, 1978.

Receiving a model of the Dash-7, the aircraft to be used by Dash-Air, from deHavilland President and Chief Executive Officer John Sandford, 1979.

As director of the Ballet Opera House Corporation, at the home of its chairman, H.N.R. (Hal) Jackman and Maruja Jackman.

As hon. lieutenant-colonel of Queen's Own Rifles of Canada, with a cold beer.

Dr Danson and Isobel, after receiving an honorary doctorate from the Royal Military College in Kingston, Ontario, May 1988: "the pinnacle of my academic career."

As an "old sweat" at the 50th anniversary of D-Day in Normandy, 1994.

Induction as an officer of the Order of Canada by Governor General Romeo Leblanc, 1996.

Becoming an officer of the Order of Merit of France, 1995.

My last face-to-face meeting with Pierre Trudeau, Ottawa, 1998. Marc Lalonde is in the background.

For Barney,

Pierre E. T. 1988

Receiving the Vimy Award from Governor General Adrienne Clarkson, November 2000.

The author
and Prime
Minister Jean
Chrétien,
2000, shaking
hands on the
agreement for
government
support for
the new
Canadian War
Museum.

To my friend Barney, with my best wishes, Jean Chrétien

With Isobel
and Casey
(the one in
the middle),
the real star
of our family,
at the cottage,
2001.

when I didn't feel that I was on top of my responsibilities. I felt comfortable with the troops and I think that they felt comfortable with me. There is no question that my wartime army experience gave me the background to absorb complex briefings which dealt with the current equipment and operational needs of the Canadian military. And the fact that not only was I at home in my job but that I understood the troops definitely gave me credibility with them.

As I look back on these years now, my chief regret concerns something over which I had little or no control, namely, the general lack of interest in military matters in peacetime on the part of most of my colleagues in government, the media, and the public at large. Apart from the sometimes overheated and acid rhetoric that emanated from the opposition benches at Question period, both sides of the House treated military subjects in a non-partisan manner, when they discussed them at all. Quite often, the MPs' only interest related to the closing of bases in their constituencies and then only for economic rather than military considerations. In the media, I can recall only four reporters, Peter Ward, Jo Ann Gosselin, Doug Fisher, and Peter Worthington, who wrote on and were knowledgeable about military matters, and this state of affairs prevailed only because most Canadians were indifferent to the whole business. I wish that I could have sparked a debate on military issues, both in Parliament and outside it, for I believed that these issues were of critical importance to the future of Canada and our place on the world scene. Recently, there has been a new interest in our history, and awareness of our military history in particular has been enriched by gifted and dedicated historians such as Jack Granatstein, David Bercuson, Desmond Morton, and Terry Copp. So far, however, apart from the ranks of a dedicated few, public knowledge of our armed forces is still superficial.

Set against this are a number of things in which I take some satisfaction. One is the CF-18 itself, a magnificent aircraft whose performance decades later justifies our decision to select it over the competition. On the larger stage, though I was never a militant Cold Warrior, I did believe strongly that Soviet totalitarianism had to be contained by making the consequences of expansion too costly in military and economic terms to attempt. This required constant awareness and readiness to respond, which the Allies demonstrated year in and year out. NATO must surely rank as the most successful military alliance in the history of the world, for it ultimately achieved victory without a shot being fired. How different the history of the twentieth century would have been had Western powers stood up to Nazi Germany in the same way in the 1930s. Finally, back in Canada again, when I took on the job of defence minister, morale was low, partly because of budget cuts and partly as a result of the insensitive way in which unification had been implemented. From the beginning, I made it a priority to restore a sense of worth among the men and women in the military. The greatest compliment I ever received was when one senior officer told me that I was the best minister of defence since Brooke Claxton. That touched me: Claxton, a titan of the King and St Laurent cabinets, was one of my political idols.

My years at Defence were indeed a good time for me. I suppose I made my share of mistakes, but I think I got many things right. And I loved every minute of it.

Chapter Seven
Endings and Beginnings, 1979–2001

By the spring of 1979, I had been in Parliament for eleven years, six as a backbencher (including two years as parliamentary secretary to the prime minister) and five as a cabinet minister. I loved the House of Commons as much as ever and my job at Defence was, as I've said, endlessly fascinating. Indeed, I thought that I was beginning to get the hang of the portfolio and that if I stayed there another few years I would be able to leave a firm imprint. Unfortunately for me, the democratic process intervened and the voters decided otherwise.

During all my time in politics I never believed that I would not have a fighting chance of winning an election — if I had I would not have run for anything — but neither did I ever think that victory was in the bag; election after election, I superstitiously tried to ensure success on voting day by following a set routine: buying a new pair of socks, taking a steam bath, and, as a way of preparing myself for defeat should it happen, drafting a concession speech. I then waited until the last vote was counted before breathing a sigh of relief and savouring the result in the company of Isobel and my supporters. That was true in 1968, 1972, and 1974. The campaign of 1979, however, ended differently than the preceding ones — very differently: I lost. At the time I put a brave face on my defeat, joking that I would have to line up for unemployment insurance just like everybody else, but I can't deny that the experience hurt. Why did I lose? I don't think I'm being immodest when I say that my defeat had less to do with my own unpopularity in the riding than with the unpopularity of the government as a whole.

The Last Election

The difficulties I faced in the 1979 election had evolved gradually over the years since our victory in 1974. After returning to office with a comfortable majority that year, we immediately came face to face with a number of intractable problems. One was inflation. As I said in an earlier chapter, inflation had become sufficiently worrisome by the time of the 1974 election campaign — it was then running at about 11 percent — that Robert Stanfield and the Conservatives decided to run on a platform of wage-and-price controls. The Liberal position was different. We believed that the main causes of inflation — particularly increases in the price of oil — lay outside Canada and so would not be susceptible to domestic controls. Such controls, in short, would inflict rigidity on our economic system that was not yet warranted and that, in any case, would prove futile. After our 1974 victory, with Canada increasingly generating inflationary pressures independently of the international economy, we came to the view that the best response would be a program of voluntary restraint. We tried hard to make this program work but, by late 1975, it was becoming increasingly evident that voluntary measures were not having the desired effect — in October of that year, wage increases were averaging nearly 19 percent. The program's failure was a disappointment to all of us and particularly to the person in charge, John Turner, the minister of finance.

Around this time Turner suddenly resigned as finance minister. His decision left us reeling — he was a pillar of the government, and he had never let on to any of us that he was planning on stepping down. That is not to say that he was a happy camper. On several occasions he had made strong interventions in cabinet on the need to get our spending under control, but he was always a team player and public supporter of the prime minister — even when he had grave reservations about Trudeau's leadership and the government's direction. It is reported that he and Trudeau were completely at odds on the government's economic management, and so, when he offered his resignation, Trudeau didn't resist. It is a report I'm inclined to accept. Whatever the truth of the matter, John Turner acted in the best tradition of our parliamentary system. When in office you support your leader and if, in clear conscience, you can no longer do so, you either convince the prime minister that your view is right or resign. This is a painful position for any minister. What you can't say outright is that, if the leader doesn't agree with you, you will resign. You don't threaten the prime minister, and wise prime ministers and wise ministers try to avoid this crucial confrontation at all costs. Conviction and often pride are key factors. In effect, you say to yourself that, if the leader doesn't have enough confidence in me to accept my deeply held position, I had better get out. As the saying goes in politics, "The boss may not always be right, but he's always the boss." In any event, while it is rumoured that Trudeau offered Turner alternative portfolios or a seat in the Senate, Turner was adamant. His views were based on his best judgment as minister of finance, and he was not prepared to compromise.

Turner was succeeded by Donald Macdonald, who made one more effort to coax the private sector — business and unions alike — to put the brakes on wage-and-price increases. Again, however, it was to no avail. And so in October 1975, after long and often heated debate in cabinet, we reached the view that mandatory wage-and-price controls were necessary. Trudeau cautioned that he was going along reluctantly and that we should all be prepared for the negative consequences. I have often described this decision as one that Trudeau took "kicking and screaming."

On Thanksgiving Day, 1975, the prime minister went on national television to announce that the government was introducing a system of wage-and-price controls, as well as embarking on a program of significant cuts in its own expenditures. Over the course of the two and a half years the controls program was in place, it did succeed in taming inflation: by 1977, the inflation rate had been cut to about 8 percent. Clearly, Canada was in much better shape economically by the end of the decade than it was before wage-and-price controls had been introduced. The inflationary beast had not been vanquished, but it had been tamed. Yet, politically, there can be no doubt that the imposition of controls cost us dearly. Our reversal in policy regarding controls made us vulnerable to charges of deception. Hadn't we just said in an election campaign that such controls were a bad idea? We could have responded by explaining that circumstances had changed, that the causes of inflation were now as much in Canada as elsewhere, that we had tried voluntarism and it had not worked. In fact, we said all these things, but not as effectively as we should. The result was that, from this point on, the perception began to take hold that the Liberal government was not to be trusted. All Liberals were tarred by that brush, even though, to our minds, we had acted in good faith according to our considered judgement of how best to respond to changing circumstances.

As if this were not enough, the country was then straining under the weight of its national-unity problems. Over the course of 1975, a government task-force report proposing to allow the use of French by pilots and air-traffic controllers led to angry protests by the unions representing those groups. These protests in turn prompted Quebec pilots and controllers to form their own breakaway union, L'Association des gens de l'air. Inflammatory rhetoric was the order of the day — the use of French in the skies, it was said, would imperil airline crews and passengers alike — and quickly became part and parcel of the ongoing resistance to the government's official-languages policy. Like other members of the government, I was convinced that we were on the right track, that bilingualism in the air made as much sense as it did on the ground — indeed, I thought, the future of our country depended on whether or not we could make francophones feel as much at home in Canada as the rest of us did. I also believed, as did my colleagues, that while much of the resistance was based on real or perceived grievances, for many it was a pretext to vent their intolerance. We could not see how airline safety was jeopardized by allowing French-speaking pilots to use French, in those regions where the size of the French-speaking population warranted it, when communicating with French-speaking air-traffic controllers, and vice versa.

The controversy escalated in the summer of 1976 when the unions opposing the government's plans called a strike. Realizing that a compromise had to be found if the country was not to be torn apart, the government announced that the matter of bilingualism in the airline industry would be temporarily deferred until a commission of inquiry had investigated the issue. Shortly afterward the strike was settled, but only by the government agreeing to further concessions that had the effect of making the introduction of bilingual air-traffic control unlikely in the foreseeable future. This development infuriated the minister of transport, Jean Marchand, who had until recently been responsible for the file. He resigned in protest. The whole experience left us angry and not a little saddened — Marchand was highly regarded by all his colleagues. It also left us licking our political wounds; the hysterical outcry over bilingual air-traffic control left no doubt that many people in English-speaking Canada had little use for our vision of the country.

There was more bad news a few months later. On 15 November, René Lévesque's Parti Québécois, which had not hesitated to use les Gens de l'air controversy to stoke nationalist fires, came to power in Quebec. Though Trudeau was not shaken by this development — he went on television to reassure Canadians that the PQ was elected not to pursue its separatist agenda but simply to provide good government — the country was clearly at a crossroads. In my own case, at the time of the Quebec election, I was not in Canada but in London attending my first NATO meeting. Being distant from the scene, however, made me more anxious, not less. Over the next few years I remained optimistic about the country's future, but, as long as there was such a great lack of understanding and raw intolerance in large parts of Canada and a government in Quebec actively planning a referendum on separation, my natural optimism was always tempered by some concern. It certainly didn't help my spirits that the government's response in these years to the challenge of Quebec separatism — a sustained effort to achieve constitutional reform, pursued through a succession of federal-provincial conferences — fell afoul of the provinces' seemingly insatiable appetite for more powers. The public didn't blame us for this failure — on the contrary, there was increasing impatience with the provinces — but, paradoxically, it also showed signs of weariness with the whole business of constitutional reform. There was a growing sense in the country that too much attention was being paid to constitutional issues and not enough to the country's social and economic needs. This perception didn't do wonders for the government's popularity, to say the least.

Trudeau's personality, sometimes infuriating and other times endearing, was yet another ingredient in the political mix of that time. Today, in the wake of the vast outpouring of grief over Trudeau's death, it almost seems as if everyone loved him all of the time. But it wasn't so. By 1972, as I have already related, the country's love affair with Trudeau had lost its bloom. There were as many people in the country, particularly the west, who hated him as admired him. His popularity recovered somewhat during the minority Parliament of 1972–74, but no sooner were we returned to office in 1974 than the old animosity to him revived. By the late 1970s, Trudeau had become a lightning-rod for discontent. Some saw him as "ramming French down their throats"; others saw him as yet another eastern politician intent on exploiting the west, when he was not just ignoring it; and still others, while admitting that he was interesting and colourful, felt him to be insufferably arrogant and not as focused on social and economic issues as he should be. The hostility to Trudeau was a slippery thing that was hard to get a handle on but it was palpably real all the same — and, in politics, perception is reality. Of course, as the prime minister's lustre faded so did the government's, opinion polls showing steadily declining Liberal support and a corresponding increase in the popularity of the Conservatives, now led by Joe Clark, throughout the late 1970s. For the prime minister personally, life was made even more difficult by marital problems. Everyone knew by now that he and Margaret were having troubles, but few if any us appreciated how serious these troubles were until March 1977, when their separation was officially announced. This announcement came immediately after a cabinet meeting where the prime minister was obviously in some distress; he didn't say anything about what was coming, but there was clearly something very wrong — he was visibly exhausted and agitated. The meeting was quickly adjourned, and then the news broke. We were all terribly saddened by this tragic personal development.

By the spring of 1979, we were into the fifth year of our mandate. With the polls showing us in desperate shape, we had put off the day of reckoning as long as possible, but now there was no longer any room to manoeuvre; an election was mandatory. In my own riding of York North, a poll indicated that I, too, would be defeated, but I didn't believe it. I knew that I was personally popular in the riding and was convinced that I would be one of the few Liberal ministers to be returned. I'm sure other ministers about to be defeated felt the same way. I was wrong. With an election called for May 22ⁿᵈ, I returned to my riding to throw myself into the electoral battle, my opponent this time being not Steven Roman but a newcomer, John Gamble. A politician never expects to love an opponent, but usually one has a grudging respect for those, regardless of party, who put themselves on the line politically. It was difficult for me to be even grudgingly respectful towards Gamble. I was thus taken aback to discover that many people in the riding whom I had come to count on were supporting Gamble, a number of them explaining that, while they still liked me well enough, they just couldn't stand "that Trudeau." They were like rats deserting a sinking ship, I thought at the time, an ominous signal in politics. As the campaign wore on, I realized that I was in a tough fight, but nothing prepared me for the extent of the loss that unfolded on election night when Gamble won by some 7,000 votes. I had been soundly thrashed, no doubt about it. As the magnitude of my defeat became evident, I was deeply disappointed though not in total shock. I had seen the possibility of defeat coming but still thought I could escape it. My supporters and workers, however, took it very badly. For their sake I tried to keep a stiff upper lip. I thanked them for all their efforts. It was not the end of the world, I told them; there would be new battles to fight and they had done all that the party and I could expect. I then pulled myself together sufficiently to make my way to Gamble's victory party to congratulate him, an obligatory process full of hollow phrases on both sides.

What made the night a bit more bearable in a perverse way was the knowledge that I was not alone. We were out and the Conservatives were in; the final standings were 136 Conservatives and only 114 Liberals. No fewer than thirteen cabinet ministers were defeated. And *all* the Toronto-area cabinet ministers were swept out of office. We had been routed, pure and simple. With the NDP holding twenty-six seats and the Créditistes six, the Tories would be in a minority position, but they would be the government all the same.

Following my defeat, I received a phone call from John Diefenbaker, who offered his condolences; as I have said, I was one of the few Liberal MPs he seemed to have any use for. I thanked him and others who called, wrote, or approached me in public to commiserate, and set about vacating my parliamentary and ministerial offices and reorienting my life. With regard to the dramatic events that soon followed — Trudeau's resignation as party leader on November 21st, the quite avoidable defeat of the Clark government in a budgetary vote in the House on December 13th, Trudeau's return as leader on December 18th, and the Liberal victory in the election of 18 February 1980 — I was an interested observer but not an active participant. In the period immediately after the election of May 1979, I didn't rule out entering politics again, but I had no immediate plans to do so. I was fifty-eight and wanted to get on with my life rather than spend the rest of my days as a political wallflower. And to tell the truth, I didn't even believe at the time that the results of the election were a disaster for the country. The Liberal Party, I privately thought, had been in power for a long time, and its weariness was showing, as was the prime minister's; it was time for a change. I thought that Clark was a decent man, and that his Conservatives deserved to have their chance at governing the country. As for myself, I wanted to take some time off, lick my wounds, reflect, and think about the future.

That summer Isobel and I sold our Ottawa house (to Jean Chrétien, incidentally) and took a holiday in Europe, spending most of it in Portugal, where I knew no one, no one knew me, and, as I said at the time, I could move around freely and not have people walking up to me on the street to offer their sympathy. Reinvigorated, we returned to our new home in Toronto. This was a rented apartment, not a house. I wasn't interested in tying myself down to another house since I wanted the flexibility to move to wherever the next challenge presented itself. The one place I did want to tie myself down to, however, was our summer place on Georgian Bay. In one of my wiser moments, I had purchased the land on either side of my cottage site at what would now be considered a bargain-basement price. I began making plans for another cottage on our land, which could then serve as a sort of family compound. The place has become what I call my "spiritual home."

Later, when Trudeau resigned in November, I was saddened but not surprised, and I even thought that his decision was a good one, both for him and the party. I still had the highest regard for him, but I felt that the moment was ripe for a new leader. If a leadership convention had been held, I would have supported Don Macdonald. But I never got the opportunity, of course. With other Canadians, I watched in astonishment as the dramatic events of late 1979 and early 1980 unfolded. When another election was called, my old riding association in York North asked me to run again, and for a time I was sorely tempted. By this time, however, as I will recount in a moment, I was involved in a business venture that required a full-time commitment; my associates had earlier asked me whether I would abandon them at the first opportunity to re-enter politics, and I said, no, I had closed the door on politics for good. I kept my word. Yet I also have to admit that, if Trudeau had asked me to run, I would have; there was no way I could turn him down — such was my admiration for him. But he didn't ask, and I wasn't surprised; he never did that kind of thing, whether for me or for others. It just wasn't his style. And so I stayed on the sidelines — even though, if I had run again, I probably would have won. Indeed, Gamble's campaign manager called me to find out if I was running, since many of his workers had indicated that they would not work for him if I was to be a candidate. As it turned out, Gamble was returned, though a few years later, after he had tried to mount a palace coup against Joe Clark, his own riding executive refused to allow him to run again as a Tory. Later still, it was rumoured that his overtures to the Reform Party were rebuffed.

I wasn't around, then, for the triumphant return of Pierre Trudeau and the Liberal Party. When Trudeau made his victory speech in the Chateau Laurier — announcing "Welcome to the 1980s!" — I was back in Toronto, busy with other things. My political life was over. It had been quite a ride, full of excitement, challenges, and rewards. I can't remember a single boring day, whether in my years on the backbench or in my time in the cabinet. There was always so much to do: decisions to be taken, issues to be studied, people to meet, trips to be taken, and — the top priority of any MP — looking after the needs of constituents. The day-to-day round of activities provided an adrenaline rush that few other jobs can match. Looking back on those years now, I deeply miss the action and often wish I were back at it, but that is not to be. Still, I am deeply grateful for having had this extraordinary experience. I saw parts of the world I otherwise would not have seen, met numerous larger-than-life figures on the international stage, and made friendships both in Canada and abroad that endure to this day. Through it all, I came into contact with people who left an indelible mark on me, chief among whom was Pierre Trudeau, one of the most remarkable people I have ever encountered. All good things must come to an end, of course, and the world of politics offers no job security. A political career is a privilege, not a right, and anyone who thinks that it will last forever is deluding himself. In my case, I have no regrets and wouldn't have missed the experience for anything.

Dash-Air

At the time of my defeat in 1979, I was still a fairly young man and had no intention of riding off into the sunset. Retirement could come later, if ever; there were still a lot of things to do — though, for a while, I was hard pressed to say what they should be. Politics had been the focus of my life for so long that it wasn't at all clear what new direction my life should take. I had time to build a new career and source of income (parliamentary pensions weren't what they are today), but most of all I wanted to do something interesting and challenging. Even if I could have afforded it, I couldn't — and still can't — think of anything worse than waking up in the morning wondering what I was going to do that day. Nor could Isobel. In politics, my need always to have something on the go had never presented a problem, and even in business I would awaken with five or six things I had to do that day. I made it a habit to keep a pad and pencil beside my bed so that, if I woke up with a new thought, I simply made a note of it and went back to sleep rather than tossing and turning, exploring it further and waking up exhausted. Actually, there were occasions when that didn't suffice — the thought was too stimulating — and I would go into another room and write for an hour or so. Some of my best work was done at 4:00 o'clock in the morning.

Politics was no longer an option, and the plastics industry was long behind me, but I knew that there were lots of exciting opportunities right here in Canada. One involved aircraft. When in cabinet, I had always been fascinated by the discussions on the new STOL (Short Take-Off and

Landing) aircraft — the latest version known as the Dash-7 — developed by deHavilland in Toronto. The technology was leading edge, at the time, and the fifty-passenger Dash-7 was ideal for a commuter airline on heavily traveled medium-range routes such as the Toronto-Montreal-Ottawa triangle. Dash-7 aircraft were selling well in the United States, and interest outside North America was significant. In Canada, however, only Time-Air in Alberta was running a successful commuter service, in this case between Calgary and Edmonton. The government had supported STOL development at deHavilland to the tune of some $100 million, and when deHavilland's owner, Hawker Sidley of England, indicated that it was not prepared to continue to give deHavilland the priority it needed, the government bought out Hawker Sidley's interest and deHavilland became a Canadian crown corporation. As minister of national defence, I authorized the purchase of two Dash-7s for the armed forces based in Germany, where they would become familiar sights in the skies and at the airports of many of our NATO allies.

By 1979, I couldn't think of a more appropriate challenge than to investigate the feasibility of a new commuter airline providing frequent and reliable service to the downtown central business areas of Toronto, Montreal, and Ottawa, without the expensive, time-consuming trips to the major airports that were then the norm. Eric Acker, my executive assistant at both Urban Affairs and Defence, was also out of a job, and we developed a plan for a STOL Dash-7 service that deHavilland agreed was both feasible and potentially quite profitable. In this planning stage, we received a great deal of assistance and advice from professionals in the air industry — particularly Rhys Eyton, then president of Canadian Airlines in Calgary, and Canadian Airlines' lawyer, Jack Major (later a justice of the Supreme Court of Canada), who acted as our counsel — investment underwriters Nesbitt Thompson (now BMO Nesbitt Burns), led by CEO Brian Steck, and the Canadian Imperial Bank of Commerce. Some personal friends and I put up the operating cash for the new Dash-Air Inc., and we placed deposits on options for seven Dash-7s from deHavilland. We proposed to have the service up and running within two years. For airports, we planned to use Uplands Airport in Ottawa and the Toronto Island Airport. While in Montreal we proposed to build on site of the old Victoria Airport in the harbour area. Upgrading the Toronto Island

Airport to accommodate our hangars and maintenance base would cost about $10–15 million, depending on our final choice of landing systems, and building the new Montreal airport would require another $10 million. It was our estimate that these costs, to be shared by us and the three levels of government, could be recovered in about ten years.

Others soon jumped on the bandwagon. We had serious competition for the licence to operate — in those days, prior to airline deregulation, the Canadian Transport Commission (CTC) was responsible for the licensing of new airline services — from Canavia Transit of Montreal, City Centre Airlines (now Air Ontario) of London, Ontario, and Bradley Air Services of Carp, near Ottawa, but we were the only ones with options on Dash-7 aircraft. There was powerful opposition, too, from Air Canada, which argued that the service wasn't necessary, and from certain political quarters. The Ontario government liked the plan for a STOL service, but the federal government, first under the Conservatives and then under the Liberals, dragged its feet on the issue of improvements to the Toronto Island Airport and the building of a new airport in Montreal. In addition, while the Metropolitan Toronto Council (under Paul Godfrey's chairmanship) was supportive, there was considerable opposition to the project on Toronto City Council, which had voted against many similar proposals in the past. Opponents, led by John Sewell, soon to be mayor, argued that a STOL service would seriously damage the quality of life on the Toronto Islands and in the Habourfront area, particularly if it was followed by jet flights. For our part, we specifically undertook never to introduce aircraft noisier than the Dash-7 to the Island, noting that the Dash-7 was a far quieter plane than the private aircraft already using the Island Airport. Speaking from a personal perspective, I emphasized that, as someone who had helped Harbourfront come into being, the lakefront was precious to me too, and I would never consider doing anything that had the potential to harm it in any way. The critics were not convinced.

The process of trying to obtain governmental approval for a STOL service proved to be a slow one, indeed far, far slower than I had anticipated. Our company submitted its formal application to the CTC on 13 November 1979. Commission hearings on the project were under way by early the following year, but we were still awaiting a decision when, on 19 October 1980, Toronto City Council, with John Sewell as mayor, voted to oppose the project. Shortly afterwards the CTC put the matter on hold because of Toronto's opposition and the refusal of the Department of Transport — my "friends" in the Liberal Party were now back in power — to commit money to the upgrading of the Island Airport. Having spent hundreds of thousands of dollars of my own money and that of my friends on the project, and after having waited so long for a decision that, it seemed to me, could have been made much earlier, I was deeply frustrated. A few months later, however, the skies brightened. A new Toronto City Council, under a new mayor, Art Eggleton, was more receptive to the STOL idea, and I encouraged this change of thinking by commissioning Gallup and Goldfarb polls which showed a large majority of voters everywhere in the city to be support-ive of a Dash-7 service, and an overwhelming majority in favour in the four wards adjacent to the Island Airport. My efforts paid off when, on 13 February 1981, council voted to withdraw its earlier opposition in principle to a STOL service, on four conditions, namely, that no new runways would be built; that jet aircraft would be barred; that noise lev-els would be strictly controlled; and that no bridge or tunnel would be constructed to the mainland, leaving us dependent on the almost as adequate ferry service. We then sat back to await the outcome of nego-tiations between city staff and the Department of Transport; the latter finally had a made a verbal promise to the city that it would spend $2.5 million upgrading the airport and another $5.6 million installing spe-cial microwave-landing equipment, necessary for safe, reliable opera-tion of the service and which would largely be repaid in landing fees. We also waited for the result of an appeal of the earlier decision by the CTC.

Astonishingly, there was no outcome in either case. The negotia-tions among the bureaucrats dragged on and on, and the CTC showed no signs of making a decision. (Once, a decision did seem imminent, but then the chairman of the CTC's Air Transport Committee took off to Europe for the summer.) The final straw for me was when a repre-sentative of one of our competitors, Canavia, told me that if the CTC ruling was not in their favour, they would appeal. I now saw this busi-ness stretching on interminably with no end in sight. And to make matters even worse, the projects' finances were starting to look increasingly shaky because of escalating interest rates (18 percent by 1981) and a general economic slowdown. Enough was enough. We pulled out, and Dash-Air was disbanded. Subsequently, under Lloyd Axworthy as minister of transport, the airline industry was deregulated and Air Otonobee of Peterborough started a commuter service operating out of Toronto Island. Yet it was nothing as ambitious as what we had envisioned, and it certainly did not employ the state-of-the-art Dash-7. Some years later, Air Canada, in conjunction with Air Ontario, instituted a similar service with the deHavilland Dash- 8. But by then I was long out of the picture.

All in all, it had been an unhappy experience for me. Not only had I lost about $100,000 of my own money (not pin money for me — particularly at that time), but also I had come very, very close to beginning a business that, in my mind, clearly would have had a great future — only to fall short. Apart from the excellent service it would have provided, our Dash-Air commuter airline would have been a showcase for deHavilland and would have benefited the aviation sector as a whole through substantial investments and industrial spin-offs. Our failure to get Dash-Air Inc. off the ground confirmed my instinct, born during my years in politics, that it was hopeless getting into a business that was so dependent on government action, unless you had very deep pockets. I should have known better, but, then again, I have always been an optimist. Isobel calls me her Don Quixote, always tilting at windmills.

Uganda

Towards the end of 1980, in the midst of the planning and manoeuvring on behalf of Dash-Air, the secretary of state for external affairs, Mark MacGuigan, asked me whether I would be interested in becoming part of a Commonwealth team that was to monitor democratic elections in Uganda, the first in that country for eighteen years. I leapt at the opportunity. The mission, conceived by the Commonwealth's secretary general, Shridaih (Soni) Ramphal, clearly was of vital importance to the future of democracy in this part of Africa, and besides, it was bound to be fascinating. I had never been to Uganda before and was eager to see it, a country known both for its beauty and for its hideous suffering under the recently deposed dictator Idi Amin. December wasn't a bad time to be in a tropical climate and, at the very least, it would be a welcome break from the endless waiting and political bickering of the Dash-Air business that, at the time, was in abeyance until the new year in any case. With Isobel accompanying me, I left for London on 20 November and the next day I joined the other members of the Commonwealth Observer Group (COG), which, in addition to its chairman, E.M. (Kojo) Debrah of Ghana, had eight members in all, representing Canada, Australia, Botswana, India, Barbados, Britain, Cyprus, and Sierra Leone, as well as a support staff numbering about seventy. Further meetings and delays followed as the terms of reference were hammered out with the reluctant Ugandans.

On the 24th we departed for Uganda, stopping first at Nairobi, Kenya. Our high commissioner in Kenya, Jeff Bruce, who was also accredited to Uganda, advised us that it would be unwise for Isobel to go to Uganda, since the country was then chaotic and highly dangerous and accommodation was uncertain. He and Mrs Bruce invited Isobel to stay at the High Commission residence until it was thought safe for her to join me in Kampala. We took his advice. Isobel remained in Nairobi with the Bruces; she did not join me in Uganda until near the end of my work there, and then only briefly. Isobel arrived in Kampala shortly before election day, but there was considerable evidence of escalating violence and all foreigners, except our group, were advised to depart on any planes landing at Entebbe Airport. An unscheduled Sabena flight en route to Brussels was then touching down at Entebbe for refuelling, and Isobel managed to get aboard. We ultimately managed to catch up with one another in London, where my highest priority was a hot bath, a shampoo and haircut, and then dinner at Scott's, a very good (expensive) restaurant.

Arriving in Kampala on the 25th, we met immediately with the head of the Military Commission then running the country, General Paulo Muwanga, and further meetings followed with diplomatic personnel stationed in Kampala, faculty and student leaders at Makerere University (the leading university in central Africa), and others. In our conversations with Ugandans, outside the governing circle, we encountered deep anxiety and suspicion regarding the possibility of free and fair elections, feelings that were balanced, however, by a high degree of political awareness and interest and an intense desire to have, at long last, a stable and honest government, a prosperous economy, and a secure and free environment. Concerns about fairness seemed well founded. The Military Commission obviously backed and was closely tied to one of the two parties contesting the election, the Uganda Patriotic Congress (UPC), led by a former president, Milton Obote (whom, as I have already recounted, I had met earlier at the Singapore Commonwealth meeting of 1971, when Amin, taking advantage of Obote's absence from Uganda, deposed him). The UPC's main rival, the Democratic Party (DP), led by Paulo Semogerere, had considerable support in the country, particularly among the ethnic Bugandans of the Kampala region, but it faced an uphill battle, as did the other two parties contesting the election, the Uganda Peoples Movement (UPM) and the monarchist Conservative Party. The Election Commission, which was supposed to be responsible for the running of the elections, was adopting a hands-off approach as Muwanga and his colleagues took a range of outrageous actions, from putting government vehicles, facilities, and personnel at the disposal of the UPC to suspending fourteen of thirty-three district commissioners (who were also election returning officers) and removing the chief justice. State-controlled media coverage was also blatantly slanted in favour of the UPC.

On 3 December with elections set for the 10th, we divided ourselves into four teams, each responsible for a specific district. Our task was daunting, for there were about 5,000 polling stations in the country separated by hundreds of miles, with only the most primitive roads connecting them. We set out by light aircraft and vans for our assigned areas, mine being Kabale in the southeast, close to the border with Kenya. What we saw both encouraged and alarmed us because, though people were obviously working hard to ensure that the elections came off smoothly, there was considerable disorganization. We spent one day driving to Kisori on some of the worst roads I have ever experienced through some of the most beautiful, lush, mountainous country I have ever seen. On the 6th we were back in Kampala, where we met for the first time with Obote, who expressed scepticism about our value but admitted that we were having a calming effect. Incredibly, he complained about what he saw as the partiality of the Election Commission and assumed the role of the oppressed underdog.

By now long-awaited Land Rovers had finally arrived and so on 8 December we were able to drive to polling stations in each of the three constituencies in the Kabale district. In Tororo, the district commissioner's headquarters and the hub of the election effort, we found ballot boxes but no ballots on the 9th — one day before election. We spent that afternoon driving over often-treacherous roads to remote areas to meet officials at the polling stations. Most of these were in rural schools but other buildings such as community centres were also used, and, in one case, a mud-walled, grass-roofed chicken coop, chickens and all, served the purpose. Incredible ingenuity was displayed in constructing voting booths with corrugated metal, grass, woven mats, and anything else that came to hand. Enthusiasm was high but it was only towards the end of the day that the ballots arrived. Not seeing how these could be delivered to the polling stations by 8 AM the next morning, we resigned ourselves to disaster.

But our worst fears were not realized. At 7:50 AM on voting day, we reached our first poll to find voting already in progress. Literally thousands of people were lined up, some having arrived the night before and most having been in place for at least two hours. Officials and party agents were on the job and working in complete harmony. Women were in separate lines, virtually all of childbearing age, many with babies on their back or sides or nursing infants. Each voter had his or her hand stamped so they could not vote more than once. There was some congestion and in one case I had to call in an additional police squad to restore order so that the interrupted voting could resume. (These civil police, dressed in British style forage caps, and khaki uniforms and equipped with First World War rifles, were treated with respect and, knowing their communities, had little difficulty doing their job. Certainly, they were far more effective than the Tanzanian army troops, who were supposedly acting as peacekeepers but by now had become something of a renegade army repeating the excesses of the totally discredited Ugandan army they had replaced.) Somehow, however, a miracle had occurred overnight and the election was proceeding without overt irregularities. We travelled from poll to poll joining in the serious but still festive spirit. The level of interest in the election was extraordinary; the voter turnout, it was later reported, was 90 percent. We questioned voters, party candidates, agents, and officials freely and did not detect any situation where unfairness was evident or the secrecy of the ballot compromised.

In the late afternoon, we returned to Kampala to prepare the COG's interim report. Just before we were to cable that report to London — its conclusion being that, in the main, the process had been a fair one so far, subject to the count and recording process — we learned of an astonishing development: Muwanga, apparently alarmed by premature reports that Obote's victory was in doubt, had announced that voting was to be extended until 2:00 PM the next day and that returning officers were to report to him directly and secretly, on penalty of a large fine and five years in jail. Immediately releasing our interim report, we protested Muwanga's action and informed him that, if it were not rescinded, we would leave the country immediately. He relented. I have no doubt, however, that his change of heart was the result of further reports that Obote had indeed won. If it had become clear that Obote was going to lose, Muwanga would likely not have been so compliant. That night more gunfire erupted on the streets of Kampala. I could hear it all too well from my hotel room in the dilapidated Speke Hotel, and I attributed it to UPC supporters either celebrating their victory or attempting to intimidate their DP opponents.

Before leaving for Nairobi, the COG met again with Obote and impressed upon him the necessity of working harmoniously with all elements in Uganda, refraining from reprisals, and returning his nation to peace and dignity. We stressed that he had a unique opportunity to rebuild his shattered country. He said all the right things in reply, none of which, as it later became apparent, he had any intention of acting upon. In 1985 his repression and corruption was to produce a military revolt that resulted in the much respected Yoweri Kaguta Museveni of the UPM assuming the presidency the following year. He still occupies this post today, though he has claimed that Uganda's most recent elections, in March 2001, will be his last. Finally, the democratic process seems firmly entrenched in Uganda. As for Obote, he was an inscrutable, untrustworthy, and, as it turned out, venal and ruthless man, certainly not the kind of leader that Uganda needed at this critical point in its history and little if any improvement over Amin.

As I reflect now on my visit to that country in late 1980, I remember many things — the beautiful countryside, the soldiers and armed thugs who seemed to be everywhere, the frequent gunfire at night-time in Kampala, the broken-down state of Kampala, a city in which nothing seemed to work, except the impressively modern and efficient Bata shoe factory, which seemed to be operating at peak efficiency when all else was crumbling. (The local water was so unfit to drink that we had Evian bottled water flown in from London. The supply of local water was so unreliable that we used our Evian water for washing, shaving, and even, on occasion, flushing the toilets.) But most of all I recall the spectacle of a proud, dignified people lining up in the thousands to vote, to put their tragic past behind them and make democracy work whatever the obstacles. They deserved better than the fate that befell them in the years immediately following the election.

Boston

Back to Canada. After the demise of Dash-Air, I was appointed by the government to the board of directors of deHavilland (ultimately I became its chairman). This appointment came about as a result of my interest in STOL aircraft and because of the knowledge of the industry I had acquired while minister of defence and while pursuing the Dash-Air project. In many ways it was fascinating work and the president, John Sandford, was a superb CEO and a delightful person to work with. The difficulty was that, since deHavilland was a crown corporation, all major decisions were turned over to the government. The advantage of this arrangement was that the crown, as the government is fondly known in bureaucratic circles, in effect guaranteed financial commitments. These commitments were huge, for development, manufacture, and sales in the aircraft business cost enormous sums of money and occur over long periods of time.

Ultimately, the government, which also owned Canadair in Montreal, realized that it had to come to grips with these two companies and brought them under the wing of still another crown corporation, the Canadian Industrial Development Corporation, or CIDC. This, made the role of separate boards redundant and also led eventually to Bombardier of Montreal assuming control of Canadair and deHavilland and infusing them with the disciplines of the private sector, something that all too frequently eludes crown corporations. Bombardier's management efficiently coordinated the operations of both these companies and those of their other aircraft-related operations, such as Short Brothers in Belfast, achieving world-class success in the process.

By the time Bombardier came into the picture, I had moved on to a much more gratifying job. In the spring of 1984, Prime Minister Trudeau, who was aware of my frustrations at deHavilland, offered me the post of Canadian consul general in Boston. This was the result of long-past conversations when I had expressed my view that, if I was ever to live in the United States and had my choice of location, Boston would win hands down. I had visited the city on a number of occasions during my years in the plastics business, and I liked it immensely; not only was it rich in culture and history, but it was also a short drive away from the ocean and the magnificent countryside of New England. I accepted the offer immediately — or, to be more accurate, after doing a selling job with my initially sceptical wife. She ultimately came to delight in our decision once she saw the area's superb ski hills.

We settled into the consul general's official residence in suburban Weston. My responsibilities covered not just Massachusetts but also all of New England and included a range of issues for which my government and business experience was invaluable training. High-tech and defence industries in New England were an important market for Canadian suppliers, but in fact the full range of business and investment made New England and Canada major trading partners. This included the fishing and fish-processing industries, a sector where we were often contenders in fishery-boundary disputes. I had the task of encouraging trade between New England and Canada and working on whatever irritants were impeding it.

At the same time, Boston was a particularly neat fit for me because of the political associations it offered through the Conference of New England Governors and Eastern Canadian Premiers. At these conferences, all the governors and premiers came together to thrash out their differences and identify areas of mutual interest where they could work together, particularly in trade but also other areas such as energy, fishing, tourism, and the battle against acid rain. John Sununu, the governor of New Hampshire and the sole Republican of the group (and later chief-of-staff to President George Bush I), was usually the odd man out. He staunchly defended President Ronald Reagan's policy of maintaining a "hands off" approach to any issue, such as acid rain, that others thought called for government intervention. On a personal basis, my closest friend among the governors was Michael Dukakis of Massachusetts, later a Democratic presidential nominee; he and his wife, Kitty, remain good friends to this day. As for the Canadian premiers who attended the conferences, John Buchanan of Nova Scotia had the closest association with Boston, seemingly spending almost as much time there as he did in Halifax. Brian Peckford of Newfoundland had been my "Newfie" counterpart when I was in Urban Affairs, and Richard Hatfield of New Brunswick, Tim Lee and his successor, Joe Ghiz, of Prince Edward Island, and René Levésque and his successor, Robert Bourassa, of Quebec were also acquaintances from earlier political days.

My other political contacts in Boston included a number of federal congressmen and senators from the New England states. By far the most colourful was the legendary "Tip" O'Neill, speaker of the House of Representatives. Tip, a thoroughly delightful, powerful figure, was larger than life, reeling off political anecdotes endlessly. Many Canadian federal ministers found their way to Boston, too. One former prime minister, Pierre Trudeau, and one future prime minister, Jean Chrétien, were our guests and were well received by local political and business leaders as well as by the large and prestigious academic community. At the time, there were a number of highly respected Canadian studies programs in the New England area — at Harvard, M.I.T., Tufts, Northeastern, the University of Massachusetts, Dartmouth, Brown, and the University of Maine — and I saw all of these programs first-hand. Harvard in particular was always an attractive forum and the interest in Canada there was considerable. A great Canadian presence at Harvard was John Kenneth Galbraith, an American most of his life and an icon on both the local and the national scene, who genuinely enjoyed his Canadian associations and participated in our activities whenever he was able. Tom Axworthy, brother of Lloyd and former principal secretary to Prime Minister Trudeau, was then cutting quite a Canadian swath at Harvard and we met frequently. John McArthur, a remarkable Canadian, was dean of the renowned Harvard Business School and a particularly helpful friend. Finally, the people of the region, many of whom had their origins in Canada, particularly Quebec, were always welcoming. Unless you spend time in the United States as a resident rather than just as a casual visitor, you really don't sense what a genuinely open and hospitable people Americans are. With their family values, their impressive dedication to the education of their children, and their absolute commitment to the democratic process, you couldn't find better friends and neighbours. Certainly, Canada and the United States have many areas of disagreement, but in spite of this, we could not choose finer people to differ with.

Our two years in Boston were rewarding but all too short. The Conservatives under Brian Mulroney came to power shortly after my appointment to Boston, but, despite the change of government, I had excellent relations with the PMO and External Affairs. Then, in early 1986, without warning, I received a call from Ottawa informing me that I was to be replaced, even though the usual term for a consul general was four years and I had served only two. I was surprised; "at pleasure appointments" such as a consul generalship, once made, are not normally subject to political whims. I was also concerned, because I was then in the midst of treatments for bladder cancer. I requested, and was granted, an extension of a few months to complete my treatments — a reprieve that was largely the result of the intervention of a Boston friend, Bob Shea, an old buddy of Brian Mulroney from St Francis Xavier University. By June I was back in Toronto. It was a momentous day in my life as, on the drive home, I gave up smoking for the last and final time.

Ballet and Opera

I wasn't idle for long, because Ephraim Diamond, an old friend and former Dash-Air backer, asked me to become director of the Ballet-Opera House Corporation, of which he was chairman. This corporation was a joint venture of the National Ballet of Canada and the Canadian Opera Company. Its goal was to build a new ballet and opera house in Toronto to replace the current facility, the O'Keefe (now Hummingbird) Centre, which everyone agreed was inadequate (particularly acoustically). There was already a site for the new building, the Ontario Conservative government of Bill Davis having made a promise that it would donate a piece of prime downtown real estate at Bay and Wellesley streets. My job, nominally part-time but in practice virtually full-time, would be to coordinate the lobbying and fundraising campaign, under the direction of Hal Jackman, later lieutenant governor of Ontario, who succeeded "Eph" Diamond as the corporation's chairman. Another major part of the job would be to oversee the architectural competition. I accepted the offer on the condition that I would move on in two years. I had no wish to become a cultural bureaucrat, no matter how dedicated I was to the project.

As dynamic as Eph Diamond and Hal Jackman were, neither would deny that the general director of the Canadian Opera Company, Lotfi Mansouri, was a driving force in the campaign. Lotfi was totally dedicated to the project, but when he became convinced that it was not likely to come to fruition soon, he accepted a comparable position with the San Francisco Opera. Nor should one discount the role of Anne Moore, the director of development, who had the determination of a bloodhound, with absolutely incredible acuity when she set her sights on a donor. Anne could smell a potential donor's pocketbook before the victim realized that he or she was a potential donor, and before long they found their name assigned to some important part of the planned grand structure and with a much depleted net worth.

Within a couple of years, we had made considerable progress. After visiting opera and ballet halls in Europe to determine the kind of facility we wanted, we staged an architectural competition that ultimately was won by Moshe Safdie. Putting the final financial package together proved more difficult, despite Herculean efforts on our part. Key were financial commitments from the three levels of government, each of which was waiting for a firm commitment from the others. The city of Toronto was dragging its feet and, in fairness, just didn't have the financial resources of the provincial and federal governments. They, in turn, were playing cat and mouse with each other — the province claiming that its contribution of land was sufficient, the "feds" protesting that it was really a local matter. Still, we did raise, or have firm commitments for, a lot of the money needed and had received promises of more by the time I left the corporation in 1988. In fact, I was feeling confident that the project was a *fait accompli* when in 1991 the newly elected NDP government in Ontario, under Bob Rae, announced that it was withdrawing the offer of the Bay/Wellesley site and would not be directing any money to project. This caused the federal government to withdraw a commitment that, after much coaxing, it had finally made. All our hard work had apparently been in vain. Today, the battle continues to build an opera house (a combined opera-ballet facility is no longer envisioned) of which Toronto — and all of Canada — can be proud. Personally, I am certain that, if the facility we had been on the verge of building in the late 1980s had seen the light of day, Toronto would have had the best opera and ballet facility in the world, bar none.

No Price Too High

My next foray into the world of fundraising occurred in the early to mid-1990s and involved another branch of the arts-film. In 1992 CBC-Television broadcast a three-part documentary film on Canada's participation in the Second World War. Produced by Brian and Terrence McKenna and entitled *The Valour and the Horror*, it presented a revisionist appraisal of three subjects, the fall of Hong Kong, the Allied bombing of Germany, and the Normandy campaign. The film managed to outrage large elements of the veteran community, their families, and most historians. I particularly recall watching the segment on the bombing of Germany, when Isobel, a war bride from London who had lived through the "Blitz," walked into the room and exclaimed, "I can't believe what I'm seeing! Did those people not remember who started all of this? Have they forgotten London, Coventry, Liverpool?" An immediate and infuriated response. To me, it was not only a warped view of history but bad television in that, among other things, it insultingly caricatured some of our leading military figures. As George Bain, a bomber pilot in the Second World War, wrote in *Macleans*, "the film diminished all of us who participated in the war, portraying us as stupid or criminal or both." What upset me most of all was its lack of context. It did not give anything close to an accurate picture of why and how the war had started and how close we had come to losing it. I expressed my feelings in a letter to the *Globe and Mail* on 4 July 1992. I wrote that *The Valour and the Horror* "left the impression for bereaved families and future generations" that "we had been duped," and that the film dishonoured the memory of the "all too many friends with whom we enlisted, trained, served, fought and, in a very special way, men we loved, who died and who we will never, ever forget."

Nothing that I have ever written or said produced such an astonishing response; I was deluged with letters and phone calls from across the country expressing wholehearted agreement with my views and thanking me for speaking out. This was gratifying, but it was difficult to know what to do next, if anything. The Senate was conducting hearings on *The Valour and the Horror*, where veteran's organizations and military historians vented their outrage. While this focused public attention, more needed to be done. The National Film Board had earlier produced a balanced documentary film, *Canada at War*, but it was by now long forgotten. In these circumstances, my overriding concern was to make certain that *The Valour and the Horror*, as the latest film treatment of the subject, didn't come to be seen as the definitive television record of Canada's role in the Second World War. But how could this be accomplished? The answer came unexpectedly from a Penetanguishene journalist, Anderson Charters, who, after reading my letter to the *Globe*, contacted his friend Richard Nielson, a documentary filmmaker. Together, Charters and Nielson had developed a proposal for another TV-film treatment of Canada's role in the Second World War — tentatively entitled *No Price Too High* — and they sent it to me to see if I was interested in becoming associated with the project. I liked what I saw and invited them to visit me at my Georgian Bay cottage. From the start, I liked them both as people — they struck me as serious, thoughtful, practical, not "showbusiness" types at all (Nielson had an established reputation as a fine documentary-film producer) — and was just as impressed with their film proposal. I agreed to raise the money for the project and to help find a broadcaster willing to show it, saying, "I don't intend to die until this thing is produced."

The first objective was easily met. I assembled a number of prominent people from the worlds of business, politics, and the professions, virtually all of whom were veterans themselves, to form the No Price Too High Foundation. With me as chairman and my old friend and colleague (and former naval officer) Alastair Gillespie as vice-chairman, the Foundation had a ten-person board of directors and a seven-person advisory committee. I was largely responsible for the fundraising. Eventually, I raised $1.2 million in the private sector, the largest portion from foundations led by Hartland Molson and the Molson Family Foundation, supplemented with $600,000 from Telefilm Canada and the National Film Board. The next step was to find a broadcaster, which proved to be far more difficult than we anticipated. CBC was not interested, no doubt because showing our film might leave the impression that *The Valour and the Horror* had been a mistake. Neither were Global or CTV. Peter Herndorff of TV-Ontario expressed considerable interest but negotiations then dragged on interminably. We were starting to become discouraged when a guardian angel, in the form of Moses Znaimer of CHUM/City TV, came to the rescue. Znaimer bought the rights to the film and agreed to broadcast it on his new Bravo! network.

With money and broadcaster in place, production of the film was completed by 1995. Two separate versions were made in English and in French. Divided into six hourly segments, *No Price Too High* combined newsreel and private film footage with photographs and extracts from wartime letters and documents (compiled by Andy Charters and his wife), supplemented by commentary from the distinguished military historian Terry Copp. It provided a deeply moving, richly textured picture of Canada at war and told the story of the men and women of this generation in their own words. I and my colleagues on the Foundation loved it. This was exactly the kind of film — balanced, fair, and accurate — that we had in mind. Richard Nielson and his great young team at Norflicks Productions had done a superb job. The reaction of others was the same. When the film was shown on Bravo! in September 1995, it received universally rave reviews; Allan Fotheringham, not an easy guy to please, writing in the *Financial Post*, called it "magnificent," and the *Globe and Mail*'s John Haslett Cuff wrote that it was "arguably the most comprehensive and genuinely affecting portrait of Canadians at war ever made for television."

We still wanted the film to reach a wider audience, however, and Moses Znaimer, though holding the broadcast rights, was fully cooperative. I approached an executive with WGBH, the Boston affiliate of the Public Broadcasting System, whom I had known during my days as consul general, and he suggested that I start with the PBS station in Buffalo, WNED, which had a large audience both in upper New York State and in southern Ontario. He put me in touch with WNED executives, who were immediately enthusiastic and, after viewing the film, agreed to show it; the contrast with the response of Canadian broadcasters couldn't have been greater. WNED broadcast *No Price Too High* in September 1996 and subsequently most other PBS border stations across the United States did so as well. A book based on the film, written by Terry Copp, was published in 1996 by McGraw Hill Ryerson, which also distributed the videotape of the series, and a couple of years later even the CBC followed PBS's lead, giving *No Price Too High* the national prime-time audience we had always wanted. For this, a great deal of credit must go to the then president of the CBC, Perrin Beatty. Our hard work had paid off; the record of Canada's quite remarkable role in the Second World War had been properly documented, and the memory of those who fought, and especially those who died, had been honoured. As a result of the renewed interest in Canadian military history that *No Price Too High* helped spark, the NFB's *Canada at War* enjoyed a CBC revival.

An interesting sidelight to this story is worth mentioning, if only because it provides me with a great opportunity for some high-level name-dropping. Earlier in this book, I described my role on a guard of honour for the king and queen in 1939. This was also the subject of a segment in *No Price Too High,* and so I thought it would be appropriate to give a copy of the video to the queen mother, then in her ninety-sixth year. Roy MacLaren, our high commissioner to the United Kingdom, arranged an invitation for lunch with the "Queen Mum" at Clarence House. Besides Isobel and me and Roy and his wife, Lee, the guests were the Duke and Duchess of Wellington, whom I had never met before, and two former politicians whom I had known, Lord Callaghan, a former Labour prime minister, and Lord Carrington, a former foreign minister and subsequently secretary general of NATO, who I had met in my political days and for whom I had an especially high regard. The Queen Mum was her usual delightful self, speaking warmly of her first visit to Canada and of Montreal's Black Watch and the Toronto Scottish regiments, of which she was colonel-in-chief. Sadly, she didn't seem to recall me from the guard of honour.

A rare opportunity for one-upmanship arose when, over pre-lunch drinks, the conversation turned to Lord Nelson. Isobel and I ski near Collingwood, Ontario, where our friend Major-General Richard Rohmer had a portrait of Admiral Collingwood in his home. Richard had told me that the good admiral was Nelson's second-in-command at Trafalgar, a tidbit of knowledge I tucked away. Well, one of the lords — or was it the duke? — mentioned the name of an admiral whom he said was Nelson's deputy, and I interrupted to say that that could not be true because Collingwood was Nelson's second-in-command. These British nobs looked startled to hear a mere colonial correct them on a matter of their country's history and acknowledged the error. It was, to be sure, the only bit of British history on which I could have corrected them, but they did treat me with great respect for the rest of the luncheon.

Aside from this matter of great historical import, I remember Lord Carrington, apropos of nothing in particular, speaking about the pervasive gloom in Great Britain in the months following the outbreak of the Second World War. They felt all alone, as they scrambled to organize their military for a war with a very formidable enemy. Then, a bit more than three months after the declaration of war and just before what promised to be a bleak Christmas, the First Canadian Division arrived in England. "You can't imagine what that meant to us," Lord Carrington said, and the others agreed in turn.

John McCrae's Medals

While lobbying for the broadcasting of *No Price Too High*, I became involved in another project, an initiative to secure the recently discovered medals of John McCrae, the celebrated medical officer of the First World War who wrote the immortal poem *In Flanders Fields*. The medals had mysteriously appeared in the catalogue of an auctioneer of military memorabilia in London, Ontario. It had been thought that they had been lost after McCrae's death when the ship carrying his effects was torpedoed en route to Canada. Newspaper reports indicated that they might sell for $20,000, and I was concerned that they would fall into the hands of some anonymous collector and possibly be moved out of the country. They were standard First World War service medals, and one of them was a reproduction, but their connection with this legendary figure made them important. Phoning the Canadian War Museum to determine if it was going to bid for them, I spoke to Dan Glenney, the director of programs and collections, who was the acting director of the museum following the recent resignation of the director, Victor Suthern. Dan, whom I immediately liked and soon came to respect greatly, informed me that the museum had no funds for acquisitions, which shocked me. He did, however, confirm that the Museum had checked the medals and confirmed their authenticity.

I then contacted a few of my *No Price Too High* connections to see if I could raise the necessary funds to bid for the medals successfully and make certain that they had a secure and appropriate home with public access in Canada. The logical place was either the Canadian War Museum in Ottawa or, perhaps more appropriately, in McCrae's hometown at the Guelph Museum's McCrae House. I was convinced that McCrae House was the best location for the medals, as not surprisingly did Lawrence Grant, its director, but they didn't have the money either. Initially, I thought that $20,000 would be easy to raise — McCrae, after all, was an icon of Canadian military history — but the considerable media attention led to a steep escalation in the price. Fortunately, I had donors as interested in the medals' fate as I was, including Guelph's 11th Field Artillery Regiment (McCrae's father's regiment) and (to my surprise) the Remembrance Masonic Lodge of Toronto, which wished to commemorate one of its members, Percy Galloway, who had willed his estate to the lodge for purposes it deemed worthy. By auction day, Saturday, 24 October 1997, I had over $200,000 in commitments, a figure I kept secret. It was a sum large enough to make me feel secure, at least until the bidding got under way.

The auction was held on a Saturday morning at the Primrose Hotel in Toronto. As the bidding escalated past the $100,000 mark and rose rapidly, I realized that I might have to exceed my committed funds. I gave up when it passed the $200,000 figure, while two other bidders kept right on raising each other. Finally, the successful bidder, Arthur Lee, secured the medals for $450,000 plus a 10 percent hammer fee for the auction house and GST for the benevolent government, making a total figure of $560,000. The final second-place bidder surreptitiously disappeared out of the room and down the stairs to the exit before anyone could identify him in spite of a half-hearted chase by the media — half-hearted because they were more anxious to film and interview Arthur Lee. The new owner of the McCrae medals was completely unknown to all of us, as was the other bidder and indeed the previous owner, whose name the auctioneer refused to reveal. Lee, a native of Hong Kong and a successful clothing manufacturer in Canada, said that he had no particular interest in the medals but came to the auction sale simply as a matter of curiosity and then got carried away by the competitive spirit. When asked what he was going to do with the medals, he replied that he had not thought about it yet. He just wanted to do something for Canada. I then asked if he would give them to McCrae House and he immediately agreed. While we lost the bid, we won the medals. They had found their rightful place of honour in Canada, thanks to Mr Lee, who was fêted in Ottawa by Prime Minister Chrétien and Governor General Romeo LeBlanc. Ultimately he was awarded Canada's Meritorious Service Medal by the governor general at a gala ceremony at Government House in Ottawa in May 1998.

The Canadian War Museum

By now, my work on *No Price Too High* had given me a degree of credibility in the veterans' community where I had not been previously involved in any visible way. In addition, the incident of McCrae's medals caught the attention of my former and successive colleagues in government, who were under heavy fire from all sides over a dispute that had arisen over a planned addition to the Canadian War Museum that was to include a Holocaust Gallery. Veterans groups and many historians protested angrily, claiming that the modest extension that was planned should be devoted exclusively to the War Museum's own collection, most of which was in storage. I agreed. Though I certainly believed that the Holocaust should be properly memorialized, I also thought that adding a gallery to the War Museum would not do the Holocaust proper justice. A freestanding Holocaust museum was needed, not an appendage grafted onto the War Museum.

In the fall of 1997, Sheila Copps, the minister of Canadian heritage, asked if I would fill a vacancy on the board of trustees of the Canadian Museum of Civilization, the parent body of the Canadian War Museum, and chair a new advisory committee of the War Museum which would provide the input necessary for government to deal properly with the issues raised by the expansion plans. I agreed with enthusiasm.

Without question, my greatest accomplishment — in conjunction with the chair of the Museum Corporation, Adrienne Clarkson, now Canada's governor general — was to persuade the distinguished military historian Jack Granatstein to reconsider his earlier refusal to become director and chief executive officer of the War Museum. Jack gave drive, enthusiasm, and considerable national profile to the museum. The advisory committee was comprised of representatives of all the major veterans' groups — the Royal Canadian Legion, the Army, Navy and Air Force Veterans, the National Council of Veterans Associations (which included the War Amps) — as well as several military historians and representatives of the Canadian military.

It soon became evident to Jack Granatstein and the committee that the expansion of the War Museum was a "band-aid" solution. What the War Museum really needed was not an extension but a completely new building to house and display its collection; the existing structure was notoriously inadequate — dilapidated and much too small to exhibit more than a tiny portion of its holdings, including a magnificent collection of war art, which, with 15,000 works, was second in size only to the collection of the Imperial War Museum in London. The fact that thousands of works chronicling Canada's military past were consigned to storage in a ramshackle building called Vimy House, formerly a streetcar barn, that was prone to flooding — and that many of these works had not been displayed for decades, if at all — was, I thought, a national disgrace.

Yet we soon agreed that the museum had to be more than a collection of art and artefacts to be preserved and displayed — it had to be seen in the context of Canada's history, of which the military was a significant and proud part. Indeed, it was thought by many that this could best be expressed by a change in name to the Museum of Canadian Military History. While few objected to this in principle, some veterans were vociferously opposed and we agreed that a name change at this stage would create controversy that could well affect the momentum we were achieving. The matter of the museum's name could wait until we had our new building built and dedicated. Instead, we kept our focus squarely on the museum's purpose. We saw our priority as fostering remembrance, preservation, and education. The importance of remembrance and preservation were fairly obvious, but we believed that education was no less vital if our military history was to be understood and future generations were to put their remembrance in the context of our history and the critical role the military has played in times of crisis and at tragic cost. With the aid of new communications technology, we envisioned every Canadian and every schoolroom having access to our collections over the Internet. What we were proposing, then, was not just a new and more efficient building but also an entirely new and expanded resource for all of Canada, excitingly presented in the nation's capital, with linkages for loans and exchanges of portions of the collection with regional military museums across the country. Our recommendation of a completely new museum and broader concept was accepted by the board of trustees, which directed us to develop a plan for submission to the government for approval.

While all of this was taking place, I personally lobbied the prime minister and other friends in cabinet, senators, and MPs on both sides of the House, briefing them on the total inadequacy of the expansion plan and the need for an entirely fresh approach. The Friends of the Canadian War Museum, with Jack Granatstein's superb inspiration, engaged in a prodigious lobbying and public-relations campaign. Everyone listened attentively but no firm commitments were made; nor were such commitments expected until we had a firm proposal for Sheila Copps to put before cabinet. Sheila was an enthusiastic supporter but, like all effective ministers, she wanted to have all her ducks lined up and the timing right before she was ready to make her pitch to her colleagues. Art Eggleton, the minister of national defence, went a step further than anyone, offering a parcel of the old Rockcliffe airbase lands for the new museum's site; subsequently, this was supplemented by additional land from the National Capital Commission, giving us a total of thirty-five acres on a majestic site close to the National Aviation Museum and overlooking the Ottawa River and Gatineau Hills. Though some ten minutes by car from downtown Ottawa, it was the only parcel of land adequate for our purposes except the old vacant LeBreton Flats site in central Ottawa, which we had seriously considered but discounted because of soil pollution and traffic patterns which would cost as much or more to remedy as we estimated for building the entire new museum. Rockcliffe, in contrast, was a happy compromise. The land was free to us, the site was magnificent, and its proximity to the Aviation Museum — as well as the fact that it was the home of the RCMP Musical Ride — made it a destination where families and school groups could spend an entire day. There was also the great plus of adequate parking, which was non-existent at the museum on Sussex Drive, and there was ample room for outdoor displays, ceremonies, and picnicking. What it lacked was a central presence near the parliamentary precinct and the National War Memorial. But the important thing was that we had a site and a plan — a bird in the hand!

This left the matter of money. The total cost was estimated at $80 million. We committed to raise $15 million in the private sector, and the Museum of Civilization committed $7 million, making our net request $58 million plus the land. Over the next year and a bit, we mounted an intensive fundraising campaign through the Friends of the Canadian War Museum's Passing the Torch Campaign, headed by former CDS General Paul Manson, a man with whom I had a long association and for whom I had immense respect. The Royal Canadian Legion enthusiastically pledged over $500,000, and a number of corporations and charitable foundations made substantial commitments, though they stipulated that no cheques would be written until the federal government made its own intentions known. Extracting a promise of money from that quarter took time, but eventually, in 2000, the government of Canada, through Sheila Copp's Heritage ministry, promised $58 million for the project, on the understanding that we would raise the remaining $15 million in the private sector.

By now, I had a tough decision to make since my eyesight was deteriorating badly and simple tasks were becoming more difficult. I enjoyed the museum work and was excited about my subsidiary job as chairman of the building committee, an area in which I had some experience, particularly with the Ballet-Opera House in Toronto. But with the new War Museum now approved, I decided that I had to concentrate on those things that no one else could do — such as writing my memoirs — and I knew there was a great team that could bring the new Canadian War Museum to fruition. In any event, my first and principle objective — securing a commitment by government to the War Museum — had been accomplished. My vice-chairman, General Paul Manson, agreed to replace me as a trustee of the Museum of Civilization and chairman of both the advisory committee and the building committee of the War Museum; this made for an extremely heavy workload, but Manson, dedicated, talented, and respected, was no ordinary volunteer. The project was in good hands and I could resign with a clear conscience and some sense of achievement but not without a degree of sadness.

Then came a surprise. With planning well under way for construction at Rockcliffe and a short list of architects about to be announced for the final architectural competition, rumours began to leak around Ottawa that the prime minister didn't care for the Rockcliffe site. Because the War Museum would be representing an essential part of our history, it should be located, he thought, at or near the other important buildings and symbols and within reasonable walking distance of Parliament and particularly the National War Memorial and its Tomb of the Unknown Soldier. This would not only enhance the museum's visibility, it would also offer easier access to visitors and tourists, which could well double the attendance at the museum. The only available and adequate land in downtown Ottawa for the museum was the LeBreton Flats site that we had earlier rejected as too costly.

Prime Minister Chretien phoned me to wish me a happy birthday, my eightieth, and in our conversation he said that the LeBreton site would have to be developed one day in any event and the government would have to cover the cost. He was thinking of recommending to cabinet that they do it now and turn over the LeBreton site, pollution free and road system in place, without cost to the War Museum. If this proposal had been presented to us two years ago, we would have jumped for joy, but so many people had invested so much time and energy into the Rockcliffe site that many of us had become deeply attached to it. Our greatest worry was the delay such a decision might cause — and the fear that few veterans would be alive when the new museum became a reality. The prime minister was conscious of my concerns in this regard and assured me that I would be around for the opening. Since the purpose of his call in the first place had been to wish me a happy birthday and many more, I wasn't sure whether I was getting good news or bad. In any event, the rumours cast a pall on many of those involved and, since all of our proposals were based on the Rockcliffe plans (we had already raised close to $10 million of the $15 million goal), our fundraising came to a halt. Then in April 2001 the government announced that the LeBreton site was ours, clear of pollutants and with improved traffic access and additional funding for an expanded public area to accommodate the anticipated increase in visitors and adequate indoor parking. The outcome was a good one, but it's now back to the drawing board for a new plan, for a new superb site.

Today, I continue to be involved in the museum's private-sector fundraising and often offer unrequested advice without any responsibility for the consequences. I fully intend to be in attendance at the ribbon-cutting ceremony, which is currently targeted for 8 May 2005, the sixtieth anniversary of VE Day.

Peacekeeping, Peacemaking, and Conflict Avoidance

All of this may leave the impression that my time since 1979 has been mostly taken up with committee meetings and raising funds for worthy causes. That is not the case. In fact, since leaving the Defence portfolio,

I have continued to pursue one of my greatest interests, Canadian military policy. I have retained a regular consultative association with most of the ministers who succeeded me, none more so than David Collenette and Arthur Eggleton. Occasionally, too, I have written articles and spoken in public forums, focusing particularly on the need to define Canadian's military role with more precision.

My views, of course, reflect the perspective of one without responsibility or the tremendous disciplines imposed by budget allocations and political realities. As well, the world has changed since 1979. Most dramatically, the Cold War has ended. When I was minister of defence, my job was relatively straightforward. We had a serious potential adversary in the Soviet Union. Our military policy had a clear focus and in the end, with the fall of the Soviet Union, proved triumphantly successful: the enemy was virtually destroyed without loss of life on either side. Now, the Cold War is behind us and, for the moment, we thankfully have no apparent single adversary, but we do have a disturbing number of localized disputes resulting in incredible disruptions and appalling loss of life. NATO still exists but its mandate is unclear to most and Canada's role in it is significantly diminished; we have no troop formation serving in Europe and a rather fuzzy military posture. In the midst of this we are left trying to keep our skills fine-tuned and to maintain some capability in a variety of air, land, and sea roles. Our most visible and effective role is in our valued and traditional peacekeeping commitments, but even here we are reaching, or perhaps have reached, the limits of our capacity. Our forces, as well as budgets, have been stretched to an unsustainable extent, and our ability to respond at home or abroad to disasters is tenuous.

In these circumstances, I have argued, and continue to do so, that we should carve out clear roles and capabilities that we can carry out credibly with well-trained and well-equipped forces. To play an effective role in any military mission in which we choose, or are obliged, to participate, such as another Kosovo or Yugoslavia, we should maintain a fully equipped, trained, ready force, capable of being airlifted to any point where it is required on short notice. This applies to the army and air-transport command, but well-focused roles will also need to be defined for the air force and navy. Since it is virtually unthinkable that we would ever be required to act without the support of our NATO allies or others outside NATO, such as Australia (as in East Timor), both our strengths and limitations should be clearly understood by all and our assets coordinated with those of others. For example, heavy-armoured support cannot be readily airlifted but our light-armoured personnel carriers can. Thus, if heavy armour is required for rapid response, it should be supplied by prior agreement with other countries closer to the scene. Reinforcement or training battalions along with an enriched militia can provide the nucleus necessary to respond to emergencies when the quick-response, highly mobile brigade is deployed outside the country.

We simply cannot respond positively to every peacekeeping request that comes along, as we have been inclined to do in the past. Well-trained and well-equipped troops make us respected peacekeepers and give us credibility in the international community, and, by doing what we choose to do very well, we have the right to call on others to support us in those tasks we are not able to do. We just cannot do everything nor can we be expected to do so. This is true of all nations with the exception of the world's sole remaining superpower, the United States, and even it is frequently not the appropriate nation to be engaged directly in peace-keeping. That is precisely why alliances are needed and why they work.

A key element of my thinking on such subjects — one that I have been writing and talking about since 1980 — concerns the need for an international peacekeeping staff college and resource centre. In the past, Canada's quite admirable peacekeeping record has added to our stature in the world community. Yet budgetary imperatives might force us to reduce this participation at the very time when regional tensions demand an enlightened, experienced, and innovative international response. Today, the nature of regional tension and conflict requires a different response than traditional green-line peacekeepers enforcing or monitoring agreements reached between protagonists. We must better understand and anticipate smouldering tensions which can erupt into apparently senseless killing — sometimes mass slaughter, as in Rwanda, or ethnic cleansing, as in the former Yugoslavia. If some of these cases appear to defy solution, it is no reason to avoid *seeking* solutions. We must learn from the mistakes of the past and the present. We must develop the preventive diplomatic skills to anticipate conflict and develop methods of conflict resolution once conflict occurs. And we must develop a network of institutions, civil and military, government and non-governmental organizations, equipped to initiate and coordinate the international response. For all these reasons, a central, innovative international peacekeeping staff college seems of vital importance.

Any nation that chooses can conduct training for peacekeepers and many have, sometimes by government initiative; examples are the International Peace Academy in New York and Canada's relatively new Pearson Peacekeeping Centre at Cornwallis, Nova Scotia. What is lacking, however, is a system of linkages to coordinate and cross-pollinate these initiatives among all interested nations. This should be created under the wings of one institution. Such an institution should be established by national governments to give it the imprimatur and support of nation-states and to facilitate the commitment of resources. And no nation is better qualified than Canada to establish a peacekeeping centre of world calibre and excellence, in concert with other like-minded countries. In doing so, we would be building on our strengths and credibility while at the same time enhancing our position on the international stage, building support for an activity that already has national approval while adding to our effectiveness as a leader in the fields of peacekeeping and peacemaking.

The complexities of peacekeeping demand a broad range of skills and resources in addition to the military. These include preventive or anticipatory diplomacy to mitigate tensions before they erupt; the resolution of conflict once begun with monitoring of agreements; the delivery of aid in its many forms, particularly food, water, and medicine, to disrupted regions; the creation of command-and-control procedures and rules of engagement with flexibility to deal with changing circumstances; the understanding of different cultures, religions, and political systems of nations where an international presence is, or may be, required, be it civil or military; and electronic-surveillance and communication systems to monitor troop movements and facilitate arms control. Training in all these areas could be provided through an international peacekeeping staff college. Such an institution could involve NGOs, such as CARE, the Red Cross, and Médecins sans Frontières, and study how best to coordinate their work. It could also determine how to supervise elections and establish or re-establish legislative bodies; how to train print and electronic journalists and assist in building communications facilities and infrastructure in areas where they have been destroyed or where they did not previously exist; and how to promote skills training through organizations such as CESO (Canadian Executive Services Organization), which has counterparts worldwide to assist in building and rebuilding viable economies at the practical, grass-roots level. Lastly, it is difficult to conceive any scenario where a well-trained and appropriately equipped civilian police force will not be required after the military has restored order (a role that our own police forces, particularly the RCMP, is playing in many countries). Such a force, however, will often need to be created and trained from scratch and, here again, the training of civilian and police leaders in a staff college would prove invaluable. To cite an example in Canada itself, one can only speculate on what might have evolved in Quebec during the Oka crisis of 1990 if, after military intervention had served its purpose, a trained civilian police force had been introduced — a force with experience in the functioning of a native community and with the capability to train and establish an indigenous police authority.

The proposed college would be a facility of multi-disciplinary study with a small but diverse student body. Its faculty and students would be representative of many nations, cultures, and stages of political development. It would be closely linked to a major university with departments of political science, strategic studies, and international affairs. It would conduct research and training in preventive diplomacy, conflict resolution, political development, aid, health assistance, and the use of state-of-the-art communications technology to deal with the current and emerging tensions in our evolving world. It would have linkages with other such facilities domestically and internationally. It would not be exclusively military in orientation but would have a major military component.

Training at the college would be for senior-level leaders from a wide range of countries who would subsequently train their own personnel in applying peacekeeping procedures to hypothetical situations. It is unlikely that any real-life situation will precisely match any of those practised, but most will have many of the same components, which can be adapted to actual circumstances. The result would be that each new situation would not be faced from a standing start. Ideally, the ranks of both potential antagonists and peacemakers would include people who had been trained in the same techniques by the staff college or its linked counterparts elsewhere in the world. Indeed, the training process and interchange of people, ideas, and procedures at the college would develop strong personal and professional bonds, which would facilitate communication and negotiation. Adversaries and peacekeepers alike would figuratively be speaking the same language and singing from the same song sheet.

Under the aegis of the college, peacekeeping-training centres could be established in a region in conflict. Even in such conflict-ridden places as Northern Ireland and the Middle East, there are voices of moderation. Once governments have agreed to seek peace, these moderates could train together at such peacekeeping-training centres to develop modes of operation on which both sides can agree. Troops or civilians who have trained together, lived together, and relaxed together on the playing fields, in discussion, or "on the town" almost always develop personal and professional bonds. They could man border points jointly, perhaps initially with a third party from a country acceptable to both, and trained in the same procedures, until full confidence is restored. They could be a restraining influence and role model in their own communities, while also assuming both policing responsibilities and many of the bureaucratic functions necessary to provide essential services. (One can only speculate what would have happened in the Middle East if peace negotiations had evolved sufficiently to reach this stage.) None of this will work, of course, if there is not the political will on both sides to make it work. It is not guaranteed to work flawlessly. But nothing will happen if we don't try.

The college could maintain an inventory of manpower and other resources around the world that is available to be deployed to meet any foreseeable situation. These resources could be drawn upon in the creation of the international team best suited to the geography, culture, religion, and language of the region in crisis — and thus most likely to be effective and acceptable to the indigenous population. The United Nations, and increasingly NATO, would have great interest in such an impressive inventory for many of its missions. As a political body, the UN does not have the role either of research or of leadership training, and it is not realistic to expect the UN to have a force of its own with sufficient scope and diversity. By having strong linkages with the college and tapping into its expertise, its regional network, and its inventory of resources, however, the UN could more rapidly and effectively respond to emerging crises or intervene where conflict has already erupted.

Canada could take the lead in an area of international activity — peacekeeping — that has always reflected our most basic values. We would not be alone, but, with imagination and political will, we could be the catalyst for the development of an important element of a truly new world order. While the cost of such an initiative has not been established, it is obvious that it must be within the limits of current budgets. Then it becomes a matter of priorities. But it should not be assumed that all costs should be assumed by the defence budget alone; the Department of External Affairs, including the Canadian International Development Agency, would have a major involvement in the college. Out-of-country costs and those of most foreign students studying at the college would be borne by the nations involved, or perhaps, in some cases, the United Nations. The existence of the college would mean, however, that Canada could withdraw from some of its peacekeeping commitments with the knowledge that more nations would have the capacity to respond than is the case now. In the past we have engaged in some missions because this country had the skills needed that others either did not have or would not provide.

Recently, I have been heartened by the news that Britain is proposing an institution much like the one I have in mind and that the United Nations is studying the idea in its assessment of Lakhdar Brahami's report on UN peacekeeping. I believe, however, that while strong linkages with the UN are essential, making the college and its affiliated global network dependent on the UN or having it take its direction from the international body would be a serious mistake. Such an arrangement would inhibit the college's effectiveness and introduce many of the difficulties that plague the UN.

The only concrete step taken so far has been the founding of the Pearson Peacekeeping Centre in Cornwallis, Nova Scotia, which is associated with the Canadian Institute of Strategic Studies. This institution is addressing many of the objectives set out above. It does not, however, have the prestige and clout of government to which it is subcontracted nor a budget to perform its global role properly. It lacks a functional linkage with a major university and, because of its remote location, it cannot easily attract expert guest lecturers and lacks the essential cosmopolitan environment necessary to recruit the very best staff and students. In fairness, since the initial proposals for a staff college in 1980, Canada other countries and the United Nations have undertaken some initiatives similar to the ones I have outlined. These initiatives have had varying levels of success. Nothing has yet emerged, however, that has the capacity to bring either substance or coherence to international peacekeeping.

Summing Up

Such are some of my activities over the last two decades. It is by no means an exhaustive list but rather a mixed bag of highlights. It was never my intention to write a book that resembled a résumé. Besides, burdening the reader with, for example, summaries of the boards on which I have sat was never my intention. Nor do I want to give the impression that my life consists of nothing but work, which would be off the mark. Today more than ever, it is my family — my wife, Isobel, my sons and their wives, and our grandchildren — that I think about the most and that give me the greatest joy. Isobel and I have a full life, and indeed we seem never to stop: travelling frequently on vacation; regularly going to concerts, the opera, and the ballet; relaxing at our Georgian Bay cottage; boating (these days with someone else driving); gardening; tennis for Isobel; skiing throughout the winter at Collingwood and elsewhere — Isobel bombing down the hills, while I do cross-country, most often with my beautiful partner, Kitty Griffin, in her ninetieth year, and a bright-jacketed friend as guide in front; enjoying the company of old friends; and walking and playing ball with my "best friend," Casey, an Airedale. As I look back on my earlier life — in the army, in business, in politics, and in my "retirement" (perhaps better described as a condition without a regular or paying job) — I know that I have much to be thankful for. I also never cease to wonder, as I said at the outset of this book, why I have been so blessed while wartime friends — Freddy Harris, Gerry Rayner, Earl Stoll, Harlan Keely, and many, many others — had their lives cut tragically short. I like to think that I have kept my promise to those friends to be part of efforts to make Canada a better place. That is the least I could have done, both to honour their sacrifice and to show my gratitude for all that I have received. Certainly, life has been good to me, but if there is one important lesson I have learned and would choose to pass on to my grandchildren, it is that you get out of life only as much as you put into it.

I had initially planned to end the book here, but, on re-reading the manuscript now, I feel that there is much more than this one truism that I want to pass on to my grandchildren. Today, it is our grandchildren, some of whom are young men and women themselves, who provide the most excitement in our lives. We know that we will not see them all reach adulthood but the fascination of watching them develop is endless (which mightn't be the case, I admit, if we still had to shoulder the strains and responsibilities of parents). Of course, I want them to realize that they will get as much out of life as they put into it, but I also want them to have values and principles, many of which have become clichés but are valid nonetheless. It may sound corny, but the Golden Rule of doing unto others as you would have them do unto you must be high on the list. So must Shakespeare's timeless advice: " ... to thine own self be true, and it must follow, as the night the day, thou canst not then be false to any man."

There are other things that I feel deeply about. For example, it is not a sin to fail; the great sin — or, if not a sin, certainly a tragic waste — is in not trying, not using your full potential in anything you undertake. Absolutely essential, too, is to be deeply committed to people and, most of all, to the freedoms we so often take for granted, like freedom of religion, freedom of expression, and the freedom to vote by secret ballot, that precious exercise of a person's mandate in a democratic society. To my grandchildren, I say that there have been times and may be times again when you are challenged to preserve these freedoms even at the risk of life itself, and, if they are not part of your very being, life itself is shallow. I urge you as well to give your lives richness and meaning through music, art, science, and reading — seek out your own heroes and heroines. I never cease to marvel at the genius and versatility of Leonardo da Vinci, the wisdom and spectacular language of Shakespeare, the incredible talent and breathtaking productivity of Mozart. But there have been other giants in our world: you should discover them yourselves.

Life is like the universe, absolutely limitless, to be experienced and savoured. My deepest wish is that my grandchildren will have the wisdom to select one or more aspect of this universe for which they have a special inclination and become especially knowledgeable, perhaps expert, about it, exploiting to the fullest extent their God-given potential — never, however, without being conscious of and sensitive to others, particularly those less fortunate.

Afterword

Before 11 September 2001, I envied my grandchildren growing up in an era of constant and instant communication, with access to information sources which, if available earlier at all, required a prodigious effort to locate and access. These sources are now accessible from almost anywhere, virtually at the push of a button. At the same time, we enjoy relatively inexpensive travel to the most remote or culturally rich destinations on earth and soon, perhaps, beyond. New technology and new services are opening exciting and rewarding vistas of prosperity and fulfilment.

My generation helped lay the foundations of a truly great society. Certainly, there were weak spots both domestically and internationally but they were increasingly manageable through social-safety nets and international institutions. It was not a perfect society by any means, but it was light years ahead of that of earlier generations. We were leaving a rich and proud legacy. Or so we thought.

The world of 10 September 2001 was a much different place from the one that emerged on the 11th, when hideous, concentrated destruction and murder shattered all our concepts of a civilized society. Virtually nothing was secure any longer. In spite of our remarkable technological advances, we could take nothing for granted. The greatest military power ever seen in world history could not protect itself, let alone others. The most advanced anti-ballistic defences in space became redundant before they could prove their effectiveness (or ineffectiveness). Unlike the wars of the twentieth century, in which my generation was prepared to risk life itself if necessary, we now confronted a new shadowy enemy who gloried in the martyrdom of suicide to inflict death and havoc on whatever random targets they or their fanatic masters chose. It was now easy to imagine the potential for destruction through chemical and biological aggression, which would carry little cost for the perpetrators themselves but cause massive destruction to their real or imagined enemies.

With massive economic and military resources, the United States, for the first time in recent history, found itself in an international arena where the old certainties were nowhere in evidence. In such a world, even loyal allies and neighbours had to be treated with care — something the United States has not always done. After "9/11," as that horrible day quickly came to be known, a new era of international policies and practices began emerging, the new ground rules of which are not yet clear.

What I have written in this memoir remains largely valid, particularly that portion on peacekeeping, but everything must be adjusted to the new realities that, at the present time, make the realities of September 10th, as we perceived them, seem relatively safe and simple.

The legacy we leave our grandchildren is indeed uncertain.

Index